In-Between God:

Theology, Community and Discipleship

Stephen Pickard

2011

National Library of Australia Cataloguing-in-Publication entry: (pbk)

Author: Pickard, Stephen K

Title: In-between God : theology, commmunity and discipleship / Stephen Kim Pickard.

ISBN: 9781921817106 (pbk)

Notes: Includes index.

Subjects: Church of England--Doctrines.
Theology.
Christian life.
Christian sociology.

Dewey Number: 230.3

Cover design by Astrid Sengkey
Original painting by Yvonne Ashby

An imprint of the ATF Ltd
PO Box 504
Hindmarsh, SA 5007
ABN 90 116 359 963
www.atfpress.com

In-Between God

Contents

Preface and Acknowledgements

The essays collected in this book represent a number of key themes that have occupied my thinking, teaching, preaching and writing over the last decade and a half. They cover three main areas: theology, community and discipleship.[1] This present volume gathers these themes in one place. It contains a number of previously unpublished essays; however, the majority of essays have already appeared scattered in journals and book chapters in Australia and overseas. I felt it was time for the scattered seeds to be planted in one garden. Of course there are always dangers in such an exercise; the seeds might not grow happily alongside each other and the result may produce an unbalanced crop. I hope that is not the case but the reader can make his/her own judgement. A great deal of my own thinking and writing is concerned with the practice of Christian life in challenging and changing contexts. How we might inquire into and engage with such concerns in such a way that will help to repair and benefit what has become broken is a major question for the Church of Jesus Christ today. These essays hopefully contribute to such a project.

Each chapter includes a brief background statement to introduce the essay. Chapter one is an extended essay unfolding the logic of the book. The three themes addressed—theology, community and discipleship—represent three vital and interrelated strands in the Christian tradition. I am reminded of the ancient wisdom from Ecclesiastes: 'And though one might prevail against another, two will withstand one. A threefold cord is not quickly broken' (4:12, NRSV). For the purposes of the present volume the three strands are differentiated and ordered sequentially. However, as I hope will be displayed throughout the book, the themes intersect and complement each other.

1. A fourth area of my concern over the last decade is ministry; see Stephen Pickard, *Theological Foundations for Collaborative Ministry* (Farnham, UK: Ashgate, 2009)

In times of significant social fragmentation and an anxious search for communal life the church has to rediscover resources to both draw upon and offer to society. The fundamental resource of course is the Holy Triune God who can be neither owned by the church nor managed by its leadership. The church's vocation is to bear witness to the remarkable ways in which this God is woven into the fabric of the world. This witness takes the form of a story of the life of Jesus: his living, dying and rising into the world. The resurrection of Jesus in the power of the Spirit gives shape and texture to the narrative of Christian faith and life with God in the world. This is the story the church is called to interpret in each generation. In this sense the theological task is to listen for and give voice to the deep rhythms of faith. This is always an ecclesial exercise undertaken in the company of others who share this faith and those who do not. In this sense it is a witness that is always reaching beyond the known boundaries of the community of faith. As the Jesus story is shared and practiced new communities of disciples emerge and the joy of God expands. Theology, community and discipleship are indeed three tightly woven strands that breed strength and resilience in the midst of the pain, joy and violence in the world. Of course much more can and ought to be said about such things. This book hopefully makes its own small contribution.

The short title 'In-Between God' reminds us that we are never alone in this world; that God is in-between all things, mediating and sustaining life. There is no space left untouched by the Spirit of Jesus who is the Lord and giver of life. However 'In-between God' is not simply a spacial category but has temporal significance. All things exist and have their being in between the eternal God, the alpha and omega. Furthermore within this wider temporal frame the church bears witness that we live between the rising of Jesus and the final consummation when God will be 'all in all'.

I am grateful to editors and publishers of books and journals for permission to publish the following:
Chapter 2 in *Risk and Uncertainty: Multidisciplinary Perspectives*, edited by Gabriele Bammer and Mike Smithson (Hamburg: Earthscan, 2008); Chapter 3 in *Essentials of Christian Community: Essays for Daniel W Hardy*, edited by David F Ford and Dennis L Stamps (Edinburgh: T&T Clark, 1996); Chapter 4 in *The Task of Theology: Doctrines and Dogmas*, edited by Victor Pfitzner and Hilary Regan (Adelaide: ATF Press, 1998); Chapter 5 in *Agendas for Australian Anglicans: Essays in Honour of Bruce Kaye*, edited by Tom Frame and Geoff Treloar (Adelaide: ATF Press, 2006); Chapter 6 in *Missionalia*, South African Journal of Mission Studies,

Volume 21 August (1993); Chapter 7 in *Journal of Anglican Studies*, 2.2 (December 2004); Chapter 8 in *Journal of Anglican Studies*, 7/1 (May 2009); Chapter 9 in *'Into the World you Love': Encountering God in Everyday Life*, edited by Graeme Garrett (Adelaide: ATF Press, 2007); Chapter 10 in *Karl Barth: A Future for Postmodern Theology*, edited by Geoff Thompson and Chris Mostert (Adelaide: ATF Press, 2000; Edinburgh: T&T Clark 1999); Chapter 11 in *Pacifica* 9/2 (June 1996). The essays are published here as they originally appeared with slight changes to the chapter titles in some cases. I would also like to record my thanks to Canon Professor Martyn Percy, Principal of Ripon College Cuddesdon for a generous Visiting Fellowship for the academic year 2010/2011 during which time I benefited from a faculty seminar I gave on 'The Passions' (chapter 12) and completed the manuscript. Thanks are also due to Hilary Regan at ATF and Robyn Cadwallader, editor.

I also thank my colleagues in the Public and Contextual Strategic Research Centre (PACT) of Charles Sturt University, Australia, of which I am a member, for their support and in particular those colleagues who have commented on various chapters in this book

The final essay in the book reflects on the story of the road to Emmaus. This story forever remains an essentially unfinished journey for disciples of Jesus. Luke offers a discipleship without shortcuts or dead-ends. I am grateful for all those Emmaus road companions I have travelled with over the years. I am especially mindful of those who have helped me avoid the tempting short-cuts and dead-ends. Their friendship has given me joy, courage and strength on the way. This book is dedicated to Jennifer with whom I continue to travel to the farthest and deepest places on a remarkable journey of friendship and love; and to Ruth, Andrew and Miriam who fill me with joy and thankfulness.

I am also aware that we are constantly surprised by the One who walks as a stranger among us; whose presence is etched into our hearts and minds. This risen Christ is woven into the geography of our shared lives through the work of the eternal Spirit of Love who surrounds and holds all creation past, present and future.

Stephen Pickard
September 2011

Chapter One
Seeding Communities of the In-Between God

Beginning in-between

I recall a comment of Stanley Hauerwas that the appropriate location for Christian ethics was always 'in the middle' of things. His point was that we did not have the luxury of beginning outside or at the periphery of life. This resonated with my own instincts in relation to the theological enterprise. We begin and proceed encompassed by the God who is our beginning and end and who is the holy presence in and through all things. The work of theology ought not take place at some remove from the circumstances of our life nor ought it presume to deliver purified statements for DIY application. Theology begins 'in the middle' of our lives, their complex and often painful circumstances and joyful celebrations. This gives theology an inescapable ecclesial flavour; it is a work undertaken in and by the human community. The most rigorous intellectual work of theology is always framed and informed by our life together in God's world.

Human community, like theology, does not come neat and finished but is complex, constantly changing, remarkably creative and often in need of repair and renewal. It is no surprise then that Christian discipleship exhibits similar characteristics. It is also no surprise that in company with all peoples and communities the Christian disciple and the community of faith can at times feel quite overwhelmed. Try as we might it is difficult to avoid this. Indeed there are no shortcuts. It's 'in the middle' or nowhere at all. Theology, community and discipleship take place in between the many tensions and possibilities of our life on this planet. They take place in between the God of our beginnings and endings for God is a God of the in-between. We might say, following John's Gospel, that 'God so loved the world that he sent his Son into the middle of things' . . . And it is precisely here that we can expect to find the abundance of God's presence and activity. It is in the middle of things in company with God that the seed of faith is planted, new things sprout and the kingdom grows.

From small beginnings

From 2007 to 2010 I had the privilege of joining with a number of colleagues in ministry each Thursday in the chapel of a cavernous old Anglican church at Port Adelaide in Australia. A short while after I began as Assistant Bishop in the Diocese I was made Archdeacon of the Port and Locum Tenens at the parish church. The halcyon days of the parish in the first half of the twentieth century had long since passed; the demographics of the area had changed significantly, it was an aging and relatively poor area, unemployment was high and nearby new apartment dwellings were sprouting up for a new generation of the unchurched. The congregation had dwindled to a very small but resilient and extremely dedicated band of people. And it was a mixed bag indeed, including long-term members of the congregation and refugees from Africa and Asia with limited English. What was to become of us? Some voices harked back to the glory days. Others looked to a new future but had difficulty envisioning what it would look like. We all knew we needed each other and that the future belonged to God even if we were a bit in the dark. Believing for a new future was the key issue.

Compared to other congregations and parishes I had known the people in the Port weren't opposed to change. I had realised some years before that there were congregations for whom the pain of dying was far preferable to the cost of living. I had known priests who considered that their particular calling was to help congregations die peacefully. It is one thing to fight against the principalities and powers in ways that are futile but it is quite another to simply capitulate for the sake of peace and harmony. It never seemed to me to be the way of the Jesus of the gospels nor indeed the story of the early church. The congregation at the Port seemed to recognise that something new was required. But exactly what? And in which direction ought we go?

The senior associate priest and I decided that when in doubt—and we knew about that—the best way forward was to begin to pray. We could have found a congenial lounge room or coffee shop in which to meet. Nonetheless the lady chapel of the large cold and empty church seemed to be the right place. We felt we had to pray in that place as a sign of faith and belief for the future. The first week, I remember, I turned up but my colleague forgot. The next week, the tables were reversed. It was not the most determined start. But after that we began in earnest. Morning prayer was often interspersed with rambling reflections of a personal kind in response to the lectionary readings; our prayer traversed wide territory and it unfolded each week in an unhurried manner. We had one unspoken rule: those that pray together eat together. Prayer in the chapel was always followed by a stroll into the Port Mall to Coco's where we became familiar Thursday customers. The conversations that began in morning prayer overflowed into our breakfasts.

Over time the two prayers grew to three then four. Some weeks it was more, others less. A new priest was appointed, I ceased my responsibilities for the area, the previous priest moved into another ministry and others also joined the cell of prayer. A seed of prayer was planted on those Thursday mornings. We had to learn to believe into a new future even before we could see it. We didn't have a strategic plan. We didn't have many resources. In fact it was a struggle to make ends meet. Over the same period the congregation slowly grew; one person invited another. We were a motley bunch and a real testimony to the variety of the body of Christ. The Thursday prayer and breakfast was only one aspect of a diverse ministry undertaken by the small band of disciples at the Port. There was an emerging sense among the people that we were on a new journey together. What made the difference? What kick started it? Was Thursday prayer the catalyst? Who knows? I put it down to the work of Spirit who binds people together. 'The wind blows where it wills; you do not know where it comes from or where it is going, so it is with everyone born of the Spirit.' The life of the congregation probably doesn't feel that it is what some may term a 'fresh expression.' And there have been challenges and difficulties to deal with at the interpersonal level. A new congregation has not been intentionally planted though some re-potting has been taking place. The parish is not wealthy, far from it. The Op Shop expanded and people from the Port flowed through the church hall. The parish began a magazine aptly named *Reach Out*. What we were about was growing the kingdom of God. God of course gives the growth but growing is what we are about.

Port prayer and life is itself a parable of the kingdom. It begins over and over again as seeds are sown and nurtured. There are so many parables in the gospels about the kingdom of God growing and expanding. The accent is always on growth and life from insignificant beginnings. Questions of structure are located within an environment of growth and renewal of energy. And it is not the kind of growth that feeds off competition, success, and performance, nor is it fixated on the numbers game nor rigid adherence to tightly controlled strategic plans. Rather it is growth that is more at home with sowing seeds, tiny mustard seed beginnings and patient labour in the field. The accent is on a growing environment rather than quantitative growth. Strengthening and energising faith is the primary concern; numerical growth follows (Acts 16:6). Such an approach is the hallmark of an ecclesially intelligent community and leadership.[1]

On planting theological seed

The garden of faith needs hardy theological seed that can survive in adverse and unfriendly conditions. I am reminded of the Australian gum tree that can often be seen growing out of a rock face on road cuttings. How on earth did such a tree ever find root, let alone eke out an existence with minimal soil and nutrients half way up a wall of rock? The seed must be robust to say the least, and the root system extensive. I often think of theology in the church as such a gum tree on a rock face. Its survival is a wonder, particularly given the minimal attention it receives in an anxious and outcomes-driven church. For some the theological enterprise is a means of shoring up the dominant ideology of whatever flavour. For others theology has value in the practical life of the church somewhat akin to the support cast for the leading actors in the show. Alas, for others theology is simply a luxury the church can ill afford. There is some truth in these depictions, if only because theology requires an engagement of the mind (as well as heart and soul) and ought to aspire to the most rigorous intellectual standards and be subject to the highest scrutiny. As a result it can often become a slave to ideological interests. Vigilance is required in this. Furthermore theology ought to serve a practical wisdom for living without forfeiting its critical function. And resources do seem to be stretched. Planting the theological is indeed a fraught business: the seed may not take root; the soil may be barren or under-prepared; growth may be stunted due to lack of attention and care. The parable of the sower (Mark 4:1–20, Matthew 13:1–23, and Luke 8:1–15) is really a parable about the fate of the seeds and the even more remarkable fact that some seed does take root and flourish in such unpredictable and hostile environments. Sowing theological seed is an ecclesial responsibility because

1. See Stephen Pickard, 'An Intelligent Communion: Episcopal Reflections Post Lambeth', in *Journal of Anglican Studies*, 7/2 (2009): 127–37.

the gospel of Jesus has to be constantly re-interpreted for every generation and context. It is a dynamic process which ossifies and dies when the critical and constructive theological voice is muffled or neglected.

The essays on theology in this volume identify the different kinds of environments in which the theological seed has to be sown. In an uncertain and risk-averse world, religion can often be promoted as the antidote offering certainty and solace (chapter 2). This gives 'uncertainty' a bad name and creates an environment in which innovation and creativity are frowned upon as contaminating influences upon religious purity. However, familiarity with the long tradition of Christian theology indicates a very different story in which adaptation, innovation, creativity and venturing into unknown and disturbed areas of life has proven over and again to be part of the nutrient for the theological seed. This is not to bless every theological whim and fancy but it is to say that uncertainty is not an enemy of religion and that doubt is not inimical to faith but part of its inner dynamic—'I believe Lord, help thou my unbelief'.

The remarkable thing about theology is that as it responds to new and surprising events, it is called to dig deep into its own soul—to the sacred scriptures, the centuries of intelligent interpretation of the word of God, the human capacity for finding wisdom, the liturgical enactment of the gospel story, the myriad practices of discipleship. What this abundant inner resource reveals is an abiding trinitarian pattern to the church's thinking, believing, teaching and practices. What can be observed is a trinitarian dynamic in Christian belief that is resilient and creative (chapter 3). This does not mean we have a fail-safe guidance mechanism—the church has erred and no doubt will continue to do so—but it does mean that there is wisdom in the body that ever calls the church to continually refer its life and struggles to the deeper wisdom of the God and Father of our Lord Jesus Christ. Such referring is undertaken under the agency of the Spirit of wisdom. God's heart is greater than our heart; God's wisdom is greater than our wisdom (1 John 3:20).

If the DNA of the theological seed is trinitarian, what then is the task of systematic theology—a relatively recent term to signal a long-standing preoccupation? Perhaps staying on task is the critical matter for theology (chapter 4). Minimally, this means not giving up on the responsibility to articulate a rational and intelligent account of the ways of the Triune God with the world. This task has, in the modern period and under the pressure of immense diversification in the disciplines of knowledge, become both difficult and urgent. Theology itself has diversified into many areas and the coherence of the enterprise has more often been lost or only faintly seen. The theological seed has been scattered. How do they all cohere; how do they contribute to grow faithful disciples and what after all is this thing we name Christianity? Systematics asks such questions and does so in the context of an explosion of new knowledge in the world, knowledge that can enhance our understanding of God's ways. The theological seed has to take root within a large field where other seed is also being sown. The separation of fields of knowledge generates intense scrutiny of particular areas of life but danger occurs when the connectivity between fields is lost. The internal coherence of theology cannot be forged in a stand-alone religious field but actually requires engagement with the work of God throughout the whole interrelated complex of knowledge and wisdom. Under such conditions is it possible for a new wisdom to be forged that grows out of God's rich and dynamic presence? This is a tall order but it is the peculiar task of systematics.

The scattering of the theological seed referred to above can be observed in the recent history of my own Anglican tradition in Australia. The modes of theological engagement have diversified and all contribute in their own way to the larger theological task of unfolding the character and ways of God with the world (chapter 5). As the Australian experience bears out, this work is significantly influenced by the location and context of the church in society. This points yet again to the inescapable ecclesial character of theology. It also highlights the nature of theology as witness, in the tradition of John the Baptist. It is an ecclesial deed undertaken in order to give testimony to God's remarkable presence and action. To the extent that this is the case we ought to expect a deep resonance between the work of theology and the church's evangelistic responsibility (chapter 6). Alas, this has not often been the case, and at a practical level the separation of these two forms of Christian witness has only served to diminish the church's witness to the gospel. Those who bear witness to the God of the gospel cannot but be caught in the slipstream of praise, for such a God is worthy of our highest praise. Theological seed is planted for the praise of God.

On growing new communities

When good quality theological seed is planted alongside a robust and compassionate evangelism one consequence is that new community begins to sprout: 'first the stalk, then the head, then the full grain in the head'

(Mark 4: 26–28). This always takes us by surprise, sometimes sneaks up on us, and is always regenerative of personal life and relationships and connections in the world. The great Roman Catholic theologian Karl Rahner once said that 'a Christian has to be an ecclesial Christian'.[2] He was pointing to the inescapable reality of human life given and nurtured by an interpersonal God. From another point of view Dietrich Bonhoeffer spoke of God and community being given in and with each other:

> Social community is in essence given with community with God. The latter is not what leads to the former. Community with God is not without social community, nor is social community without community with God.[3]

The trinitarian theology of the fourth-century Cappadocian theologians gave voice to this truth from early times.[4] What then will the social form of Christianity look like? What does it mean to confess belief in the one, holy, catholic and apostolic church? Part two of the book focuses on such ecclesiological matters.

We are all too aware of disturbances in the world and in human life that cause fracture, disintegration, isolation and loneliness. We are also reminded from time to time of the remarkable power for life that emerges through healthy social networks where respect, recognition and compassion are the chief characteristics. What then does it mean to discover our sense of place in such a world (chapter 7)? How might this place include not simply human beings and their social life but also the landscape and environment? Further, how might a sense of place and human dwelling with God be influenced by the nature of the physical environment? These are important questions for many people today and particularly for the people of an island continent the size of Australia located at the underbelly of the globe. Finding our place with each other in God's world belongs to the human project and it is a pressing need where communal life operates at such impoverished levels in many areas of the world. This points to the liminal nature of the places we occupy: at the intersections

2. Karl Rahner, *Foundations of Christian Faith: An Introduction to the Idea of Christianity*, [1976] translated by William V Dych (New York: Crossroad Publishers, 1978), 345.
3. Quoted in E Feil, *The Theology of Deitrich Bonhoeffer* (Philadelphia: Fortress Press, 1985), 8.
4. See Catherine LaCugna Mowry, *God For Us: The Trinity and Christian Life* (New York: HarperCollins, 1991).

between living and dying; wealth and poverty; yesterday and tomorrow. This liminal space is well captured by George Steiner when he refers to human life as 'the long day's journey of the Saturday'.[5] It is a way of being placed in the world that lies between the pain and suffering of the world (Good Friday) and the triumphs and utopian dreams symbolised by Steiner in Easter Sunday. To learn to live as new community enables people to find their place within such a world of tragedy and triumph. It is an in-between place and finds resonance with the God who entered the in-between places of life through Jesus and the Spirit.

How then might people live together in society marked by liminality, stress, fracture and glimpses of new possibilities and joy (chapter 8)? Under such conditions chaos will always be unfolding new creative forms of life. The dynamism and unpredictability characteristic of such life requires above all else the cultivation of patience to live well. Sowing the seed of that ancient virtue of patience is vital for growing new community. The way of patience is a way of living faithfully in the unresolved and ambiguous nature of our world. As the ecclesia of God nurtures patience a community of resilient disciples becomes a possibility once again.

Of course such thoughts remain a pure fantasy unless they are incarnated in real community life. What then might the emerging church of the coming kingdom learn from the ancient way(s) of monasticism (chapter 9)? I do not advocate a naïve return to an imagined communal past but I do believe we ought not ignore the wisdom, energy and witness associated with Christian monasticism in its many and varied forms. This is made more urgent when there is so little wisdom at present about how community life works and what justifies our life together beyond a purely utilitarian motive. Perhaps what we need is a new style *monasterium*. Such communities provide locations and forms for engagement with God in an uncertain and often disturbed world.

Disciples on a common journey

The Spirit at work in growing new communities is the same Spirit that gives energy and direction for disciples of Jesus. Not surprisingly there are myriad ways to live as a disciple. There is no one blueprint for discipleship. The seeds for Christian discipleship sprout a richly varied and abundant

5. George Steiner, *Real Presences* (Chicago, IL: University of Chicago Press, 1989), 231–32.

harvest. But is there a common bond that informs the nature and path for disciples? In this respect Dietrich Bonhoeffer has an intriguing essay in *The Cost of Discipleship* simply entitled 'The Individual'.[6] It is a title that hardly does justice to the radical nature of Bonhoeffer's proposal regarding the place and significance of God's presence in human life. Writing in the fourth decade of the twentieth century Bonhoeffer sought a way beyond the iron cage of the individual as an autonomous self-sufficient agent. Such a conception was for Bonhoeffer both idolatrous and disastrous. In the light of the life, death and resurrection of the Messiah the deepest truth of the world is that all relations are mediated through the presence of Jesus Christ. There is in fact no such thing as a direct relationship with anyone. All relations are mediated and to this extent indirect. Christ 'has delivered them [disciples]' from immediacy with the world, and brought them into immediacy with himself. We cannot follow Christ unless we are prepared to accept and affirm that breach as a fait accompli.'[7] As a result,

> we now learn that in the most intimate relationships of life, in our kinship with father and mother, brothers and sisters, in married love, and in our duty to the community, direct relationships are impossible . . . Between father and son, husband and wife, the individual and the nation, stands Christ the Mediator, whether they are able to recognise him or not. We cannot establish direct contact outside of ourselves except through him, through his word, and through our following of him. To think otherwise is to deceive ourselves.[8]

The recovery of a proper reference of human life to God through Christ's work as mediator provides the basis for a new community (Ephesians 2: 13–16). Indeed the same Mediator who makes us individuals is also the founder of a new fellowship. He stands in the centre between my neighbour and myself. He divides, but he also unites. Thus although the direct way to our neighbour is barred, we now find the new and only real way —the way which passes through the Mediator.[9]

6. Dietrich Bonhoeffer, 'The Individual', in *The Cost of Discipleship* [1937] (London: SCM, 1959), 84–91.
7. Bonhoeffer, 'The Individual', 84.
8. Bonhoeffer, 'The Individual', 86.
9. Bonhoeffer, 'The Individual', 90.

Bonhoeffer's account of the individual presumes an ontology of persons-in-relation established and mediated through Christ.[10] The practical consequences are far reaching for the nature of Christian discipleship. The dialectic of the either/or approach to life and faith characteristic of religious fundamentalism is exposed as a cruel distortion of faithful life with God. There is no one single way to be a disciple of Christ. Rather the reality is a rich and diverse practical discipleship. This is generated from the abundance of a divine life mediating ever-new possibilities for life in the world. The simplicity of God has, on this account, a rich and complex triune character. This kind of divine simplicity is the deepest foundation for the rich and diverse nature of those who are God's friends and followers (chapter 10). Christ the mediator is grounded in the eternal work of the Word, through whom 'all things came into being' (John 1:3). The incarnation instantiates this eternal work of God in Christ. It is the way of God with the world, for as Daniel Hardy states, 'the incarnation is the concentrated historical occurrence of the dynamic relation between the mystery and revelation of God and humanity which pervades all history'.[11] Furthermore this is transformative through the agency of the Spirit of Christ who raises all things. Christ in-between all things gives everything a new place and significance; all things are reconnected in new ways; all things are enmeshed in the One who is 'all in all' (Ephesians 1:22b). This is the work of the Spirit of the in-between God.

So what kinds of options open up for discipleship beyond the fundamentalisms that beset us? The mystical way is one such shoot that has proven to be resilient through the history of Christianity and indeed the religions of the world (chapter 11). It has particular appeal in Western Christianity in the modern era, the reason being that the latter has invested significant resources in structure and institutional arrangements and less in tapping the sources of sacral energy. In such a context the mystical turn offers a way of undercutting and critiquing the powers associated with the status quo and at the same time provides more direct, unmediated routes into divine life and energy. There is nothing between the believer and God; a new immediacy is established through the Spirit. This is the work of the in-between God. Is there a particular Christian way in

---

10. Such an approach clearly requires the agency of the Spirit but this was not on Bonhoeffer's horizon.

11. Daniel Hardy, 'A Magnificent Complexity: Letting God be God in Church, Society and Creation', in *Essentials of Christian Community: Essays for Daniel Hardy*, edited by David Ford and Dennis Stamps (Edinburgh: T&T Clark, 1996), 334.

mysticism which can act as seed for fresh discipleship and community? One of the great English mystics, William Law, is an interesting case study in this regard.

The mystical turn is both full of promise and inherently dangerous. Negatively the whole enterprise may become self-referential; communion with the Divine may end up in self-delusion of a Feuerbachian kind. This should not surprise anyone, given the power of the basic human drives to skew life in unhealthy and dysfunctional ways. The disciple does not live in a hermetically sealed bubble insulated from the stresses and strains of human life. There are no short cuts of a spiritual kind for the human project. Some of the greatest battles take place within the human heart as we engage with the passions that exercise such power over us. The ancient tradition of the passions has undergone various mutations in the course of human history and in the West has reappeared on the agenda of psychology, DIY self-help industry and as a whole range of methods and processes for dealing with the challenge of being a person in the world. Revisiting the passions may be a timely reminder that the greatest challenge facing humankind is ourselves (chapter 12). The Christian disciple has to rediscover that finding one's life is a fraught and time-consuming business which only occurs through learning to lose one's life for the sake of Christ.

But what is involved in a life of giving up in order to find life? Like a red thread through the two millennia of the Christian tradition there are three intertwined themes: word, sacrament and witness (chapter 13). These three together form a threefold cord that cannot be quickly or easily broken. These three operate in a dynamic way giving energy and direction to Christian discipleship in the world. All three refer the disciple beyond the self to the voice of God which requires attentiveness; to the sacrament of bread and wine which nourishes and heals; to Christ who comes into the present as testimony is offered in faith and hope. There is an outer-directed dynamic in these three elements of the Christian life. Through word, sacrament and witness the disciple proves again and again that to lose one's life for Jesus has a gift-like character for others and for self. The Emmaus road story reveals itself as a two-way journey for discipleship. It remains an essentially unfinished journey for a travelling people following the footsteps of Jesus.

Planting theological seed, growing new communities of faith, joining on a common journey as disciples of Jesus, these are the themes of the essays of this book. They are the marks of discipleship following the God who is 'over all, through all and in all' (Ephesians 4:6). This is the in-between God 'to whom all hearts are open, all desires known and from whom no secrets are hidden'.[12]

12. From the *Prayer of Preparation* at the beginning of the service of Holy Communion in the Anglican tradition.

Part One:

Theology: Seeking the Rhythms of Faith

Chapter Two
Uncertainty, Religion and Trust[1]

At the Perimeter

This essay focuses on the wider cultural and philosophical issue of uncertainty. This is a fundamental feature of our contemporary world and as such is the late modern context for religion and theology. We seem to be increasingly risk-averse in direct proportion to our fear of living with uncertainty. This essay begins the conversation at the outer perimeter of theological concern and at the interface with other disciplines and social and cultural life. Uncertainty is an all-pervasive feature of our world. How might theology engage with this issue? And might it be possible to provide a positive theological account of uncertainty? The essay leads to a reflection on the nature of trust and patience within communal life, a matter I return to in part two of the book.

Towards a positive account of uncertainty in religion

In the popular mind uncertainty is rarely associated with religious claims, particularly in an age of religious fanaticism and fundamentalism. This chapter examines the nature and function of uncertainty in religion. It does so by way of ten provisional theses: five general theses regarding religion in contemporary society and five theses exploring uncertainty from within the Christian tradition. In Part I the theme of uncertainty is considered against the background of fundamentalism and the accompanying lust for certainty; the impact of appeals to certainty with the rise of the modern sciences from the seventeenth century and the religious response; and the relationship between faith, doubt and uncertainty. Part I highlights the essentially negative way in which uncertainty has operated

1. Originally published as 'Uncertainty and Religion: Ten Provisional Theses', in *Risk and Uncertainty: Multidisciplinary Perspectives*, edited by Gabriele Bammer and Mike Smithson (Hamburg: Earthscan, 2008), 55–69.

for religious traditions in the modern period in the West. Part II offers a constructive and positive account of the nature and role of uncertainty from the perspective of Christian theology. Critical here is the link between uncertainty and the long tradition of innovation and creativity that has generated such diversity and richness in the modes of expression of faith. This very diversity opens up new problems and 'undecidables' and imports a great deal of uncertainty into the religious life. This positive account of uncertainty calls attention to the need for communities of fundamental trust wherein uncertainties can be held and life can be lived with hopefulness and faith.

Part I: Five general theses

Thesis 1: *The denial of our desire for certainty is the root of our problem*

In March 2005, in a column in *The Canberra Times*, the Bishop of Canberra and Goulburn, George Browning, discussed the 'drive for certainty in human affairs' both political and religious.[2] The implication of his column was that part of the art of living involved learning to live either beyond or without certainty in many areas of social, political and religious life. Apparently for the bishop, to live with uncertainty in matters of religious faith and practice was neither unusual nor something to be avoided. In contrast to this position, a recent edition of the *Griffith Review* offered an intertesting commentary on the lure of fundamentalism in contemporary religion.[3] One feature of most religious traditions is the emphasis upon certainty, which appears very much at odds with Bishop Browning's view. Two other articles from the *Griffith Review* caught my attention. The first, 'Beyond the Cathedral Doors', was by the Melbourne journalist, historian and prominent laywoman in the Anglican Church of Australia, Muriel Porter. Porter examined recent developments in the Anglican Diocese of Sydney and argued that a fundamentalist mentality could be observed.[4] She referred to the definition of fundamentalism by the UK scholar James Barr, noting the emphasis on the 'inerrancy' of the Bible, 'hostility' to modern critical study of the sacred text, and an 'assurance' that views differing from the fundamentalist position were in error and those who

2. George Browning, 'As I see It', in *The Canberra Times*, 6 March (2005).
3. *The Lure of Fundamentalism, Griffith Review*, edited by J Schultz (Meadowbrook, Australia: Griffith University, 2004).
4. Muriel Porter, 'Beyond the Cathedral Doors', in Schultz, *The Lure of Fundamentalism*, 178–84.

shared them were not true believers. These three key words struck me: inerrancy, hostility and assurance. A symposium on uncertainty would probably be off limits!

The other article was by John Carroll, Professor of Sociology at La Trobe University, entitled 'Nihilistic consequences of humanism'.[5] Carroll reflected on the rise of fundamentalism in Islamic, Christian and Jewish traditions. He noted that the motive in each case was a reaction against 'Western modernity', 'which combines the material progress that has been generated by capitalist industrialisation and the humanist culture that framed it'.[6] Carroll proposed that the 'bleak view' of Nietzschean nihilism had generated in humanist modernity a 'range of reactions against itself', of which fundamentalism is one. Thus 'from believing in nothing there is a leap to the opposite—fanatical attachment to a body of doctrine that is claimed to be absolute and universal'. Yet this move masks a 'fragile faith' that harbours significant insecurity. Carroll's own scepticism regarding religion emerges; fundamentalism 'is merely the general church orientation magnified'. Yet the crisis of modern society—the lonely, anonymous and restless individual, and the lack of social cohesion—suggests that one of 'the most tempting of antidotes is certainty. In particular what beckons is the certainty provided by belonging to a strong community with fixed boundaries, and the certainty of dogmatic, unquestioned belief'.[7] Carroll thus concludes that fundamentalism is one of humanism's pathologies and 'will continue as long as we fail to rediscover from within our own culture persuasive answers to the central metaphysical questions'[8]—where do I come from? What should I do with my life? What happens to me at death?

Carroll's brief reflections are illuminating because the themes of certainty and fundamentalism are so closely linked. Not simply fundamentalism but the need for certainty itself might be one of humanism's pathologies. Or perhaps it is the modernist denial of the need for certainty that masks the real issue. Until our society recognises its own drive for certainty—and it cannot as long as it denies this primal need—we will virtuously shun certainty and in so doing ensure that the drive re-expresses itself in new forms. Religion is just one such form. Uncovering the desire for certainty as a feature of the human condition and learning to come

5. John Carroll, 'Nihilistic consequences of humanism', in Schultz, *The Lure of Fundamentalism*, 46–48.
6. Carroll, 'Nihilistic consequences', 46.
7. Carroll, 'Nihilistic consequences', 47.
8. Carroll, 'Nihilistic consequences', 48.

to terms with this may be a precondition for living with uncertainty. Indeed finding a way to live with uncertainty may be a therapeutic response drawing on the deeper resources of humanism and religion.

Thesis 2: *Religion in modernity seeks certainty and suppresses uncertainties*

The language of certainty/uncertainty is relatively recent in religious usage. It can be traced to the period usually referred to as the Enlightenment, with its origins in the early to mid seventeenth century. In particular we can identify the rise of modern science in the seventeenth century as a key factor in the development of an empirically based knowledge. This was associated with the emergence of an epistemology that recognised different degrees of knowledge. This could range from those enterprises of human inquiry that offered the most sure and certain knowledge (for example mathematics), through disciplines that accorded various degrees of probability, to more speculative and unsubstantiated knowledge.[9]

Stephen Toulmin, in a provocative and important book, *Cosmopolis*, traced the emergence of modernity from the Renaissance humanism of Erasmus, 'who lived in times of relative prosperity, and built up a culture of "reasonableness" and religious toleration'.[10] Toulmin identified a second origin in the seventeenth-century rationalists from Descartes

> who reacted to times of economic crisis—when toleration seemed a failure and religion took to the sword—by giving up the modest skepticism of the humanists, and looking for 'rational' proofs to underpin our beliefs with a certainty neutral as between all religious positions.[11]

The quest for certainty takes on a new and virulent form in the areas of politics, science and religion from this period. The Cartesian programme of philosophy 'swept aside the "reasonable" uncertainties and hesitations of sixteenth century skeptics, in favour of new, mathematical kinds of "rational" certainty and proof'.[12] Older notions of certainty—Latin *cer-*

9. BJ Shapiro, *Probability and Certainty in Seventeenth-Century England: A Study in the Relationship between Natural Science, Religion, History, Law and Literature* (Princeton, NJ: Princeton University Press, 1983), 109.
10. Stephen Toulmin, *Cosmopolis: The Hidden Agenda of Modernity* (Chicago, Illinois: University of Chicago Press, 1994), 81.
11. Toulmin, *Cosmopolis*, 81.
12. Toulmin, *Cosmopolis*, 75.

tus, meaning settled or sure—now operated in a new climate marked by aversion to speculation, preference for abstract and timeless propositions, disconnection from context, and resistance of certainties to interrogation or revision.

The application to theology of the mathematical and experimental natural philosophy had political consequences such that by the eighteenth century 'the ability to construct formal demonstrations of religious doctrines . . . was less a way of carrying intellectual conviction than an instrument of ecclesiastical persuasion and apologetics'.[13] The change in theology from the High Middle Ages to the late sixteenth century was a change from a more relaxed and adventurous mode of engagement to a tighter and more controlled environment.

Medieval theologians were spared the Vatican monitoring and censorship to which Hans Küng and Charles Curran are subjected. Nicolas Cusanus taught doctrines for which Bruno was to be burned at the stake; Copernicus gave free rein to his imagination in ways no longer permitted to Galileo; Aquinas took up and reanalysed the positions of Augustine and his other predecessors, and reconciled them not just with each other, but with the texts of such non-Christians as Aristotle and Cicero.[14]

The academic freedoms of the church ceased to exist in the highly conflictual and bloody era of the seventeenth century. What emerged was a sanitised and rational religion exemplified in England by John Locke. In his famous work *The Reasonableness of Christianity*,[15] Locke followed the principles of his empiricist epistemology and proposed a form of religious life that eschewed mysteries and theological systems that generated social conflict. This was replaced by a rational Protestant religion which screened out the intrusions of fallible human judgement by an emphasis upon the sacred texts of faith with minimal extrapolation and theological commentary. This was the sure and safe way in matters of faith where knowledge was necessarily of a probable kind rather than certain. Thus, whilst religious faith did not attain a certainty accorded to demonstrable proofs associated with mathematics, it could claim a high probability of truth on the basis of miracles and prophecy attested to in the sacred text. In a later age, when miracles and prophecy no longer commanded such authority, Locke's reasonable religion looked a pale reflection of a much earlier vibrant Christianity. However, what is important for our reflections

13. Toulmin, *Cosmopolis*, 77.
14. Toulmin, *Cosmopolis*, 77.
15. John Locke, *The Reasonableness of Christianity* [1695] (London: Adam Black, 1958).

is that Locke, in keeping with the enlightenment programme, was keen to find a way by which the substance of religion could be erected on as sure a theological and philosophical footing as possible. Certainty might have been beyond reach but it did provide the bar in relation to which the viability and credibility of religious faith was to be judged. Uncertainties had been removed from the religious radar screen.

Thesis 3: *Neither rational religion nor 'religion of the heart' secures the certainty craved for*

The suppression of the 'religion of the heart' was never entirely successful in Western Christianity. The continued appeal of mysticism in most religious traditions testifies to the deeply held belief that the quest for certainty through a rational reduction of religion will only generate new forms of faith that open up what has been closed down. Yet the mystical element in religion shares some common assumptions with other forms of religious belief grown in the soil of the Enlightenment. Principally, both rational and mystical religion retain an enduring commitment to a way of knowledge that generates certainty. The urge to achieve certain foundations either through rational deduction or via a mystical experiential foundation that appears irrefutable has continued to be a feature of the modern period. The 'Father of modern Protestantism', Friedrich Schleiermacher, in his famous *Speeches on Religion* of 1799,[16] identified the poverty of rational religion and the shifting sands upon which it was constructed. He appealed to the affective domain of human life as the location and mode through which the religious capacities and instincts of humanity were most fully present and active. The subjectivity of faith was here taken to new depths. Had Schleiermacher saved religion from the clutch of modernity? Or was he simply bearing testimony to the stranglehold of the quest for certainty in modern culture, philosophy and religion? Contemporary forms of 'heart religion' presuppose some primal experiential grounding that resists interrogation and claims authority. This strategy belongs to a wider cultural preoccupation with the autonomous self and the drive for self-authentication.

16. Friedrich Schleiermacher, *On Religion: Speeches to its Cultured Despisers* [1799] (London: Harper & Row, 1958).

Thesis 4: *The craving for certainty banishes doubt and subverts faith*

When Bishop John Robinson's famous religious best-seller *Honest to God* was published in 1960,[17] he received over 4000 letters in response. When Robert Towler analysed the responses he identified at least five contrasting ways in which people could be religious.[18] One of the most important and interesting aspects of the study was the insight it offered on what the author, Robert Towler, called 'the lust for certitude'.[19] Towler noted that 'the quest for religious certainty is an agonising affair'. The 'agony of doubt' and the 'thirst for certainty' was a key feature of the respondants to Robinson's book. This craving for certainty was related to the desire for order, meaning and control. However, Towler helpfully distinguished between religious knowledge 'as it normally occurs' and that 'marked by certainty'.[20] He stated that 'faith is not the same as doubt, but it is clearly different from certainty', explaining his position thus: 'To have faith in someone or something suggests trust, confidence, reliance, and when one acts in good faith one expects to be trusted'.[21] This accorded with religious knowledge as it occurred in 'conventional religion' and contrasted with the enjoyment of certainty in the 'assurance of conversionism' and the 'knowledge of gnosticism'. In these latter religious types, what they gain 'in certainty they lose in faith, for the two attitudes of mind are mutually exclusive'.[22] Towler further commented that

> if faith is less sure than certitude, it more than makes up for this lack of sureness by being aware of the inherently complex and problematical character of the events or experiences demanding explanation, and thus it is a more sensitive form of knowledge.[23]

17. John Robinson, *Honest to God*, fortieth anniversary edition (Louisville, KY: Westminster John Knox, 2002).
18. Robert Towler, *The Need For Certainty: A Sociological Study of Conventional Religion* (London: Routledge and Kegan Paul, 1984). Towler identified five types: exemplarism, conversionism, theism, Gnosticism and traditionalism.
19. Towler, *The Need For Certainty*, 99.
20. Towler, *The Need For Certainty*, 105.
21. Towler, *The Need For Certainty*, 105.
22. Towler, *The Need For Certainty*, 105.
23. Towler, *The Need For Certainty*, 106.

The problem with certitude is that it did not allow for the possibility of further discovery. This was quite different from faith, which implied a 'continuous act of aspiration'.[24]

Faith on this account was concerned with

> a vision of the truth which has constantly to be reviewed, renewed, striven towards and held on to; the vision is never beyond doubt and never firmly in one's grasp, for if it were it would have ceased to be a vision and it would have ceased to be faith.[25]

Thus for Towler, doubt 'is an intrinsic part of faith, and since certitude is marked by the absence of doubt, or the attempt to escape from it, this places the two in sharp contrast'; for this reason certitude 'overshoots faith, craving for sureness'.[26] Towler identified the lust for certainty with being religious in a 'degenerate sense' such that 'certitude is a stunted growth compared with faith'.[27]

It is interesting to set this discussion alongside the statement by the Reformer, Martin Luther, that 'The Holy Spirit is no Sceptic, and it is not doubts or mere opinions that he has written on our hearts, but assertions more sure and certain than life itself and all experience'.[28] Luther's own agony and wrestling with doubt and depression is well known. He was one who craved certitude. But the certitude desired may have had more to do with a heartfelt religious conviction than the calculating assent of the rational mind. That such conviction, for Luther, did not dispense with doubt is clearly evident from his own biography. But it did give remarkable energy for life and a vision of faith. It reminds me of the response of the South American liberation theologian Gustavo Gutiérrez, whose struggles for justice in his own country were always fraught with danger. When asked if he ever felt he might be wrong in his convictions, he replied 'every morning'!

However, it is also true that 'the assumption that faith requires certainty permeated the writings of theologians who have conceived of faith

---

24. Towler, *The Need For Certainty*, 107.
25. Towler, *The Need For Certainty*, 107.
26. Towler, *The Need For Certainty*, 107.
27. Towler, *The Need For Certainty*, 107.
28. EG Rupp and PS Watson, 'Luther and Erasmus', in *Free Will and Salvation*, edited by EG Rupp and PS Watson (Philadelphia, PA: Westminster Press, 1966), 109.

in primarily propositional terms as well as of those writers who have conceived of faith in primarily affective terms'.[29] 'Rational religion' and the 'religion of the heart' are both forms of religious foundationalism seeking certainties that cannot be interrogated. The appeal of certainty within such 'framework belief' for the religious is understandable but, as one philosopher has recently argued, it may be based on a misunderstanding of Wittgenstein's conception of certainty, which 'allows for primitive doubt as the ground on which a language game may lie'.[30] Verbin concludes that being 'uncertain about God, being confronted with God's hiddenness is part of the very nature and possibility of having faith, coming to it, and losing it'.[31] For this philosopher of religion, certainty 'does not characterise the life of faith. The life of faith is characterised by doubt, uncertainty and disagreement'.[32] Interestingly she goes on to argue that this

> does not mean that the believer is always devoid of certainty, nor does it mean the believer's commitment to God is conditional. A believer may be certain at various points in her life that God exists, that God is a Just Judge, or that a certain event was a miracle . . . However, such certainties are ordinarily surrounded either at a personal level or at a communal one with uncertainty.[33]

Verbin's account of the relationship between faith, doubt and certainty is important and insightful. For her, doubt, uncertainty and disagreement 'are not accidental, peripheral features of religious discourse but, rather, constitutive of its very nature'.[34]

Verbin's and Towler's handling of faith, doubt and uncertainty in relation to God have particular relevance for our contemporary situation. The drive for certainty has some serious costs, most especially in its capacity to undermine true religious faith and betray the fragile ecology of human life lived in relation to God and the world.[35] Fundamentally, such a com-

29. NK Verbin, 'Uncertainty and Religious Belief', in *International Journal for Philosophy of Religion*, 51 (2002): 1.
30. Verbin, 'Uncertainty and Religious Belief', 1.
31. Verbin, 'Uncertainty and Religious Belief', 32.
32. Verbin, 'Uncertainty and Religious Belief', 33.
33. Verbin, 'Uncertainty and Religious Belief', 33
34. Verbin, 'Uncertainty and Religious Belief', 33.
35. For a recent discussion see J Young, *The Cost of Certainty: How Religious Conviction Betrays the Human Psyche* (London: Darton, Longman & Todd, 2004).

plex of relations requires openness and capacity for assimilating the new and surprising without thereby domesticating it. The same is true for art and play as much as in the field of religion.[36] Faith as fundamental openness to the world and the Divine is dangerously subverted by a craving for certainty, which banishes doubt and generates closure. In the process our humanity is lost and so is the possibility of finding the deeper truths by which we live and die. Where faith operates healthily, human beings discover a remarkable heuristic for negotiating the complexities of life and discovering things seen and unseen, things hoped for yet not fully present nor apparent.

Thesis 5: *Religion beyond modernity entails a move beyond certainty*

In regard to the matter of uncertainty the late-modern or post-modern period the scene is radically different from the nineteenth and earlier centuries. This is observed most clearly in the sciences where the assured certainties of Newtonian physics and mathematics have undergone a revolution in the twentieth century. The quantum world opens up regions of the unknown where science reaches the boundaries of knowledge. Recognition of uncertainty becomes a key feature of the new world of science.[37]

Our present age is also a period of the shaking of the foundations of life and knowledge; a desire to return to origins and an interest in uncovering primal traditions long since forgotten or suppressed by modernity. We struggle with the idea of a meta-narrative; we are acutely aware of the fragility of knowledge and the inevitability of our 'interests' shaping the kinds of knowledge and forms of life we recommend. We are also in a period that gives more attention to the 'local' and places high priority on a participatory approach to knowledge and community. Our present times are complex and this very complexity has the potential to draw people together in a common quest to better understand the world we inhabit. This is the new situation for religion and it is exciting and challenging.

Whilst most religious traditions unsurprisingly contain voices which view the present chaos of thought and belief with alarm and try to reassert their religious certainties in new and more aggressive forms, there are other voices that speak in different cadences. Are we to rejoice in our uncer-

36. See D Bayles, and T Orland, *Art and Fear: Observations on the Perils and Rewards of Artmaking* (Santa Cruz, California: The Image Continuum, 1993), 19–21; P Kane, *Play Ethic* (London: Macmillan, 2004), 55, 62, 63.

37. David Peat, *From Certainty to Uncertainty: The Story of Science and Ideas in the Twentieth Century* (Washington, DC: National Academy Press, 2002).

tainties? Can we be uncertain in some things and quite certain in others? Perhaps certainty and uncertainty are inadequate categories to depict our present religious situation? To the extent that these categories are merely creatures of a more recent period of our history (and one which seems to be fading) they may no longer help us. The German theologian Dietrich Ritschl offers religious voices a helpful way forward. Ritschl refers to questions that require answers, problems that demand solutions and mysteries that invite probing. Our inquiries have to be appropriate to the subject matter; it is not one size fits all.[38] The religious life covers all three modes of inquiry, and they are interrelated. Of course what we are finding is that many other disciplines operate with similar schema. Ways of knowing are necessarily correlated to the matter in view. Epistemology and ontology are dynamically related. Quantum physics and theology are perhaps at this level in common cause. The reality to which they both point is highly resistant to thematisation. In its deepest and most profound aspects it evidences elusive and uncertain properties (if 'properties' is the right word). Yet for some reason both disciplines (quantum physics and theology) evoke awe and wonder among those who enter such imaginative worlds.

Religion beyond modernity may offer an opportunity to recover some richer veins of life than hitherto recognised. Indeed, it may evoke a deeper faith that does not need to claim its self-generated certainties. The different religious traditions will all offer their own spin on this. And even within particular religious traditions there will be significant diversity. Uncertainty may be built into the very fabric of religion and theological reflection. Uncertainty, diversity, innovation and undecidable issues may infect religion at its deepest level. In the theses that follow I want to try my hand at giving a rationale for this state of affairs in the Christian tradition that I have been formed in and speak out of.

Part II: Five specific theses on the religious life

Thesis 6: *Uncertainty points to the innovative potential of religion*

Innovation derives from the Latin *innovare*, meaning to renew or alter, essentially to bring in or introduce something new. Hence we may speak of novel practices and/or doctrines. It is a controversial feature of the life of the church. Innovation is almost endemic to this religion and it makes for a somewhat fluid and conflictual religious life. The very nature of the

38. Dietrich Ritschl, *The Logic of Theology* (London: SCM Press, 1986), 96–97.

gospel suggests that notions of surprise and novelty belong to the life of discipleship because they first inhere in the very character and action of God. The great surprising act of God in the incarnation and resurrection of the Messiah sets the pattern for the emergence of novelty at the heart of Christianity. However, as is well known, novelty and innovation have been, from the outset, highly contentious in the Christian community. One reason for this is related to the need and importance felt by the early Christian movement to discover its own particular identity in relation to its roots in Judaism. Another reason for this innovative impulse arises from the interaction of the new faith movement with the Gentile and Roman intellectual world.

The controversial nature of innovation covered both doctrine (for example Christology, Trinity) and practice (ethical domain, organisational/ecclesiastical matters).[39] The controversies that occurred were perfectly understandable. For while, on the one hand, the gospel of Jesus Christ had generated something entirely new in the history of the world and religion, on the other hand, the very novelty of this outbreak of God's grace in the world had to be preserved and enabled to endure without deviation and contamination. The emergence of Gnosticism and the encounter with the philosophies of the Roman world all required robust theological responses in order for the novelty of the gospel to be maintained. It also accounted for the importance a church theologian like Irenaeus placed on identifying the authoritative teachers and bearers of the Christian tradition.

With the emergence of the great ecumenical creeds of the early church, the question of doctrinal innovation had the appearance of being settled. As a result it was not unusual until relatively recent times for novelty to be considered as essentially antithetical to Christianity. Novelty was thus a feature of heretical movements and a sign of unfaithfulness to the established theological tradition. The late second century theologian Tertullian encapsulated the ideal: 'Look, whatsoever was first, that is true; and whatsoever is later, that is corrupt'.[40] Constancy and fidelity to the past, rather than innovation, became the great virtue.

The appeal of such an approach is security and certainty. But it is more imagined than real. The actual history of Christianity is one of constant eruption of new and surprising elements in the community of faith, in both beliefs and practices. What are we to make of the last 1500 years of

39. Frances Young, *From Nicea to Chalcedon* (London: SCM Press, 1986), 63–64.

40. Tertullian, *The Prescription Against Heretics*, edited by A Roberts and J Donaldson, in *The Ante-Nicene Fathers*, volume 3 (Edinburgh: T&T Clark, 1989), 258.

faith and practice? Perhaps some innovations generate such conflict and diversity of views that the community of faith cannot decide what course of action to take. Perhaps the uncertainties that attend our innovations mean that some things are essentially undecidable!

Thesis 7: *Innovation in religion generates uncertainties which may be undecidable*

The relevance of undecidability to our discussion is fairly clear: while some sections of the church may firmly believe that a matter is decidable in a particular way, another section may firmly believe that the matter is decidable in a manner directly at odds with the former approach. A good example of this is the ordination of women to the priesthood. This issue has been determined in some parts of my Church (Anglican) in the affirmative and in other parts in the negative. There is no consensus within the international Anglican community. The matter cannot, evidently, be resolved by recourse to Scripture. This necessary and indispensable reference in conflict resolution remains insufficient, by itself, to decide the matter. Local context and cultures of interpretation add further layers of complexity. The status of the innovation remains essentially contested and undecidable.

How then can a church make decisions regarding innovations when many of these innovations appear practically undecidable within the ecclesia, regardless of how theoretically decidable (abstracted from the ecclesia) we might like to think such matters are?

The immediate horizon for the discussion of undecidability is the recent philosophical contribution of Jacques Derrida, who introduces the notion to highlight the essential disjunction between preparing for a decision and the actual decisions we make.[41] There remains, argues Derrida, an elemental risk, requiring a leap of faith. No amount of prior preparation or consideration can provide a guarantee of a hoped-for or anticipated outcome. Derrida invokes Kierkegaard: 'The instant of decision is madness'.[42] The decision is thus 'something one can neither stabilise, es-

41. For a useful overview and discussion of Derrida's scattered references to undecidability in relation to moral decision, see J Llewellyn, 'Responsibility with indecidability', in *Derrida: A Critical Reader*, edited by D Wood (Oxford, UK: Blackwell, 1992). I am grateful to Dr Winifred Lamb for references and discussion on this issue and a copy of an unpublished paper by Jack Reynolds, Australian National University, 'Habituality and undecidability: A comparison of Merleau-Ponty and Derrida on decision'.

42. Jaques Derrida, *The Gift of Death*, translated by D Wills (Chicago: University of Chicago Press, 1995), 65–66.

tablish, grasp [*prendre*], apprehend or comprehend'. Derrida is reflecting at this moment on the sacrifice of Abraham.

Derrida has been criticised for the way in which his appeal to undecidability avoids the necessity of responsibility in the public sphere.[43] His 'philosophy of hesitation' seems to offer little assistance for facing the practical realities that confront us in our public, political and ethical life. This may or may not be the case, though it is hard to deny that the philosopher has identified something quite fundamental for our times. We are unsure of our footing; it is not always, if ever, clear what course of action to follow. More particularly, there exist significant disagreements in our communities regarding the ethical and moral dilemmas we face. Furthermore, the dilemmas actually look quite different depending upon our context. If we hesitate, we might not be lost; we might simply be bearing witness to our very humanity. Undecidability may be a given of our existence. If this is the case, it points to the importance of a degree of faith and 'courtesy' being extended to others when we make our decisions.[44] From this perspective, undecidability points to the impossibility of control over outcomes and scenarios. Innovations generate a variety of responses and the hesitant society may be a natural outcome. Perhaps instinctively we recognise that to decide is an act of madness!

Undecidability may have deeper roots than Derrida supposes. Perhaps there are elements in the nature of Christianity itself—alluded to earlier—that generate a 'natural undecidability' about many matters of faith and morals. Here we are in the region of ontology and specifically that which has to do with the being and action of God in the Christian tradition. As Richard Hooker said some five hundred years ago, the essential character of the Divine might be identified as 'riches', 'abundance' and 'variety'.[45] Hooker was bearing witness to something quite central for a Christian theology of God. This can be put simply as the concept of divine abundance—for example creativity, grace, forgiveness—that is shaped and substantiated by the life of Jesus and the Spirit in the world and the people

43. See the discussion by Simon Critchley, *The Ethics of Deconstruction: Derrida and Levinas* (Oxford, UK: Blackwell, 1992).
44. Courtesy is the style of interaction with the 'other'. It is characterised by thoughtfulness, respect, graceful speech and attentive listening. George Steiner refers to both the 'yearning' and 'fear' of the other necessarily involved in courtesy. For discussion see Graeme Garrett, 'Open Heaven/Closed Hearts: Theological Reflections on Ecumenical Relations', in *Faith and Freedom: A Journal of Christian Ethics*, 6 (1998): 63–80.
45. Richard Hooker, *Of the Laws of Ecclesiastical Polity* [1593] (London: JM Dent, Everyman edition, 1907), 1.1.4.

of God. The characteristic theme here might be overflow or abundance.[46] On this account, undecidability may have ontological weight. Diversity of understanding, multiple perspectives, and possibilities for new and surprising responses—all of these things may in fact belong to the character and ways of God in the world. Therefore if the religious community finds new problems, situations, and moral and ethical dilemmas it should not be surprised that this is accompanied by an inability to reach consensus. It may be that the significant differences of interpretation of divine intentions and desires are precisely what one should anticipate in the Christian tradition. This also suggests that the church urgently requires an ethic of creativeness in order to practise wisdom and discernment in the practical affairs of its life and mission.

Thesis 8: *Vagueness and ambiguity are our lot in the religious life*

Of course there is a variety of other reasons for undecidability connected to issues of cultural mores, social life, different value systems and human sin. However, it is not so easy to disentangle these, and one wonders whether it is ever finally possible or appropriate. What it does mean is that our religious life is often messier than we would wish. This is difficult for us to tolerate, and we mostly desire clarity and sharp boundaries as a means to preserve and nurture personal and communal identity. Being vague, unsure and uncertain are hardly virtues that we hear our leaders extol. However, when dealing with the difficult terrain of innovation and the undecidables that seem to haunt us, we are in urgent need of resources that enable us to live with ambiguity and vagueness.[47] This is quite difficult given the strong views increasingly voiced these days by those from many

46. See, for example, the following New Testament references to the idea of overflow and abundance: Letter to the Colossians 1:19 and 2:9 (*pleroma*); Gospel of John, 10:10b (abundance); Paul's first letter to Timothy, 1:14 (super-abundance). In the same vein Ricoeur refers to Paul's letter to the Romans chapter 5:15–21 as 'the "odd" logic of superabundance' wherein an 'ordinary "logic" collapses and the "logic" of God . . . blows up'. See Paul Ricoeur, 'Paul Ricouer on Biblical hermeneutics', in *Semeia*, 4 (1975): 138.

47. While we seek plain and clear texts, doctrines and ethical standards, perhaps the reality is quite different. We have difficulty dealing with the 'irremediable vagueness' and indefiniteness that seems to lurk within the plainest of statements and positions. Yet this very 'vagueness' provides the conditions for diverse and new interpretations and responses. Charles Peirce's notion of 'irremediable vagueness' is interesting in this regard. See Peter Ochs, *Peirce, Pragmatism and the Logic of Scripture* (Cambridge, UK: Cambridge University Press, 1998).

religious quarters who call for sharper delineation of moral, ethical and doctrinal boundaries. The legislative impulse is powerful.

Thesis 9: *Uncertainties in religion require communities of patience*

It is clear from the above discussion that genuine community is not a simple state of affairs but a dynamic and somewhat restless feature of the life of religious communities. This is fostered and nurtured by constant innovation—new responses in new contexts that seek faithfulness to the tradition and relevance in the modern world. In other words, innovation belongs to the dialectic of the gospel. Community is also constantly threatened by innovation. Innovation is thus inherently conflictual and unavoidable. For these reasons, innovations generate uncertainty and appear in the life of religious communities as undecidable. Yet at the same time they require determination for the sake of our religious life in the world. This suggests that a key issue for religious communities is how they will operate in their uncertainties and disputes without falling into a trap of either fundamentalism or 'anything goes'. They cannot seek simple default solutions through authoritarian top-down or democratic majority bottom-up approaches. Resilient religious communities will be those that find the capacity to give freedom and space to others as well as a capability of including others in decision-making and life practices.

This discussion also highlights the fact that living with others requires patience and long suffering.[48] There are no short cuts through either political or legal manoeuvres that do not also include a moral vision of what it means to be a communion that travels, in the words of George Steiner, 'the long day's journey of the Saturday'.[49] Steiner's invocation of the Holy Saturday tradition at the end of his remarkable *tour de force* of the cultural and philosophical condition of the twentieth century provides a powerful reminder that we find ourselves in times of immense transition and uncertainty. In such a context of radical innovations and so many undecidables, a cultivated waiting that brims full of vigour, life and resilience becomes paramount. Steiner counsels neither the despair of Good Friday nor the triumphalism of Easter Sunday, but rather a hopeful waiting. It is a theme picked up by Rowan Williams's meditations in the aftermath of the

48. For a fuller discussion see Stephen Pickard, 'Innovation and Undecidability: Some Implications for the *Koinonia* of the Anglican Church', in *Journal of Anglican Studies*, 2/2 (2004): 87–105.

49. George Steiner, *Real Presences* (Chicago: University of Chicago Press, 1989).

terrorist attacks in the US on 11 September 2001.[50] In closing, Williams reflects on Jesus' writing in the dust recorded in chapter eight of John's Gospel. In this strange and enigmatic gesture Williams senses hope:

> He [Jesus] hesitates. He does not draw a line, offer an interpretation, tell the woman who she is and what her fate should be. He allows a moment, a longish moment, in which people are given time to see themselves differently precisely because he refuses to make the sense they want. When he lifts his head, there is both judgement and release. So this is writing in the dust because it tries to hold that moment for a little longer, long enough for some of our demons to walk away.[51]

Religious communities that provide resources for the long day's journey of the Saturday will be those that foster the ancient spiritual discipline of patience. It was Tertullian in the third century who considered disharmony and conflict in the ecclesia—the family of siblings—as a sign of impatience.[52] He saw the archetype of this present in the Cain and Abel story wherein Tertullian argued that 'Therefore, since he [Cain] could not commit murder unless he were angry, and could not be angry unless he were impatient, it is to be proved that what he did in anger is to be referred to that which prompted the anger'.[53] Tertullian's exegesis may be unconvincing, but his appeal to the sibling metaphor for the ecclesial family and his emphasis upon harmony and discord revolving around the theme of patience may yet prove instructive in our present context. It may be precisely through this ancient discipline that religious communities that share the heritage of Cain and Able are enabled to live with uncertainties and at the same time find a richer and resilient life together for the common good.

Thesis 10. *Patience in our uncertainties requires a fundamental trust*

A religious community that emerges out of patient and hopeful waiting in troubled and unsettled times cannot be one that can be artificially manufactured and managed. It comes as gift but requires fundamental

50. Rowan Williams, *Writing in the Dust: Reflections on the 11 September and its Aftermath* (London: Hodder & Stoughton, 2002).
51. Williams, '*Writing in the Dust*', 81.
52. J Hellerman, *The Ancient Church as Family* (Minneapolis, Minnesota: Fortress Press, 2001), 173–82.
53. Hellerman, *Ancient Church*, 178.

trust between people. Trust is not an easy matter in our present situation, though the giving and receiving of trust is basic to shared lives and genuine community. Trust has a somewhat troubled history and is difficult to establish and sustain in modern society.[54] However, a community based on trust and associated mutual respect and recognition is precisely what the Christian story invites people to embody in their life together. Such trust includes face-to-face relations, interdependent lives, openness to correction, and willingness to offer and receive wisdom. This is the stuff not of certainties but of a more humble and modest openness that resonates with the deeper wisdom that is still unfolding (Hebrews 11:1). The dynamics by which creation and human life are assimilated to this emergent yet transcendent wisdom—which is but alluded to here—is one of the most fundamental, elusive yet urgent, issues of our times.

Conclusion

It is difficult to predict how religion will handle the increasing uncertainties of contemporary life. Understanding the roots and energy of modern fundamentalism in religion will be an important project precisely because fundamentalism views uncertainty so negatively and as threat. Where religious communities approach uncertainty in life and thought more positively, there will be new opportunities for inter-religious dialogue and openness to those of other faiths and to those of no faith. However, the move from a negative to a positive appraisal of uncertainty in religion will require, among other things, a robust intellectual engagement of theology with the richest disciplines of thought available. Here I predict we will find common cause and unfolding fascination with the world and the God who is its deepest mystery. At this point uncertainty becomes the doorway into the world that still awaits us.

54. For a discussion see Anthony Giddens, *The Consequences of Modernity* (Cambridge UK: Polity Press, 1990), especially chapter 3.

Chapter Three
Trinitarian Dynamics of Belief[1]

To the centre of faith

This essay had its genesis in my early doctoral work as I grappled with the inner logic of theology. In this sense the essay moves from the perimeter to the centre of faith. Theology reveals itself as an ecclesial activity founded upon and informed by its fundamental reference to the Triune God. The essay is an attempt at faithful reasoning following the pattern of God's ways with the world.

Loss and recovery of trinitarian belief

The tendency of Christian belief to collapse into an undifferentiated form of monotheism has been a recurring feature of the Christian tradition. Karl Rahner's observation in this regard is most apposite:

> despite their orthodox confession of the Trinity, Christians are, in their practical life, almost mere 'monotheists'. We must be willing to admit that, should the doctrine of the Trinity have to be dropped as false, the major part of religious literature could well remain virtually unchanged.[2]

More recently Jürgen Moltmann, among others, has drawn attention to the impact of this loss of trinitarian belief within the wider socio/political and ecological contexts of modern life.[3] The roots of this trinitarian

1. Originally published as 'The Trinitarian Dynamics of Belief', in *Essentials of Christian Community: Essays in Honour of Daniel W Hardy* (Edinburgh: T&T Clark, 1996), 63–75.
2. Karl Rahner, *The Trinity* (London: Burns and Oates, 1970), 10.
3. See for example, Jürgen Moltmann, *The Trinity and the Kingdom of God* (London: SCM, 1981) and *God and Creation. An Ecological Doctrine of Creation* (London: SCM,

slippage are varied and complex and have their traces in the formative stages of the Christian tradition.[4] However, it is also the case that the rationalistic temper of European enlightenment thought contributed to, if not accelerated, the drift from a distinctive trinitarian form of belief into more diffuse and abstracted notions of the presence and action of God in the world.[5]

This problem has intensified from the nineteenth century under the impact of the Feuerbachian critique of religion.[6] As a result the church has had to face more directly the challenge of recovering the fullness of Christian belief in order to nourish and sustain ongoing discipleship in the modern world. This has constituted a major agenda for the church in the twentieth century and is evidenced in important attempts to relocate Christian belief and practice within a fuller trinitarian framework.[7] This suggests a new effort to identify in a comprehensive and rich way that which is most distinctive in the Christian tradition.[8] This development raises, indeed provokes questions to do with the dynamics of belief that is self-consciously trinitarian in form; for example, how is the God believed in present for faith, initiating and sustaining human believing? To what extent is it possible to embody the object of belief in beliefs? By what process does belief come to full form? How significant is the ecclesial nature of Christianity for belief? What is the function and purpose of belief? Such questions have to do with the foundation and dynamic of ecclesial discipleship witnessed to in Christian belief.

1985), especially 94–98.

4. For a recent discussion see Colin Gunton, *The Promise of Trinitarian Theology* (Edinburgh: T&T Clark, 1991), chapter 3.
5. This problem is highlighted in John Locke (1632–1704) in John Locke, *The Reasonableness of Christianity* [1695], edited by GW Ewing (Washington: Regnery Gateway, 1965). A highly reduced form of Christian belief is proposed—belief in one God and in Jesus as the Messiah—in relation to which the doctrine of the Trinity cannot but appear as a marginal and metaphysical irrelevancy.
6. The de-objectification of God has led to a radically immanentist account of divine reality. As a result God becomes the sum total of human spiritual ideas. An example is Don Cupitt, *Taking Leave of God* (London: SCM, 1986).
7. Gunton, *Trinitarian Theology*, chapter 1, notes the important developments in the doctrine of the Trinity in Barth (Reformed), Rahner (Roman Catholic), and Lossky (Orthodox) as well as in more recent theology.
8. Jürgen Moltmann, *History and the Triune God* (London: SCM, 1991), xi states: 'The doctrine of the Trinity has become important in the last ten years because it is the way in which the distinctive feature of Christianity is formulated'.

In many respects Christian theology has failed to show how belief and practice of faith nourish and stimulate each other. This has contributed to the inner dissolution of the trinitarian form of Christian belief. Ultimately it would be of great practical benefit for the Christian community to understand what it means to live in the Spirit with Christ in God (Colossians 3:3).

The following discussion offers, in brief form, a way of understanding how Christian belief arises out of, is informed by and contributes to the presence and action of the triune God in the world. What is distinctively trinitarian in the dynamics of belief will be woven into a discussion of the strategies and environment that attends faithful response to God in the community of Jesus Christ.

Trinitarian belief: its impulse and source

Uncertainty over the presence of God in the world and human society has had a major impact on Christian belief. Specifically, it has become unclear whether distinctive Christian beliefs 'reach back' to and thus mediate the presence of God witnessed to in the community of Jesus Christ.[9] As a result the long-held conviction that the Christian disciple already dwells in the truth as it is in Jesus (Ephesians 4:21b) has become problematic. It can no longer be taken for granted that Christian belief gives expression to a fundamental bond in the Spirit with the God of Jesus Christ. The problematic nature of the 'whence' of Christian belief reveals itself in the range of options in theology for identifying the source and impulse for belief.[10] An option at one extremity evidences a conventional or hard objectivism. This usually involves appeal to a strong formal authority for belief in terms of biblical warrant and/or its authoritative interpreter. In this context belief is reduced to assent to propositions. This mode of belief is usually underpinned by the assumption of a strict one-to-one correspondence between word and object.[11] Attention is necessarily transferred from what is primary to its intermediate forms. Although a form of trinitarian faith

9. For further discussion see Edward Farley, *Ecclesial Man: A Social Phenomenology of Faith and Reality* (Philadelphia: Fortress Press, 1975), chapter 1.
10. The question of the source and impulse for Christian belief is implicit in George Lindbeck's discussion of the cognitivist, experiential-expressivist and cultural linguistic approaches to Christian doctrine. See George Lindbeck, *The Nature of Doctrine: Religion and Theology in a Post-Liberal Age* (London: SPCK, 1984).
11. Lindbeck, *Nature of Doctrine*, 80.

may be vigorously espoused, it is unclear how a trinitarian dynamic actually operates in such belief. Whilst belief may come in some sense *from* God, the *way* such belief is held raises suspicions of a malfunction in the dynamic of belief. Unsurprisingly such believing usually generates a form of uncreative repetitive discourse.[12] It seems unable to generate free-flowing speech corresponding with the dynamic of God's action concentrated in Jesus of Nazareth, and continued in the energy of the Spirit. Communication that occurs within the constraints of this dynamic will necessarily generate a free and ever enriching response to God.

As a counterpoise to conventional objectivism the other extremity of the theological spectrum locates the impulse for belief within the realm of human religious subjectivity. Thus for Schleiermacher, belief arose from an 'inner relation to the redeemer', Jesus Christ.[13] To state such belief was to give linguistic expression to the religious self-consciousness as formed by the 'impression' of the Redeemer. Belief was thus a response to piety and only *indirectly* a response to God. Primary belief was that which could be identified as an immediate utterance of the religious self-consciousness. On this view, Christian belief had no intrinsic trinitarian structure; the triunity of the being of God was not, in Schleiermacher's view, an immediate utterance of the religious self-consciousness.[14]

Both the above options imply different answers to the question of the impulse and source of Christian belief. In the first option the content of belief is codified in a manner that thwarts the dynamic of belief appropriate to the triune God. The latter form struggles to avoid the almost inevitable collapse of Christian belief into a *form* of Sabellian modalism.[15]

Important attempts have been made to recover the fullness of Christian belief and avoid the above problems. Here the *possibility* and *content* of belief is located more directly in what is 'given' for faith to apprehend.[16]

---

12. This is at the heart of Karl Barth's critique of the fundamental articles of faith tradition in Protestantism. Here Christian belief becomes codified in 'irrevocable' articles of belief which are simply repeated but are no longer able to be reconstituted by the Word of God; see Karl Barth, *Church Dogmatics*, volume 1 part 2 (Edinburgh: T&T Clark, 1975), 863–66.
13. Friedrich Schleiermacher, *The Christian Faith* (Edinburgh: T&T Clark, 1928), 56. Compare 'original impression' (125); 'image' (56); and 'influence' (49).
14. Schleiermacher, *Christian Faith*, 738–51.
15. See for example, William Hill, *The Three-Personed God: The Trinity as the Mystery of Salvation* (Washington: Catholic University of America, 1982), 90f.
16. Thus Barth, *Church Dogmatics*, volume 4 part 1, 742, can say: 'Faith stands or falls with its object . . . It [faith] simply finds that which is already there for the believer and also for the unbeliever'.

Thus for Karl Barth belief is a graced response to an encounter with the Word of God, incarnate in Jesus Christ, witnessed to in scripture and proclaimed afresh in the church.[17] The impulse and source for Christian belief is located in the prevenient activity of God revealing Godself in such a way that faithful response is made possible. The possibility for belief rests here in the free and loving will of the revealer to be present for human beings, revealing the identity of the hidden God.[18] This makes possible a faithful response toward God through the power of the revealedness of God *from the side of the human being.*[19] The threefold form of God as revealer, revealing and revealedness, corresponding to Father, Son and Holy Spirit, is both *what* is given for faith to apprehend and determinative for the *way* human beings can respond.[20] In this trinitarian dynamic belief is both a gift from God and a free human response of trust in God.[21] This dynamic in faith involves both a closure of 'the circle of divine judgement and grace' in Jesus Christ and a corresponding opening of the 'closed circle' of the human being.[22]

For Hans Urs Von Balthasar belief that corresponds to the being of God involves aesthetic considerations. The mystery of Christianity has an inner form to be discerned by the light of faith as it attends to what is given.[23] Christ constitutes the 'fundamental form'.[24] The *visio Christi*—'the material heart and centre of his theology'[25]—is manifested in the 'transparency' of ecclesia's mediate forms (for example, worship, ritual, creeds and confessions, forms of discipleship) which receive their form from the

17. For Barth's discussion of the object and act of faith see *Dogmatics*, volume 4 part 1, 740–49.
18. Barth, *Church Dogmatics*, volume 1 part 2, 245.
19. Barth, *Church Dogmatics*, volume 1 part 1, 451: 'God Himself becomes present to man not just externally, not just from above, but also from within, from below, subjectively. It is thus reality in that He does not merely come to man but encounters Himself *from man*' [my italics].
20. The significance of Barth's pneumatology for faith is discussed by Philip Rosato, *The Spirit as Lord: The Pneumatology of Karl Barth* (Edinburgh: T&T Clark, 1981), 60–65.
21. See Karl Barth, *Dogmatics in Outline* (London: SCM, 1966), 17 and 139f.
22. Barth, *Church Dogmatics*, volume 1 part 2, 743.
23. Hans Urs von Balthasar refers to faith as 'the light of God becoming luminous in man, for, in his triune intimacy, God is known only by God' ('Seeing the Form', in *The Glory of the Lord: A Theological Aesthetics*, volume 1 (Edinburgh: T&T Clark, 1982), 156).
24. Balthasar, 'Seeing the Form', 576; compare 153.
25. Remark made by Donald MacKinnon in his introduction (4) to the English edition of Von Balthasar, *Engagement with God*, translated by John Halliburton (London: SPCK, 1975).

form of Christ.[26] Thus in statements of belief, what 'shines forth' is 'Jesus Christ and his invisible truth'.[27]

Barth and von Balthasar express, each in their own way, a common answer to the question of the whence of belief. Christian belief is capacitated from God. However, the correspondence implied here can never be isomorphic, for it is a correspondence with the plenitude of God's being.[28] Both theologians exemplify an effort to allow full freedom for the content of Christian belief to be determined by God in God's self revelation. Significantly this approach has fostered belief which evidences richly textured patterns consistent with believing that seeks faithfulness to 'the eternally rich God'.[29] The presupposition here is that God is present in the believing such that belief is 'spirited' along in a manner which honours the God of Jesus Christ. Belief here is capacitated from a source that is involved not only in the content of belief but also in the process of believing. What is believed and how it is believed are thus related through a dynamic intrinsic to God's own being.[30]

Trinitarian belief: a communicative process

When the accent is on belief as the *response* of faith, belief has the character of a communicative activity in which the founding reality of faith receives more concrete and determinate forms. This embodiment occurs through a variety of mediums including religious practices (for example, worship and religious rites, service and care) and explicit articulations of faith (for example, creeds and confessions, doctrine). When such belief is understood as merely a *product* of reflection upon what is given in the divine-human relation, belief, as a response from within a relation to God, is easily obscured. Christian belief cannot, on this latter view, be reduced to a merely interpretive activity somewhat secondary and distant from

---

26. Balthasar, *Glory of the Lord*, volume 1, 252.
27. Balthasar, *Glory of the Lord*, volume 1, 242.
28. Balthasar, *Glory of the Lord*, volume 1, 552. Balthasar's notion of the 'evermore' of the Trinitarian event is discussed by Gerard O'Hanlon, *The Immutability of God in the Theology of Hans Urs von Balthasar* (Cambridge: Cambridge University Press, 1990), 124–30. For Barth see discussion of simplicity in the text below.
29. Barth, *Dogmatics*, volume 1 part 1, 763.
30. This feature of belief is precisely what is missing in Alistair McGrath's inquiry in the *genesis* of doctrine. See *The Genesis of Doctrine: A Study in the Foundations of Doctrinal Criticism*, Bampton Lectures for 1990 (Oxford: Basil Blackwell, 1990).

the founding reality of faith.[31] A more adequate view regards the believer's interpretive response to the gospel as an activity intrinsic to the dynamic of Christian faith and the means for its enrichment. In this process the reality of Christian faith is brought to its full strength at the level of religious consciousness.[32] Furthermore, precisely because the response of faith occurs from within a genuine relation to the plenitude of God's own being, specifications of the content of that relation will have a necessary provisional character. Thus an expectation is raised in faith of an ongoing communicative effort in which the full truth of the one-in-Christ bond (Galatians 3:28; compare Colossians 3:11) is continually and critically uncovered in myriad contexts. From this perspective it is the strategies by which belief is realised in language that reveal the deeper dynamics of believing that is trinitarian.

The Search for Foundations

The search for foundations has been an important recurring and controversial strategy initiating faith's attempt to deepen understanding of life in relation to God.[33] The search for and identification of the substructure of belief has offered the possibility of fixity, permanence and definiteness for Christian faith. The danger of this strategy is that it tends to over-stabilise the dynamic of faith's response to God and can result in the conventional objectivism in belief identified earlier. The search for a more adequate hermeneutic of foundations will have to take account of both the contingent nature of faith and the nature of that fundamental relation between God and human beings generative of Christian belief. It is difficult to specify this relation because in the Christian tradition the mediation of this relation is a mediation of plenitude, concentrated in Jesus Christ (Colossians 1:19 and 2:9, John 10:10b) richly dispersed in the Spirit (Romans 5:1–5) and experienced by humankind as God's superabundance of grace, faith

31. See for example Daniel Hardy's discussion of John Hick in 'Theology through Philosophy', in *The Modern Theologians: An Introduction to Christian Theology in the Twentieth Century*, volume 2, edited by David Ford (London: Oxford University Press, 1989) 54–59.

32. For Bernard Lonergan, doctrine is not an alien intrusion but rather a product of the 'differentiated consciousness'. What is not so clear is how this activity might contribute to the fullness of God's presence for the believer; see Bernard Lonergan, *Method in Theology* (London: Darton, Longman & Todd, 1972), 295–334.

33. For an important recent discussion see Colin Gunton, *The One, the Three and the Many: God, Creation and the Culture of Modernity,* The 1992 Bampton Lectures (Cambridge: Cambridge University Press, 1993), 129–35.

and love (1 Timothy 1:14). It is precisely this fullness of being which has funded, among other things, a recurring trinitarian pattern in the history of Christian belief. This kind of plenitude is richness in perfection; the maximal concentration of 'God's expanding perfection'.[34]

Faithful response to a foundation construed in the above manner will generate richly textured belief and fresh possibilities for Christian discipleship. An interesting example here, from within the Christian mystical tradition, is the eighteenth-century Anglican William Law (1686–1761).[35] In Law's later Christian life he rediscovered the soul-presence of the triune God. His re-appropriation of the foundation of faith generated interior renewal, animated the fundamental beliefs of Christianity (incarnation and redemption) and broke the conventional forms of stating Christian belief in the church. For Law Christian belief was essentially a response to the 'outflow' or 'overflow' of God who was 'All Love'; in whom there could be no wrath.[36] Yet the response of faith belonged for Law to the movement of God's own vivifying presence in the believer, propelling faith into free-flowing abundant speech. The linguistic unraveling of the reality of the presence of the triune God was the way in which praise of God found its precision and wisdom.

Law is but one example that testifies to the fact that foundations rooted in God are foundations with the capacity to disrupt what is stable and conventional in favour of fresh and surprising orderings of reality. The dynamic operating in Law's believing represented the logic of God's outward directed movement of love, incarnate in Jesus Christ and continued in the regenerating activity of the Spirit. To believe in this trinitarian dynamic was to believe deeper into the divine reality.

The Appeal of Simplicity

Implicit within the search for foundations is an appeal to simplicity. The concept of simplicity is implied in any critical reduction in belief, a fact clearly evidenced in the important discussion in Protestantism of the 'es-

34. The notion of God's expanding perfection is discussed in Daniel Hardy and David Ford, *Jubilate: Theology in Praise* (London: Darton, Longman & Todd, 1984), 63, 161–67.

35. The high point of Law's later works is *The Spirit of Love* reprinted in *The Classics of Western Spirituality*, edited by Paul G Stanwood (London: SPCK, 1978). In particular 'The First Dialogue', 391–427, is a good introduction to Law's mystical theology.

36. Law, *Spirit of Love*, 429.

sence of Christianity' and the appeal to certain fundamental articles of Christian belief.

At a practical level simplicities in the faith are important (for example, catechesis, creedal statements, worship, apologetics). However, when simplicity is extolled as a virtue in itself it becomes merely a pseudonym for 'simplistic'. Simplicity as conceptual economy is thus a sign not of the seal of truth, but of transitoriness; of belief being superseded by richer and fuller belief. This seems to accord with knowledge more generally where increasing penetration of reality discloses increasingly higher degrees of complexity. Does then the danger of the lure of simplicity outweigh the benefits it promises?

The above question is of more than practical interest for at the heart of simplicities in Christian belief is a question about the simplicity of God. The concept of God as pure simplicity has been a dominant feature of the doctrine of God from early in the Christian tradition. As Karl Barth noted, theological talk of God has meant essentially 'only the simplicity of God and not the richness, at best the simplicity of riches, but at bottom only the simplicity'.[37] In Barth's discussion of the perfection of God he redevelops the concept of simplicity in relation to plenitude as the characteristic relations of the Lord of Glory:

> Consideration of the divine attributes can but move in circles around the one but infinitely rich being of God whose simplicity is abundance itself and whose abundance is simplicity itself.[38]

Consequently for Barth God's simplicity was not 'poverty': 'On the contrary, God is one in the fullness of His deity and constant in its living vigour'. In this way the doctrine of the Trinity, as co-inherence of plenitude and simplicity is the Christian doctrine of God.[39]

This discussion suggests that faithful response to the kind of God referred to above will generate communicative patterns that evidence an ongoing dialectic between highly concentrated statements of belief and extended free-flowing discourse. Something of this dynamic is present when the writer of the letter to the Ephesians asks the church to pray 'that

37. Barth, *Dogmatics*, volume 2 part 1, 329.
38. Barth, *Dogmatics*, volume 2 part 1, 406.
39. Barth, *Dogmatics*, volume 2 part 1, 326f; compare 445f.

whenever I open my mouth, words may be given me so that I will fearlessly make known the mystery of the gospel' (Ephesians 6:19). The point here is that the gospel of God's creating, redeeming and sanctifying love may not be simple but *it may be put simply*. However, as the writer suggests, finding the wisdom of simplicity in stating the gospel requires a community of intercessors seeking the fullness of the *communio* of the being of God. This discussion suggests that when the criterion of simplicity operates to thwart ongoing enlargement of faith, belief has ceased responding out of the fullness of God's presence. Within a trinitarian framework simplicity cannot be an end in itself, but rather a *recurring moment* in the communicative dynamic of Christian faith.

The Emergence of Hierarchy

When the dynamic of Christian faith is operating in a free and disciplined manner the search for foundations and the appeal of simplicity contribute to a grading in Christian belief. The grading of Christian belief represents a practical effort to prioritise for the purpose of communicating the more central matters of faith. However, to the extent that hierarchy emerges as a response to complexity *per se*—indicative of an attempt to assign relative values, select and differentiate in order to avoid what is trivial—more substantive issues are involved. From this perspective hierarchy in Christian belief is a way of responding to the richly differentiated form of God's presence. In this sense grading of belief is what happens as faith is *formed by* and comes to form *in relation to* the quite distinctive and particular presence of the God revealed in the Judaeo-Christian tradition. This dynamic in Christian belief has its roots in the long held conviction of the essential unity of Christianity. This conviction was generated out of the early Church's experience that 'God was in Christ reconciling the world to himself' (2 Corinthians 5:19). A consequence of this was the affirmation of one Lord, one faith and one baptism (Ephesians 4:5). This one faith, encapsulated in the early church's confession of the Lordship of Christ (for example, Acts 2:36: Romans 10:9; 1 Corinthians 12:3) required a fresh appropriation of an inherited Jewish monotheism.

The new and surprising relation to God through Jesus Christ in the power of the Spirit was the catalyst and guide for the reconstitution of the doctrine of God in the early centuries of Christianity. The intense conflicts that attended the development of the trinitarian pattern of Christian belief indicated just how difficult and necessary it was for the early Church to state what was of critical importance in order for belief to remain faithful to the presence of God in Jesus Christ. The 'simple' solution of Arius, for example, generated a mistaken hierarchy of belief in relation to the Father and the Son that undermined the fullness of Christian redemption.[40]

Underlying the emergence of hierarchy in Christian belief is the presupposition that God's presence and action is not marked by sameness but by rich variety evoking a response of praise as this presence is discerned and indwelt. In particular it has been the Church's experience of the crucified and risen Jesus present as life-giving Spirit that has provided the energy and direction for ecclesial existence. Discipleship formed and motivated by such a focus on God is one that evidences an emergent cruciform and transformative pattern (Philippians 3:10). This points to a reciprocal relationship between the inner dynamic of Christian discipleship and fundamental Christian beliefs.

Properly focused and graded belief ought to find embodiment in forms of discipleship that honour God's Christ-like presence and action in the world. The ongoing nature of this activity points to the fact that there is no finished hierarchy in belief as such. It is thus more correct to speak of an emergent and unfinished structure to Christian belief.[41]

The above discussion suggests that the content of belief emerges into full form through a dynamic process requiring active engagement of the human subject. Key elements in this participation were identified in terms of the search for foundations, the appeal to simplicity and the emergence of hierarchy. A distinctively trinitarian dynamic was discerned in this process of belief formation. It was a dynamic characterised by an essential interwovenness between what is believed, how it comes to form, and the one from whom believing arises. It is precisely because of the character of the God depicted in such belief, that it generates simultaneously both genuine and provisional statements of the trinitarian faith of the Church.

Trinitarian belief: the ecclesial dimension

In so far as the dynamics of belief are trinitarian they are necessarily *ecclesial*. What is being identified here is a fundamental axiom of trinitarian theology: communion generates communion. This arises from the fact

40. Thus in Athanasius' view the attribution of a creaturely status to the Son negated the possibility of full salvation, that is, deification and full immortality. For a contemporary discussion see Francis Young, *From Nicaea to Chalcedon* (London: SCM, 1983), chapter 2.

41. See for example Dietrich Ritschl, *The Logic of Theology* (London: SCM, 1986), 122.

that *faithful* response to the God identified in the economy of salvation as the God constituted eternally as a communion of persons ought ideally be a response that finds embodiment in a new communion of persons in society and the wider creation.[42]

The position adopted here suggests that it is inadequate to identify ecclesia as mere *context* for Christian belief. The church's own worship and mission is significantly determined by its attempt to express the truth of its life in the form of specific beliefs.[43] This suggests a reflexive relation between ecclesia and Christian faith. In ecclesia the truth of the bond with Christ in God receives determinate form: ecclesia is the place in which the truth of the gospel of God is embodied and maintained.

Guarding the truth in ecclesia

An important implication of the foregoing argument is that the church's attempt to state its belief becomes a critical means through which the deepest reality of its life is organised, expressed, argued about, and thus guarded. In this respect it is possible to identify the dynamic by which the ecclesial community's primary beliefs are developed and maintained. Important here are 'governing doctrines', those principles and rules which guide a community in the articulation of its fundamental beliefs.[44] An example of this in Anglicanism is Article VI of the Thirty-nine Articles of Religion 1563, 'Of the Sufficiency of the Holy Scripture for Salvation'. This article places limits on the scope of primary belief. Fundamental Christian beliefs are those that direct one to a life of salvation. There may be other truths and right courses of action which a community is not bound to teach. Not surprisingly there has been a long and controversial history of the attempt to identify appropriate rules for determination of what constitutes necessary Christian belief. For example, the eighteenth century Anglican, Daniel Waterland (1683–1740) identified fourteen such rules.

42. See Gunton, *The One, the Three and the Many*, 210–31, for a recent discussion of the question of Trinity and sociality.

43. For further discussion see Stephen Sykes, *The Identity of Christianity: Theologians on the Essence of Christianity from Schleiermacher to Barth* (London: SPCK, 1984), chapter 11.

44. 'Governing Beliefs' are discussed by William Christensen, *Doctrines of Religious Communities: A Philosophical Study* (New Haven: Yale University Press, 1987), 2, 11, 219–21, 230.

He considered most of them faulty because their application could not generate a trinitarian form to the Christian covenant.[45]

Governing doctrines guide the community of faith but such rules belong to a richer dynamic through which the right focus in Christian belief is maintained. The Reformation doctrine of justification by faith is an instructive example in this respect. For the Anglican Richard Hooker (1554–1600) the doctrine of justification by faith, whilst it did not belong to the 'few fundamental words' of the Apostolic Creed, was nevertheless the criterion by which the church's right holding to the foundation of faith could be determined. In Hooker's view the Roman doctrine of 'double justice' overthrew the foundation 'indirectly'. It was thus an 'unsound' church but not thereby heretical. Luther's focus on the justification of the sinner before God provided the hermeneutical clue for the re-appropriation of the dogmatic tradition concerning Christ and the Trinity. In this sense the doctrine of justification identified the dynamic by which the incarnate Word and the Spirit effected human transformation in relation to God. The doctrine was clearly more than a governing rule having substantive operational significance reconstituting persons in the church within the truth and righteousness of the triune God.[46]

The actual history of the Christian tradition indicates that the operational doctrines of Christianity—that is, those that identify the dynamic of revitalised faithful believing—can and do vary. In this respect the Lutheran theologian, Jaroslav Pelikan has suggested that the doctrine of the church has become 'the bearer of the *whole* of the Christian message for the twentieth century, as well as the *recapitulation of the entire doctrinal tradition* from the preceding centuries'.[47] Pelikan offers here a highly programmatic statement for the reordering and presentation of the gospel message. How might it be true? Within the Christian tradition it would be necessary to show how central Christian affirmations concerning the economy of God's salvation through Christ in the Spirit might be developed in relation to the rich reality of ecclesial life: its worship, confession and discipleship in the world. Significantly it is precisely the interweaving of a doctrine of God in the society of the church that can be discerned

45. See Waterland's 'Discourse of Fundamentals', in *The Works of the Rev. Daniel Waterland*, volume 5 (Oxford: Oxford University Press, 1843), 77–104.

46. For further see Jaroslav Pelikan, *The Christian Tradition: A History of the Development of Doctrine*, volume 4 (Chicago: University Press of Chicago, 1971–1988), 156ff.

47. Pelikan, *Christian Tradition*, 282, my italics.

in important theological efforts across the ecclesial spectrum of the late twentieth century.[48]

Recognition of the ecclesial nature of Christian belief has provided conditions conducive to a renewal of trinitarian theology and its correlatives—that is, a Christology of the humanity of Christ and a doctrine of the Spirit as life-giving presence. This renewal in the form and content of Christian belief is directly related to the contemporary search for a form of godly discipleship that is patterned after the humanity of Christ and enlivened by the Holy Spirit.[49] Ecclesia's truth concerns are best guarded, it seems, as they receive embodiment at the level of concrete practice of faith.

Christian belief as an ecclesial deed

The fact that Christians seek to guard the truth of the gospel and in doing so state what they believe is evidence of the rather obvious, but not to be overlooked fact, that the Christian community has an active and important part to play in the formation of its beliefs. In this activity the bond in Christ formative of the community now appears as a product of the community of faith. This process represents an externalising of ecclesia's one-in-Christ bond. Properly conceived, this is an energy-saving strategy which contributes to the strength of the relation to God through more efficient and higher quality communication of information in the institutional life of the church. In this way the ecclesial community's memory of the narrative of creation, salvation and final consummation of the world can endure in the form of corporate public expression. This gives a particular enduring significance to the ancient Apostolic and Nicene creeds, especially in the context of Christian worship. Public belief of this kind strengthens the self understanding of the Christian community in its calling to live a life of reconciliation and compassion patterned after God's pilgrimage of reconciliation and perfecting of creation in Jesus and the Spirit. The emergence of new forms of community in the unlikeliest places

48. See for example John Zizioulas, *Being as Communion: Studies in Personhood and the Church* (London: Darton, Longman & Todd, 1985). For a more practical ecclesial perspective see the 1994 report by the Doctrine Commission of the Uniting Church in Australia (published by the General Assembly): 'Ordination and Ministry in the Uniting Church in Australia'. Here a doctrine of ministry is developed within a trinitarian framework.

49. See for example, Colin Gunton's discussion of the theology of Edward Irving in *The Actuality of Atonement: A Study of Metaphor, Rationality and the Christian Tradition* (Edinburgh: T&T Clark, 1988), 128–37.

thus bears witness to the character of the God worshipped in the Christian community and identified in the primary public beliefs of ecclesia.

The ongoing dynamic of Christian belief

The desire for a global form of public faith has persisted in Christianity. It is evidently a deed worth pursuing, notwithstanding the conflicts and challenges that attend it. The persistence is expressive of a desire to identify communal faith that has authority as normative Christian belief. The irony of course is that this ideal actually provokes as well as resolves conflict. In this sense it might make more sense to speak of an unfinished consensus in what constitutes Christian belief. The provisional status of such belief is not simply a negative one, the result of the inability of frail human beings to agree together. Rather, the question of the unfinished nature of Christian belief is a 'given' of the mystery of the gospel which is, by its very character, both resistant to full thematisation and generative of a rich variety of authentic Christian responses. This points to the fact that there is an abundance of play in the matrix of ecclesial belief that is constrained by the love of Christ and embodied in myriad contexts of human life. Christian belief, in so far as it follows the presence of God in ecclesiality, remains a deed in process.

This conclusion derives its logic both from the nature of the gospel of God and the nature of ecclesial life. If the institution of ecclesia is to endure as an organiser of expanding complexity in order to nourish a godly form of human life, the deeds of the Christian community will require constant reconstitution in order to assimilate the new and changing environment in which discipleship occurs. Provisionality of belief is thus a sign of openness to the future and the possibilities this offers for novel and fresh forms of Christian life in the world.

The above discussion suggests that Christian belief cannot be simply repeated. To merely repeat the deed entails both a rejection of its contingent status and a dangerous sacralising of a past particular statement of faith. Pure repetition is thus a sign of infidelity rather than faithfulness to the gospel. An ongoing faithfulness in Christian belief will require a fresh discernment of the presence of the triune God in newly emergent contexts. Within a trinitarian dynamic what is required is a creative repetition in belief in which *freshness through sameness* is the ideal sought. Such communication corresponds to the creativity of God's threefold repetition in the economy of salvation.

Clearly continuity and identity in the faith cannot be construed simply, either in terms of over-formalised statements of belief or a radically relativised faith unassimilated to the tradition. From an ecclesial point of view such manoeuvres are indicative of a falsely stabilised institution, either through neglect of contemporaneity or rejection of its own history. In the former, stability is over-reached, in the latter it is underachieved. Both strategies are expressive of the lure of simplicity in a complex world. At a deeper level such developments are the result of a loss of the trinitarian dynamic of belief. Belief that is formed from and informed by God's Christ-like work through the life-giving Spirit operates quite differently. It is a Spirit in-formed belief that finds its delight dwelling in and probing further the 'depth of brightness and precision of wisdom'[50] of the God whose light has been made to shine in the face of Jesus Christ to give the light of the knowledge of the glory of God.

50. The phrase can be found in Hardy and Ford, *Jubilate*, 55.

Chapter Four
A Future for Systemic Theology[1]

A Future From the Centre

This essay grew out my earlier doctoral studies on the influence of the seventeenth century scholar John Locke. Locke's scientific empirical method in building up human understanding of the world was transferred into biblical and theological studies. He is at the headwaters of modern biblical criticism. Under the influence of Locke theology imploded into biblical commentary of a particular micro exegetical kind. Recovering the centre of theology in Scripture without the shackles of Lockean empiricism is a major challenge for Christian theology. This essay tries to uncover why there is a problem and how theology might move beyond the legacy of Locke.

Staying on task: the theologian's problem

In the 1992 Bampton Lectures Colin Gunton drew attention to the powerful influence in the Christian tradition of two ancient philosophies; the Parmenidean and the Heraclitean.[2] Whereas the former stressed the underlying unity and stability of the world, the latter gave prominence to plurality, particulars and state of flux of the world. The tradition of Parmenides provided the backdrop for the first millennium and a half of the Christian tradition and appeared to offer support to a Christian theism that gave order and meaning to the world. However, the Enlightenment framework of modern Christianity has been heavily influenced by the alternative tradition of Heraclitus, a tradition more congenial to the Enlightenment emphasis upon particulars (for example, the autonomous

1. Originally published as 'Unable to see the Wood for the Trees: John Locke and the Fate of Systematic Theology', in *The Task of Theology: Doctrines and Dogmas*, edited by Victor Pfitzner and Hilary Regan (Adelaide: ATF, 1998; Edinburgh: T&T Clark 1999).
2. Colin Gunton, *The One the Three and the Many: God, Creation and the Culture of Modernity* (Cambridge: Cambridge University Press, 1993), 11–40.

individual) and the dynamics of change in human life and society. The reasons for the emergence of the Heraclitean tradition and the displacement of the hitherto dominant Parmenidean tradition are complex and beyond the scope of this present essay. Yet the shift has had a profound influence on the course of modern Christianity and the theological enterprise that it spawns. In particular, given the influence of the Parmenidean tradition in Christianity, the complex transition from one undergirding philosophy to another was bound to exert pressure on Christian theism which eventually led to what Gunton describes as the 'displacement of God'. The implication seemed to be that the Hericlitean tradition was antithetical to Christian theism and its inherited dogmas. This conclusion seems to be given greater credence in the light of the rise of modern atheism within the same period of European history.

However, the story of this displacement (perhaps 'diffusion' of God is equally appropriate) is complex; it is a story of significant losses and some important gains that are still being evaluated.[3] In this context, to take the world of the late twentieth century seriously requires a sustained theological engagement with the loss or dissolution of God in the modern consciousness of the West. A variety of strategies—for example renewal, deconstruction and revisioning—are currently deployed to meet this challenge.[4] Yet there is a fundamental difficulty for any systematic theology, regardless of the particular strategy employed. It is a difficulty whose roots can be traced, in part, to the period of transition from a Parmenidean to a Heraclitean ontology. This transition can be observed in the late medieval nominalist philosophy of William of Ockham though it becomes more firmly established as an undergirding philosophy of the late seventeenth-century European Enlightenment. The difficulty is not only apparent in the displacement of God but also, as I argue in this essay, in the form of discourse through which theological work has been done. Specifically, in the transition from one philosophical tradition to another, fundamental suspicions have arisen about the viability of the systematic enterprise *per se*.

The task of theology has always included two elements or critical moments: a critical analytic, de-constructivist moment and a complementary

3. See for example, the assessment by David Ford, 'Postmodernism and Postscript', in *The Modern Theologians: An Introduction to Christian Theology in the Twentieth Century*, edited by David Ford (Oxford: Basil Blackwell, 1989), volume 2.
4. See Peter Hodgson, *Winds of Change: A Constructive Christian Theology* (Louisville: Westminister John Knox Press, 1994), 55.

synthetic, constructivist moment. The difficulty facing the contemporary systematic theologian is, in terms of modern educational teaching method, one of staying on task. The reason is that the synthetic, constructivist moment in theology is now under suspicion, a fact recognised in the early fifties by Paul Tillich.[5] The suspicion arises in part from the layers of meaning present in the notion of 'systematic', a word that came into theology with the emergence of the 'system' concept in the late seventeenth century.[6] At one level the word simply indicates an intention to conduct a method of inquiry in an orderly and organised fashion. Yet to do this with even minimal success requires some overall sense of the matter under investigation. This involves, as David Kelsey indicated some years ago, an imaginative act (a 'theological discrimen') on the part of the theologian in which a 'judgement must be made about how to characterise the *mode* in which God is present among the faithful'.[7] Such a *discrimen* is operating, for example, in the long discussion of the essence of Christianity. This preliminary grasp of the whole, gleaned perhaps through a constellation of constitutive images,[8] operates implicitly or explicitly in every theologian's work. The systematic theologian attempts to make explicit what might otherwise remain implicit and in doing so he or she begins to seek conceptual coherence and meaning in order 'to test the truth of statements by accounting for their connection with one another as well as with all other statements that can be of importance for their validity'.[9]

However, at some stage in this activity the systematic theologian becomes, *to a certain extent*, a theological systems builder proceeding with *some sense* of the whole, albeit from a 'fragmentary vision of existence'.[10] The danger is that this activity can lead to premature theological closures and rigid theological systems in conflict with each other and unable to undergo internal transformation. Thus it is not surprising that 'systematic' theology is quickly associated with a universalist metaphysic that carries in its bowels all the dangerous totalitarian tendencies of a past Christianity which prized uniformity and order above respect for local contexts, free play, experimentation and risk. As a result the self-understanding of the theologian as a 'systematic theologian' appears somewhat arrogant, mis-

5. Paul Tillich, *Systematic Theology*, volume 1 (London: Nisbet & Co, 1953), 63.
6. Nicholas Rescher, *Cognitive Systematisation* (Oxford: Basil Blackwell, 1979), 7.
7. David Kelsey, *The Uses of Scripture in Recent Theology* (London: SCM, 1975), 160.
8. Edward Farley, *Ecclesial Man* (Philadelphia: Fortress Press, 1975), 120.
9. Gerhard Ebeling, *The Study of Theology* (London: Collins, 1979), 126.
10. Tillich, *Systematic Theology*, volume 1, 65. Compare Hodgson, *Winds of Change*, 39.

placed and inappropriate in today's world where we are more aware of the fragmentary nature of things rather than any underlying organic unity.

For this reason Peter Hodgson prefers 'constructive' to 'systematic'; the former conveying less of a neatly organised structured arrangement and more of a sense of a heap-like configuration with a certain untidiness and ambiguity.[11] More commonly the systematic urge is denied or remains hidden in new forms of self-depiction, for example, 'contextual theologian'. Yet even here system building continues for, as Tillich pointed out, in each fragment (or particular) a system is implied; 'a system being an explicit fragment'.[12] However, in our current theological climate it is exceedingly difficult for the theologian to 'stay on task'. The effort encounters a major obstacle in so far as the nature of the theological task no longer seems to allow or include a genuine synthetic, constructivist moment that intends a provisional intimation of the *whole*.[13] As one theologian has recently stated, systematic theology appears to be 'dying as a result of the postmodern epistemic crisis'.[14]

This problem that assails theology is often expressed in terms of the difficulty the discipline has of finding and formulating its own subject matter. In the search for scholarly status the discipline can easily transpose itself into other areas of inquiry such as philosophy, history of thought,

---

11. Hodgson, *Winds of Change*, 39.
12. Tillich, *Systematic Theology*, volume 1, 65.
13. The theological problem here corresponds to some degree with the contemporary discussion in neuro-psychology in terms of left brain/right brain splits. Our culture, it seems, is excessively left brain in its deconstructivist, analytical tendency. What is required is a much healthier integration of left brain/right brain activity. From this perspective an alternative title for this essay could have been, 'The Detail of the Whole: Right Brain Theology in a Left Brain World'. The problem is masked somewhat in contemporary theology by references to works of 'systematic theology'. Yet as Peter Hodgson, notes, there is a 'growing popularity of confessional or thematic systematic theologies from a wide variety of cultural contexts and ecclesial traditions' (*Winds of Change*, endnote 11, 346f). However, he states that 'there is something disappointing about it to the extent that it reflects the loss of an ecumenical or holistic vision and of an effort to keep the boundary between cultural-linguistic systems open'. The success of Hodgson's own effort aside, his point is a good one. Systematic theology is surely rooted in and arises out of particular contexts, but from precisely that location it strains, under pressure of its own subject matter, towards that wider more encompassing vision of the whole, yet without pretending to have grasped it fully. This deeper integrative move involves a strong right brain orientation.
14. Ellen Charry, 'Reviving Theology in a Time of Change', in Miroslav Volf et al, *The Future of Theology: Essays in Honor of Jürgen Moltmann* (Grand Rapids, MI: Eerdmanns, 1996), 118.

social science and linguistics.[15] The wood of the Christian tradition has been deconstructed; all that seems left are the trees, and individual trees are all that matter for knowledge and meaning. The connections between the trees—the 'stands' and the larger wood—is not a project that sits comfortably on the agenda of modern theology. Johann Baptist Metz's notion of the theologian as the 'last remaining universalist' seems fanciful to say the least.[16]

This essay explores some of the reasons for this state of affairs in modern theology. However, it does this by means of a brief archaeological dig into the Christian tradition at a critical period in the transition from the Parmenidean to Heraclitean conception of the world. The focus for the paper is the philosophical and religious writings of the late seventeenth English philosopher, John Locke (1632–1704). Locke was no systematic theologian. However, he was a seminal philosopher and architect of the eighteenth-century Enlightenment laying down the foundations for future generations of thinkers in Europe. He was also a devout Christian who had a deep interest in matters religious and theological, a fact that has been increasingly recognised in critical work on Locke.[17] His restatement of the Christian faith in *On The Reasonableness of Christianity*, 'provided for many the locus classicus of the rationalistic reductionism of the eighteenth century'.[18] Locke's philosophy and theology were interwoven; his *magnum opus, An Essay Concerning Human Understanding* of 1689[19] not only underpinned his later theological work, it was written with a deep religious interest in mind, namely, to create a legitimate space for religious faith within the newly emerging society of eighteenth-century Europe.[20]

15. Daniel Hardy, 'The English Tradition of Interpretation and the Reception of Schleiermacher and Barth in England', in *Barth and Schleiermacher: Beyond the Impasse?* edited by J Duke and R Streetman (Philadelphia: Fortress Press, 1988), 159. Compare Edward Farley, *Theologia: The Fragmentation and Unity of Theological Education* (Philadelphia: Fortress Press, 1983), 129.
16. Johann Baptist Metz, 'The Last Universalists', in Volf et al, *The Future of Theology*.
17. See M Johnson, *Locke on Freedom* (Austin, TX: Best Printing Co, 1977); D Wallace, 'Socinianism, Justification By Faith, and the Sources of John Locke's "The Reasonableness of Christianity"', in *Journal of the History of Ideas* 45 (1984): 49–66.
18. Stephen Sykes, *The Identity of Christianity* (London: SPCK, 1984), 194.
19. For this essay see John Locke, *An Essay Concerning Human Understanding*, edited by Peter Nidditch (Oxford: Clarendon Press, 1975); hereafter references to the *Essay* are in the body of the text and given by book, chapter, paragraph.
20. John Yolton, *John Locke and the Way of Ideas* (London: Oxford University Press, 1956), 117.

The purpose of the present essay is to examine in some detail how Locke's particular empiricist and rationalist philosophy provided an early warning signal of the future fate of systematic theology. What I hope to show is that the disintegration of the systematic enterprise in theology is deep-rooted, that the 'epistemic crisis' of modern theology is not a peculiarly 'postmodern' phenomenon, and finally that some of the resources for a recovery or revival of systematics and the construction of something new in theology for a new time are hinted at in Locke's own program. Of course, much has happened since Locke wrote, and the dangers and challenges to theology are in many ways much greater than Locke could ever have envisaged. However, this essay is written on the premise that there is value in returning to one source of some of theology's ills to gain a clearer and more confident diagnosis of the problems and possibilities that attend the contemporary theological task. In the essay I briefly outline Locke's epistemology, show how this influenced his articulation of the Christian faith and conception of the theological task, and conclude by drawing out some of the implications of this case study for the task of theology today.

Groundwork for theology: Locke's epistemological reductionism

The context for Locke's philosophical and religious thought was shaped in part by the impact of seventeenth century experimental science, with its focus on observation, measurement, weighing of evidence, and human judgements. Experimentation and discovery went hand in hand with the quest for certain and sure foundations for knowledge. At the centre of this enterprise was the human agent as the one who, in exercising reliable human judgments, was inevitably thrust into the position of receiver, processor and former of truth. This context was, not surprisingly, ripe for the development of the science of epistemology. Locke's response to this new context constituted a major effort to re-found science, morality and religion in such a way as to take account positively of these developments whilst attempting to remain faithful to his Christian inheritance. His religious and theological work belonged to the larger philosophical framework developed in his *Essay Concerning Human Understanding*. Here Locke approached the problem of knowledge from the point of view of the physiology of the human understanding and his epistemology was developed in terms of a quasi-mechanistic account of human knowing.

The mechanism of knowing presupposed for Locke an objective reality, a world external to human beings, which was available to be known—

what he called that 'vast Ocean of Being' (1.1.7). Locke's foundational—if somewhat crude and undifferentiated—realism formed the basis of his empiricist philosophy. The matter was focused in Locke's concept of 'experience' as the foundation, in the sense of the 'original', of all knowledge (2.1.1–25). This inclusive category to denote the source of all knowledge was further specified by Locke to include a double aspect; *sensation* in relation to 'external objects'—'the source of most of the Ideas we have'—and *reflection*, being concerned with the internal operations of the mind. In the particularity of experience, ideas which constituted the 'materials' of all knowledge become present to the mind.

In this 'historical plain method' (1.1.2) knowledge thus began with the mind's passive reception of the 'simple ideas' given in experience. The mind could no more refuse to receive what was imprinted, nor 'blot-out' and create new 'impressions', 'than a mirror can refuse, alter or obliterate the Images or Ideas, which the Objects set before it, do therein produce' (2.1.25). This may have been a distorted or overly restricted notion of experience but, as one commentator has noted, it 'emerges from the legitimate epistemological interest in the given, the reality which is unfalsified by human influence'.[21] Locke's view of the beginning of all knowledge supposed that truth and goodness were not given neat and formed in the mind, as taught in the theory of innate ideas (1.2.1–28), but were located in nature and history in their particularity and accessed in and through experience. Experience provided the location for the generation of the mind's simple ideas; the constructive mind was responsible for the increase in complexity of the initial input (2.12.1–8). In this complex process a vast store of ideas were constructed by the mind, in which high-level abstractions could be traced back to simple ideas given in experience. In this way, for example, the complex ideas of power, freedom, beauty, infinity, eternity, and even the idea of 'a god' could, by a process of induction, be shown to be derived from simple ideas given in experience (2.23.33).

However, ideas were not knowledge itself, but rather its 'Instruments, or Materials'. The movement from ideas to knowledge constituted the final phase of Locke mechanism of knowing. It involved assigning value to the field of ideas. Here it was a question of the kind of activity involved in knowing that determined the relative status to be accorded to ideas and hence their claim to the status of knowledge. In this respect Locke spoke of three ways of perception—intuitive, demonstrative and sensi-

21. L Kruger, 'The Concept of Experience in John Locke', in *John Locke Symposium Wolfenbuttel 1979*, edited by R Brandt (Berlin & New York: Walter de Gruyter, 1981), 5.

tive (4.2.1–15). Each afforded a different degree of knowledge. Intuitive knowledge was irresistible for 'like the bright sunshine, [it] forces itself immediately to be perceived' (4.2.1). The discursive operations of reason did not intrude. Such knowledge was the basis for 'all the Certainty and Evidence of all our Knowledge'. Demonstrative knowledge involved both intuition and discursive reasoning, the latter contributing to the lack of 'lustre and full assurance' in this knowledge (2.2.6).

The results of Locke's analysis of ideas and ways of knowing were not particularly encouraging (4.3.22–31). In the intellectual world knowledge with highest certainty was located in mathematics which attained the ideal that other disciplines aspired to without chance of success. In the material world human knowledge extended as far as an intuitive knowledge of one's own existence, a demonstrative knowledge of God's existence and a sensitive knowledge of the external world which faded into the region of probabilities. This was simply a 'fact of life'. 'For the state we are at present in, not being that of Vision, we must, in many things, content ourselves with Faith and probability' (4.3.6).

Locke painted a picture of a world of probabilities in which the human task was to make high quality judgments as close to certainty as possible. The movement from knowledge through to judgment involved a successive series of reflections upon the datum of experience. Inevitably in this process of stimulus-response the focus was increasingly trained on the activity of reflection, and the initial stimulus tended to recede into the background. In fact the process entailed a progressive disengagement of the knowing subject from the particularities of experience, a consequent greater possibility for human error and therefore a move from the realm of certainty into the region of probability. The restrictions Locke placed upon the origin, process and scope of knowledge were mirrored in his treatment of the Christian faith and had significant consequences for his conception of the task of theology.

The reasonableness of Christian faith

Locke's argument for the reasonableness of Christianity flowed directly out of his *Essay* and to this extent his treatment of faith was already subject to a methodological constraint, since for him it was a question of showing that faith was compatible with reason and so could not harm it. As one commentator has remarked, 'Reason is assumed, and room must be made for faith'.[22] For Locke reason operated as the faculty through which a pure form of faith was made possible. Purity was objectively grounded in God and what had been revealed. But for human beings to be fully responsible, their assents had to be pure, unmixed with notions contrary to their God-given faculties. In this sense, reason appeared as the arbiter for assents to claims 'above reason'. Locke's empiricism meant that faith could not provide *knowledge*, his rationalist temper controlled those assents in which faith was *justified*.

What then constituted the material content of this rational Christianity? Locke's proposals were developed in 1695 in his now famous, *The Reasonableness of Christianity*.[23] Given the formal structure of faith outlined in the *Essay*, it was incumbent upon Locke to depict a 'safe' content for faith. In the interests of epistemological consistency, he had to ensure that what was assented to in faith did not 'spill over' into matters 'contrary to reason'. That which was 'above reason' had to remain 'reasonable'. This was the logic of the epistemology of the *Essay*, particularly as it had been developed in Book Four of that work.

For Locke, the Anglican Protestant of Latitudinarian sympathies, the Scriptures represented the safe repository of faith. As such he referred to them as,

> A collection of writings, designed by God, for the instruction of the illiterate bulk of mankind, in the way of salvation; and therefore, generally, and in necessary points, to be understood in the plain direct meaning of the words and phrases: such as they may be supposed to have had in the mouths of the speakers, who used them according to the language of that time and country wherein they lived; without such learned, artificial, and forced senses of them, as are sought out, and put upon them, in most of the systems of divinity, according to the notions that each one has been bred up in.[24]

This method was designed to undercut the accretions to Christianity associated with the development of 'particular creeds and systems'. Safety

22. D Snyder, 'Faith and Reason in Locke's Essay', in *Journal of the History of Ideas* 45 (1986): 197–213.

23. John Locke, *The Reasonableness of Christianity*, in *The Works of John Locke*, tenth edition (London: Churchill & Manship, 1801), volume 7.

24. Locke, *Reasonableness*, 5.

and purity were to be achieved by a return to the 'facts' as they originally offered themselves, that is, a return to the 'plain direct meaning' of the Scriptures. The truth of faith for the individual began as the scriptural revelation was received in its simplicity: unadorned, unforced and divested of any artificiality. It was a method entirely in accord with the 'Historical, plain Method' of the *Essay*. This was the method to uncover what in fact had been revealed, that Jesus was the Messiah.[25] This belief presupposed what had been required before the revelation of the gospel, that is, 'belief of one invisible, eternal, omnipotent God, maker of heaven and earth, etc'.[26] Yet belief that Jesus was the Messiah was a requirement consequent upon the fall of Adam from original righteousness. In the fall humankind 'lost bliss and immortality'. By the coming of the Messiah the human race was redeemed from its lost state and restored to life eternal. In so far as Jesus' resurrection was 'a mark and undoubted evidence of his being the Messiah', it was 'commonly required to be believed as a necessary article, and sometimes solely insisted on' and was 'necessary now to be believed by those who would receive him as the Messiah'.[27] Furthermore, the Christian covenant in which redemption was won included not only faith but repentance and good works. 'It is not enough to believe him to be the Messiah unless we also obey his laws, and take him to be our king to reign over us'.[28]

In Locke's depiction of the content of Christianity, what was revealed was 'safe' because it was intelligible. At a general level, the intelligibility of 'attested revelation' was guaranteed by God. This supposed that God gave to humankind what could be understood in a more or less self-explanatory form. Scripture encouraged this view when it was treated according to the historical, plain method, because this method yielded a certain 'matter of factness'. What was revealed could, it seemed, be more or less 'read-off' from the narrative of Scripture. In Locke's account of Christianity what was fundamental was located in the particularities of the historical process and was focused in the life of a particular human being authenticated by God as the Messiah through certain external signs. The plain direct meaning of these facts were presented in the Scripture text.

25. Locke, *Reasonableness*, 101.
26. Locke, *Reasonableness*, 16f.
27. Locke, *Reasonableness*, 20.
28. Locke, *Reasonableness*, 120.

Theological method: explication or self-evident explanation

Locke's view of Christianity led him into a lengthy dispute with the Calvinist Anglican, John Edwards (1637–1716).[29] The problem concerned the extent to which Locke's position represented a legitimate manoeuvre within Christianity and the extent to which it constituted a dissolution of the Christian tradition. In Locke's view, the primary belief necessary for salvation was plainly declared. Importantly, no 'explication' of this article was necessary: 'I think it may be doubted, whether any articles, which need men's explications, can be so clearly and certainly understood, as one which is made so very plain by the Scripture itself, as not to need any explication at all. Such is this, that Jesus is the Messiah'.[30] By contrast Edwards' articles required explication, were capable of competing interpretations and disputation, and some of them 'contain mysteries'. This ran counter to Locke's position for it supposed that 'it is necessary for many men to believe what is not intelligible to them . . . '[31]

In Locke's view a faith accessible to all had to possess a certain self-evident quality: 'As men (sic), we have God for our King, and are under the law of reason, as Christians, we have Jesus the Messiah for our King, and are under the law revealed by him in the gospel'.[32] This was the Christian faith in a nutshell. However, beyond this necessary belief everyone was orthodox in their own eyes and had their own distinct catalogue of fundamentals: 'nobody can fix it for him; no body can collect or prescribe it to another'.[33] Two implications followed. First, the attempt by Edwards to enumerate a true and complete catalogue of fundamentals was a purely arbitrary activity and doomed to failure. Such systems or creeds, the 'inventions of men', resulted in a 'narrowing' of Christianity and contributed to a fragmented and conflictual society. Second, each person had to take personal responsibility for what he or she believed. The alternative was to allow one's faith to be impoverished and imprisoned in ignorance by the 'creed-makers' and systematisers of religion. This could not be countenanced, 'for I assure you no-body can rob you of your God, but by your own consent, nor spoil you of any of the articles of your faith'.[34]

29. See *A Vindication of the Reasonableness of Christianity. From Mr Edwards' Reflections* (1695) and *A Second Vindication* (1697) in Locke, *Works*, volume 7.
30. Locke, *Reasonableness*, 178.
31. Locke, *Reasonableness*, 237f.
32. Locke, *Reasonableness*, 229.
33. Locke, *Reasonableness*, 233.
34. Locke, *Reasonableness*, 305.

Locke, following William Chillingworth (1602–44) of *Religion of Protestants a Safe way to Salvation* (1638) fame, advocated a diligent search for fundamentals in that place 'where God has placed them, in the holy scripture, and take them as he has framed and fashioned them there'.[35] In the Scripture the fundamental faith was always to be found 'safe and sound'. Thus a rightly formed belief entailed a progress from the foundation into the 'superstructure' of faith, from fundamentals into the things of 'perfection'.

At one level the Locke-Edwards controversy continued a long running debate in seventeenth century Anglicanism between conservative Calvinist/Puritan and Arminian/Latitudinarian elements. That Jesus was the Messiah was the plain fact of the gospel; it was supported by evidences and grounded in trustworthy testimony. This was rational Christianity. It was intelligible, it did not involve belief in mysteries, and it did not require explication to uncover meaning which was already transparent and self-evident. Locke's paring down of the faith had drawn into theological form the epistemology developed in the *Essay*. However, Locke's proposals had important implications for the status of doctrine *per se*, its nature, location and mode of communication.

From system to text: the impact of Locke's empiricism

These implications became explicit in Locke's argument with a formidable exponent of the dogmatic tradition, the Bishop of Worcester, Edward Stillingfleet (1635–99).[36] The latter considered that Locke's reductionism in the faith would encourage a rising religious scepticism and provide fuel for unitarian and anti-trinitarian interests, if not atheism. Stillingfleet bypassed *The Reasonableness of Christianity* and located the roots of Locke's theological reductionism in the *Essay* itself. The proposals in the *Essay* were highly threatening to the more traditional orthodoxy of Stillingfleet. Locke's notion of 'substance' as a 'substratum', the idea of which was but obscure and confused, was impossible for Stillingfleet to countenance.[37] It completely undermined a traditional rationale for the Trinity which, from Stillingfleet's point of view, required clear and distinct ideas of substance.

35. Locke, *Reasonableness*, 305.

36. See *A letter to the Rt Rev'd Edward Lord Bishop of Worcester* (1696), *Mr Locke's Reply to the Bishop's* Reply (1696), *Mr Locke's Reply to the Bishop of Worcester's Answer to his Second Letter* (1698), *in Works*, volume 4.

37. Locke, *A Letter and Reply*, 230.

Turning the tables on his adversary Locke suggested that the trinitarian notion of three persons in one was not appropriately explained by an appeal to 'substance', for 'where there are three persons, there must be three distinct, complete intelligent substances; and so there cannot be three persons in the same individual essence'.[38] For his part Locke refused to 'own the doctrine of the Trinity, as it hath been received in the christian church'.[39] The doctrine had been the subject of such dispute throughout church history that Locke confessed ignorance of how the doctrine had in fact been received. Stillingfleet's exposition was as fallible as another's. Locke could own the doctrine with an implicit faith but no further. Stillingfleet's was a short way to orthodoxy but Locke 'thought it enough to own it as delivered in the scriptures'.[40] On the Trinity and Incarnation, Locke pointed to the absence from Scripture of the propositions 'there are three persons in one nature, or, there are two natures and one person'.[41] The person who argued for Scripture containing such propositions was guilty of making 'a new scripture in words and propositions, that the Holy Ghost dictated not'.[42]

Locke did not wish to question the truth of the above propositions, at least directly, or deny that they could be 'drawn from Scripture', but he did want to assert that such propositions were not in Scripture explicitly. The 'safe' way was to 'keep close' to the words of Scripture. From this position he could affirm belief in the Trinity and Incarnation, that is, in so far as they were delivered in Scripture. It was an approach that had affinities with Socinian and Deistic interpretations of the ancient dogmas. However, at heart the doctrine of the Trinity could never be fundamental for Christianity for Locke because for him the doctrine, at least in its traditional ecclesiastical form, was simply irrelevant within the schema of Christian belief. The Trinity was a doctrine inessential for saving faith not because it might not be true but because it was evidence of just one's own judgment as to the truth of things. Such judgments might or might not 'reach back' to the truth of divine reality.

What was peculiarly modern in Locke's handling of the dogmatic tradition was not so much his minimalist statement of faith, but rather his modification of the nature of doctrine itself. When he referred to fun-

38. Locke, *A Letter and Reply*, 338.
39. Locke, *Reasonableness*, 197.
40. Locke, *Reasonableness*, 197.
41. Locke, *Reasonableness*, 343.
42. Locke, *Reasonableness*, 348

damental doctrines or articles of faith Locke, it seemed, was primarily focused on the Scripture text which provided the raw materials in which fundamental faith could be discerned. The truth given for faith was present primarily in a dispersed form; in textual particularity.

From one point of view Scripture already evidenced the reflection of human minds upon 'original' revelation. However, such 'attested revelation' also offered itself for continued reflection. From this point of view it could be likened to a densely textured repository of ideas awaiting sorting and gathering by the reflective activity of the human mind. This in fact was exactly what happened as the Scripture 'facts' were ordered, synthesised and complexified. Strictly speaking, this constituted a key stage in the formation of doctrinal statements. It was from this stage that possible candidates for articles of faith arose. The process came to its term in the human judgment in which judgements were made as to the relative truth value of ideas. For Locke this involved the minimalist claim that Jesus the Messiah was the sufficient confession to make one a Christian. This was a highly inclusivist statement of faith designed to undercut the strong oppositions generated among competing systems of Christian doctrine. It was clear from *The Reasonableness of Christianity* that Locke had precisely this kind of system rivalry in mind. In the *Essay* Locke had already developed a method to deal with the problem of system rivalry. Thus when he came to the question of the content of faith (that is, what was revealed), Locke was engaged in a movement backwards through the dynamics of religious knowing to the point of origins. Locke's method of religious purification entailed a return to the simplicities of the source. Systems were not purged but simply rendered irrelevant. In this move the complexities that attended the process of doctrinal formation were ignored. This development signaled a retreat from what has been referred to in contemporary theology as 'doctrinalisation'[43] back to that primordial stage in which high probability judgments were possible, that is, back to the 'given' of scriptural revelation.

This procedure implied a movement towards reality in its most dispersed and unsynthesised form, in the relatively simple ideas given in revelation. Complexities in ideas at this level could be tolerated only to the extent that they were free from the intrusion of the reflective human mind. For, as already observed in the discussion of the epistemology of the *Essay*, the complexifying of ideas, their gathering, ordering and the processes of

43. Farley, *Ecclesial Man*, 120ff.

abstracting and generalising that necessarily accompanied such activity, was the result of the power of the mind. Precisely because these operations involved the progressive intrusion of the human mind into the processing of truth, the possibilities for error were greatly increased. Such constructive activity represented 'the *artificial* Draughts of the Mind' (*Essay* 2.24.3; my italics). Consequently, the product of such operations had to receive great scrutiny when it came to the matter of assigning relative worth to these idea-complexes. In general, greater intrusion of human activity indicated lower degrees of probability.

Locke, it seemed, conceived of doctrines merely as high-level abstractions, the result of the complexifying of ideas produced by the constructive mind. From this perspective it was inevitable that the drive to formulation of statements of faith, and the conflicts this produced, would seem unnecessary and puzzling developments, somewhat removed from the truth of revelation in the Scriptures. Doctrine was clearly for Locke an unsafe territory upon which to trespass. The rivalry between different theological systems of the seventeenth century—for example, Calvinist, Lutheran Catholic—had left its heritage in blood. Doctrinal formulation simply represented speculative human judgments. For Locke, the uncertainties that attended human judgments and human proneness to error, rendered the traditional doctrinal form unsafe. He clearly had no conception that doctrine could *add* something to what had been revealed in the propositions of Scripture.

On this view, the doctrine of the Trinity did not require Stillingfleet's particular philosophical categories. Indeed, the doctrine appeared irrelevant for Christianity in any significant sense. By contrast, Locke's fundamental article—that Jesus was the Messiah—was first and foremost simply a 'plain fact', a given of revelation. This is what the facts of Scripture meant; all the evidence pointed to this conclusion, and this was consonant with a covenant of faith accessible to all. Locke's proposal for saving faith was clearly not intended as an abstraction, the speculative product of a theologian or a tradition. The proposition 'Jesus is the Messiah' was intended to evoke a high quality judgment involving trust in God. However, from the point of view of doctrine *per se*, the statement, Jesus is the Messiah, functions more like a 'constitutive image', providing raw material in the process of doctrinal formulation.[44]

44. Farley, *Ecclesial Man*, 118.

The particular way in which Locke effected the displacement of Christian doctrine into the region of human judgement was thus responsible for what was probably the most damaging blow to the dogmatic tradition in Christianity that was theologically possible, that is, it was rendered irrelevant. Locke's empiricist epistemology, his reticence about synthesis and his fine-tuned sensitivities concerning the human capacity for error, provided the fertile context in which a rationale for the formulation of content rich general statements of faith simply disappeared. Christianity's doctrinal structure could not but represent an unnecessary distortion of the covenant of faith. In this sense Locke becomes a pivotal figure in the eclipse of the dogmatic impulse and the development of modern biblical studies in the English tradition.[45] In this vein Hans Frei describes Locke as a 'sort of single pathfinder for hermeneutical theory of the Bible'.[46]

The doctrinal tradition could only survive as it was severed from dogmatic systems of belief and relocated in the particularities of texts. This was the logic of a view which was unable to grasp doctrine as a concentrated and highly informative medium for communication. The displacement or rather the transposition of doctrine from system into biblical text raised a question for systematics that had in fact been implicit throughout Locke's reconstructive effort in religion. What was the legitimate task of theology?

Theology as textual commentary

When Locke wrote *A Paraphrase and Notes on the Epistles of St Paul* [47] with its important Preface on Scripture interpretation, he noted that the fundamentals of the faith were present in a 'mixed' form in the Epistles

45. Certainly before Locke an important though often neglected English tradition in dogmatics can be traced. See John Dowden, *Outlines of the History of the Theological Literature of the Church of England From the Reformation to the Close of the Eighteenth Century*, The Bishop Paddock Lectures, 1896–97 (London: SPCK, 1897). More often than not this tradition can be observed in the many commentaries on the Thirty-Nine Articles, The Creed (for example, Pearson 1659) and in major works on ecclesiology (for example, Field, *Of the Church*, 1609). This tradition never disappeared after Locke, though it is questionable whether, in the light of the rise of Biblical Studies, it ever occupied the same position as before. In the nineteenth century FD Maurice saw the displacement of the dogmatic principle in Anglicanism as a positive virtue! See Stephen Sykes, *The Integrity of Anglicanism* (London: SPCK, 1978).

46. Hans Frei, *The Eclipse of Biblical Narrative* (London: Yale University Press, 1974), 101.

47. John Locke, *A Paraphrase and Notes on the Epistles of St Paul . . . with Preface*, in *Works*, volume 8, 1705.

as opposed to a clear and unmistakable form in the gospels. Any attempt to highlight unnaturally particular articles of faith in the Epistles was resisted by Locke. In fact it was precisely the tendency to treat Scripture 'crumbled into verses' as 'independent aphorisms' useful for constructing necessary articles of faith for church membership, that Locke was at pains to counteract.[48] When Scripture was treated in this way it became the occasion for system rivalry and social conflict. This had its origin in a failure to attend rightly to the revelation of Scripture, and indicated a desire to give divine sanction to human contrivances. Locke's method of Scripture analysis—of disregarding customary chapter and verse divisions and focus on the natural flow of the text—was designed to undercut the fancies of the system makers and to obtain access to the one original meaning of the text. Such a method would, said Locke, contribute 'to the peace of the church'. For Locke it was simple: 'If the holy scriptures were but laid before the eyes of christians, in its connexion and consistency, it would not then be so easy to snatch out a few words, as if they were separate from the rest, to serve a purpose, to which they do not at all belong . . .'.[49]

He proposed a way through the system back to the original sense, the 'tendency and force' of which was clear to the first recipients. This method offered a way of uncovering a sense of the 'strength and force' of the text's inner coherence. The implication was that doctrinal systems, confessions or articles of any church, were at best formed by 'extrapolation' from the text: 'Which, however, pretended to be founded on Scripture, are visibly the contrivances of men, fallible both in their opinions and interpretations. . .'.[50]

In terms of the task of theology what was interesting in Locke's discussion of Christianity was the way in which he construed the presence of God in revelation and the ideal form of communicating what had been revealed. His empiricist frame of mind kept him locked in the truth in its highly dispersed form, whether in nature, history or religious text. The theological form of this empiricism—implicit in *The Reasonableness of Christianity* and explicit in the *Paraphrases* and argument of the Preface—operated on the supposition that generalising theological synthesis obscured and distorted what was really present for faith in revelation. Accordingly, for Locke, ideal communication resolved itself into a kind of 'thick description'. In this activity synthesis was eschewed and attention

48. Locke, *Paraphrase and Notes*, 8.
49. Locke, *Paraphrase and Notes*, 8.
50. Locke, *Paraphrase and Notes*, 20.

remained in textual detail. Locke supposed that the text itself had a beauty, force and power which, when presented, would maximise opportunities for faith of its own accord.

It is possible to discern in the foregoing the impact on Locke's religious views of a tradition of nominalism or 'particularism' in philosophy; a tradition with close affinities to the ancient Hericlitian philosophy.[51] In nominalism everything exists originally in particularity, and the only universal propositions that can give information about the world are inductive generalisations which can never be more than probable. On the other hand propositions can attain certainty but only because they are concerned merely with abstract ideas. This situation resolves itself into a trade-off between informative, interesting though uncertain statements, and statements which are certain but uninformative. This feature of nominalist philosophy has important consequences when transferred into the region of theological discourse. Here the only task left for theology, to the extent that it maintains a concern for truth, is to sacrifice general and rich informativeness for concentration upon description and explanation of particulars. This can be discerned in Locke's move from system to biblical text. The vocation of theology implodes into textual commentary or, in Locke's case, paraphrasing. A corollary of this is the displacement and disfigurement of the doctrinal tradition in Christianity. Such was the fate of the systematic enterprise in Locke's handling of the Christian tradition.

The spirit of Locke and the task of theology

This brief excursion into the philosophy and theology of John Locke highlights a number of important issues for contemporary theology. Clearly, the eclipse of the systematic enterprise in theology is deep rooted within much broader changes that have occurred in the Western intellectual tradition in the last three hundred years. It is not simply the case that theologians have a certain preference for biblical studies or that the systematic task is lacking in practical application compared to other areas of theological effort, though such views have a popular appeal. This case study on Locke points to the impact of the powerful rationalist and empiricist impulse of modern philosophy, at least of the English variety although its influence is wider. Such a conclusion is commonplace. However, what

51. J Milton, 'John Locke and the Nominalist Tradition', in *John Locke: Symposium Wolfenbüttel 1979*, edited by Reinhard Brandt (New York: W de Gruyter, 1981).

this essay has intended to show is exactly how this commonplace axiom works itself out in relation to the theological task. Locke shows why it is so difficult for the systematic theologian to 'stay on task'. Ultimately, for Locke, the task was not only practically useless, it was morally suspect if not finally bankrupt. It is also not difficult to see how, in reaction to Locke's proposals, Christian theology could become overly preoccupied with apologetic of a defensive and reactionary kind. Such a response is not particularly conducive to the constructive theological task.

Ought we not then put Locke behind us and press on into the future? This is appealing, particularly for the systematician in the light of the foregoing case study. The difficulty is that we cannot simply put Locke behind us. The spirit of Locke is very much a part of our cultural heritage and expresses itself in many ways. Locke himself was vitally interested in the future cohesion and peaceableness of society. Certainly he was a minimiser with respect to religious belief but he had not surrendered the hope that what people believed could in fact bond them together. His minimalist statement of belief was thus part of a larger effort of social reconstruction in which Christianity was presumed to have a crucial role. To what extent does this hope provide the engine for our contemporary theological endeavours? Or perhaps our vision is a more modest one but not for that reason a more virtuous one. Locke at least poses a question to the theologian at this point about the scope of the theological project.

However, in another sense we cannot leave Locke behind us. His common-sense epistemological realism undergirds many flourishing varieties of religious fundamentalism. In periods of deep social and religious fragmentation the quest for certainty gathers fresh momentum and the sort of matter-of-factness associated with Lockean philosophy, when transferred into religion seems to offer secure anchors for individuals and social groups. This is part of the environment in which the theologian is called to work for the kingdom of God. To this extent the theologian is in constant critical dialogue with the legacy of Locke. Can the Christian theologian cut a reliable track through the treacherous terrain of modernity, a track that does not succumb to the dangers of fundamentalism in all its varieties, biblical, ecclesiastical and secular? This is not easy and the temptation for the Christian theologian is to resort to simplicities of various kinds and thereby forfeit the critical stance of the gospel.

For his part Locke was a thoroughgoing realist, perhaps naively so. He believed that there was a world that gave itself for reflection. Yet his brand of realism requires an important modification to guard against the dan gers noted above. To this extent the theologian will be better served by a *critical* realism to undergird the theological task. Such a view is admittedly at odds with a more popular idealist tendency in modern theology which views the constructivist theological task as essentially an inventive one and discounts any claim, however meagre, to the discovery nature of this effort. A critical realism will have to take stock of this alternative view and, following the advice of Donald MacKinnon,[52] work hard to allow the dialectic inherent in the systematic enterprise between invention and discovery to remain in fruitful tension. To prescind from this task exposes theology to the dangers of either ecclesial sectarianism or an uncritical accommodation to contemporary cultural values.

In a further important sense we ought not dismiss Locke too quickly. His empiricist approach would seem, in some respects at least, to be a plus for theology. Behind it the theologian is to hear the claim of human experience in all its particularity, richness and ambiguity—in a way far broader than Locke conceived—as a critical *location* for the systematic task. This is a highly controversial area and it is easy to end up either allowing the theological agenda to become overly preoccupied with the status of experience or fall into the trap of premature dismissal. In this respect a strong case could be made for the thesis that the difficulty theology has encountered in giving a proper account of the significance of human experience is mirrored in the failure of the Western tradition in particular to develop its pneumatological thread within the weave of Christian dogma.[53] This thesis presupposes that pneumatology lies on the underside of the issue of human experience. Locke's religious writings failed to make this link and to this extent he was unable to give a fuller account of the way in which human reflection could participate in the flow of God's own creativity. However, Locke's philosophy is a powerful reminder that the theological task cannot be reduced to imprinting on human life some preconceived theory about the ideal religious life of the Christian. This, in fact, was precisely what Locke objected to in the theory of innate ideas. Locke set out on a different path which recognised that it is through our sensate life in the world that our well being begins, is built up, enriched and sadly also diminished. Therefore, to some extent, the realm of human

52. Donald Mckinnon, *Explorations in Theology* (London: SCM, 1979), 151–65.

53. Barth wondered whether Schleiermacher's entire program might not be best understood as an attempt at pneumatology through anthropology. See *Protestant Theology in the Nineteenth Century* (London: SCM, 1972), 459f. It has echoes in Karl Rahner's efforts in the twentieth century. However, the task has hardly begun.

experience—an admittedly wide and unwieldy term—will be, almost of necessity, constitutive for the theological task.[54] Locke's empiricism is a reminder to the theologian to remain properly grounded upon the earth. Is this really important for theology? We do well to remember that the dogmatic tradition emerges out of a people's Spirit-led response to God in Jesus Christ through confession, witness, worship and discipleship in the world. In other words, primal experiences of human transformation are constitutive, in part, of the Church's dogma.

More directly this essay has offered an interpretation of the demise of the systematic theological enterprise that has its roots in an emergent eighteenth-century English enlightenment environment. I have suggested that the larger backdrop for this occurrence was the transition from the Parmenidean philosophy of order and stability to the Hericlitean tradition in philosophy, with its emphasis on change and particularism. Locke's epistemology exemplifies this wider change and the consequent tendency to atomisation that has been so much a feature of our Enlightenment heritage. One victim in this has been, in the English tradition at least, systematic theology.[55] Within the discipline of theology this development

---

54. The question for theology is not whether human experience is to be attended to in the dogmatic task, but how and to what degree? More commonly 'experience' is referred to as a 'norm' or 'source' for theology. I have referred to human experience as the 'location' for the theological endeavour. Admittedly this is hardly a sufficient designation though notions of norm and source are at best formal categories that give few clues about how human experience will be constitutive for theology, though certainly expectations are raised that it ought to be. Tillich referred to experience as the 'medium' of theology, that is, the medium through which the answers contained in the sources were received. Yet for him the medium did not contribute anything to the answers. Hodgson doubts whether this view can be sustained, though we ought to note that if it can it leaves the dogmatic tradition effectively divorced from human experience (*Winds of Change*, 27). Elizabeth Johnson makes the unsurprising, but, it seems, necessary observation that, 'consulting human experience is an identifying mark of virtually all contemporary theology, as indeed has been the case at least implicitly with most of the major articulations in the history of Christian theology' (*She Who Is: The Mystery of God in Feminist Theological Discourse* (New York: Crossroad, 1993), 61). See also her helpful endnote 2, 285. Perhaps one of the most important recent discussions of the significance of human experience in theology is Jürgen Moltmann, *The Spirit of Life: A Universal Affirmation* (Minneapolis: Fortress Press, 1993), chapter 1. Moltmann's discussion is set in the framework of a fundamental pneumatology. For Moltmann the link netween human experience and the doctrine of the Holy Spirit is clear though the implications for dogmatics requires much fuller exploration.

55. A question remains for me as to how particular this problem is to the English theological tradition which certainly has impacted on the Australian theological context in which I work. Certainly, systematic theology seems to be in a much healthier state

has contributed in part to a fragmentation and a consequent difficulty in conversation across the theological specialities. The spirit of Locke is alive and kicking in this area though there may be a new period emerging when the systematician and the biblical exegete may enter into deeper critical mutual collaboration in relation to 'the soul of theology', without the fear of exegesis absorbing systematics.[56]

In so far as the spirit of Lockean philosophy continues to exercise a dominant influence in our contemporary cultural, scientific and religious environment at least one important consequence flows for the theological task. To the extent that the theologian cannot simply jump out of her or his context it seems that the theological task is and will remain inescapably a local affair. It will be at the level of the 'local' that theology will have to take its cues. In one sense there is nothing new here though what is particularly challenging today, in the light of the impulse toward atomisation, is for the theologian to articulate with subtlety and conviction the interconnections that link local contexts to other local contexts. And to begin in this way suggests a more modest and humble theological task, willing to admit uncertainty and an appropriate provisionality in the results of theological enquiry, perhaps more so than has occurred in the past.

The basis for such an endeavour is not simply pragmatic but is a deeply theological task funded from the gospel of a God whose realm is the whole of creation and who pilgrimages with people in their radical particularity. From this perspective the theologian might well embark with a fresh confidence in the systematic task, believing that God has given human beings the capacity under grace to find a way through the trees of modernity in such a way that glimpses of the wood occasionally appear. This may sound like wishful thinking, though it rests on the supposition that there is a unity and wholeness to this world in relation to divine reality, albeit one that is scarcely comprehendible by human beings and not yet fully completed. At this point Locke stands quite firmly in the theological tradition. Furthermore, it is precisely a belief of this order that makes life in the forest among the trees possible. The transcendent is glimpsed and echoes are discerned through the particulars of time and space. What is

---

in Continental and United States theology, at least in pockets. Have they escaped the forces of Heraclitus? Do they other resources with which to resist and counter this? Or have such theologies yet to feel the full impact of this philosophy?

56. See Jose Alemany, 'Must There be a Tension Between Exegesis and Dogmatic Theology?', edited by Claude Geffre and Werner Jeanrond in *Why Theology? Concilium*, volume 6 (London: SCM, 1994).

thus sought is the deeper co-inherence of the particular and the universal, of transcendent and the immanent. The task of the systematic theologian today may be to point, in a provisional way, to intimations of that co-inherence and in so doing remain, in the words of Johann Baptist Metz, one of 'the last universalists'. Only in this way can the theologian 'stay on task', offer genuinely pastoral wisdom and provide tracks for intelligent discipleship on the pilgrim way.

Chapter Five
The Ways of Theology: Insights from the Antipodes[1]

Exploring the Centre

This essay explores different modes through which the theological task is undertaken—biblical, philosophical, theological, cultural, aesthetic, ecclesial. This exploration is undertaken through the lens of the Anglican tradition in Australia.

Theology and Christian vocation

What place does theology occupy in Australian Anglicanism? Australian pragmatism and impatience with matters of the intellect has had little enthusiasm for or apparent need of theologians in the Church. Some kinds of theological activity—overly academic, elitist and irrelevant—might only confirm such prejudice! If theology occupies a somewhat marginal place then perhaps this is as it should be. After all, in a management and market driven world what is the value of theology in the life of the Church? It is a question once addressed by that famous ex-Anglican John Henry Newman. In his preface to the re-publication of his famous essays on the *Via Media* of the Anglican Church (1879)—first published as the *Prophetical Office of the Church* in 1837—Newman identified theology as one of the three fundamental powers of the Church.[2] Theology (Newman's system of philosophy) offered a critical stance in relation to the other two

1. Originally published as 'Theology as a Power: Traditions and Challenges for Australian Anglicans', in *Agendas for Australian Anglicans: Essays in honour of Bruce Kaye*, edited by Tom Frame and Geoff Treloar (Adelaide: ATF Press, 2006). Where possible I have tried to update names and places referred to in the footnotes.
2. John Henry Newman, *The Via Media of the Anglican Church,* volume 1 *Lectures on the Prophetical Office of the Church Viewed Relatively to Romanism and Popular Protestantism*, third edition (London: Basil Montagu Pickering, 1877), 40 ff.

powers, the sacramental and worship tradition (ritual) and ecclesiastical rule (political power). Liturgy and polity required this third power as an essential hermeneutic for the ongoing faithfulness of the Church to the Gospel. Without this third power the Church was easily directed into an unhealthy sacramentalism and/or an unfettered abuse of ecclesiastical power. Church history bore testimony to the conflict that often occurred between these three indispensable elements of the life of the Church. Newman considered that the theological vocation was essential to preserve and foster a critical and reforming spirit. His position had an Anglican feel about it, even though he had long since jumped ship!

But who may presume to pursue such a vocation? In the early twentieth century the reformed theologian Karl Barth remarked that 'every Christian—in however primitive and rudimentary way—can and must be a theologian'.[3] For Barth the theological vocation may well generate scholars but he was equally clear that the theological vocation, so critical to the life and mission of the Church, was the responsibility to some extent of all the baptised. His reflections on St Anselm's famous dictum of theology as 'faith seeking understanding' provided a basis for the fundamental claim upon all the people of God to be theologians of the Church. In this way theology recalled the Church to the service of the Gospel.

Rigorous thought bent towards the practice of discipleship in the world was the kind of theology Barth, Dietrich Bonhoeffer and many others pursued, stretching minds and hearts into as yet unchartered regions of God's surprising grace. This dynamic had a long pedigree: it included the Apostle Paul exhorting the Christians at Rome to be 'transformed by the renewal of your mind' that they might know what was pleasing to God (Romans 12:3). It had resonances with the Scripture tradition: of the Deuteronomist discerning the providential movement of God's Spirit in the history of Israel; of the Psalmist seeking after wisdom to understand God's ways in the world; of Job and his 'comforters' wrestling with the mystery of evil and the goodness of God; of the parables of Jesus and the life of the new community.

Anglicans stand in this long tradition of theology as the active pursuit of wisdom and its radical and transformative impact.[4] It is clearly not an

3. Karl Barth, *Church Dogmatics: The Doctrine of Reconciliation*, volume 4, translated by G Bromley and TF Torrance (Edinburgh: T&T Clark, 1956), Part 1, 765.
4. For an important discussion of the ancient tradition of theology as sapiential knowledge see Edward Farley, *Theologia: The Fragmentation and Unity of Theological Education* (Philadelphia: Fortress Press, 1983).

optional extra, nor a luxury the Church can ill afford, nor the preserve of an elite—clergy, seminarians, the experts or 'professionals'. It is a task for the baptised enshrined in their baptismal vows and a corollary of their diverse ministries in the world. This is encapsulated in Cranmer's 1549 Good Friday Collect:

> Almighty and everlasting God, by whose Spirit the whole body of the Church is governed and sanctified; receive our supplications and prayers, which we offer before thee for all estates of men [sic] in thy holy Church, that *every member* of the same, in his [sic] *vocation and ministry*, may truly serve thee; through our Lord and Saviour Jesus Christ, who liveth and reigneth with thee, and in the unity of the same Spirit, ever one God, world without end. Amen.[5]

How, it may be asked, is it ever possible for the people of the Church to fulfil their vocation and ministry unless they are equipped to engage in critical reflection upon their vocations in order that they might more clearly embody the faithfulness of Christ in the world? To live a life of faith is to be a pilgrim seeking deeper understanding of the ways of God in the world with the intent to follow such ways after the manner of Jesus Christ. On this account theology has a significant function and therefore it ought to occupy a fairly central place in the life of the Church.

How fares Australian Anglicanism? This essay pursues this question by exploring the different levels of engagement possible for Anglicans in theology: from theology as a discipline of the Church; to a distinctly Anglican approach to theology; to self-conscious development of a theology of Anglicanism in Australia. The essay thus departs from more usual approaches which focus on theology from the perspective of the different camps within Anglicanism (Evangelical, Anglo-Catholic, Broad Church), or according to key themes and preoccupations (for example, Christology, Scripture and authority, ecclesiology). What results is a layered perspective of different possible kinds of engagements with the sacred text and

5. *Book of Common Prayer*, 1662 (my italics). This Collect from the 1549 *Book of Common Prayer* represents Cranmer's re-working of the earlier Roman rite. It presumes that all members of the Church have a vocation and ministry. The reference to 'vocation and ministry' was added in the 1549 Prayer Book and reflects Lutheran influence. This Collect points to a profound mutuality in ministry wherein each ministry bestows life and energy on other ministries.

contemporary world. In doing so it highlights a future direction for Australian Anglicans in the ongoing theological task.

Australian Anglican theology: some general trends

What place has Anglican theology played in the Australian scene? Ought it rate a mention at all?[6] It is clear from Robert Banks' survey covering the period 1915–1965, that there have been significant Anglican contributors to the theological scene in Australia over the course of the last century.[7] Bank's identified TC Hammond's modified scholastic Calvinism, Leon Morris' conservative biblical Evangelicalism, and Gabriel Hebert's scholarly Anglo-Catholicism.[8] Alongside such figures sits Ernest Burgmann's ecclesial/political theology in the line of FD Maurice. JC Wand, Archbishop of Brisbane, was a noted Anglican historian, though his scholarly work was produced prior to his episcopal ministry in Australia.

However there are other features of local theology noted by Banks that have impacted upon the nature of Anglican theology in Australia. In this respect it is commonplace to refer to the generally derivative or imported nature of theology and its strong denominational allegiances. Hammond was a Church of Ireland Protestant who settled in Sydney in 1936. Herbert came from the UK to Australia in 1953 and remained for almost a decade. Morris was unusual in being an Australian born and self-taught New Testament theologian.

It is also the case that up until recent times theology was enclosed in traditional seminary education. This has made for the isolation of theology from main-steam intellectual life and given it a strong focus on ministerial practice for clergy. To the extent that theology has served this pragmatic and pastoral emphasis it has not generated a substantive intellectual tradition. This has been the case notwithstanding the fact that there have been

---

6. Bruce Kaye notes that the Uniting Church scholar, Eric Osborn 'makes no mention of any specifically Anglican theology or Anglican contributions to Australian theology in his survey'. See BN Kaye, 'The Anglican Tradition in Australia', in *St Mark's Review*, 141 (Autumn 1990): 24–33, especially 28, note 24; and Eric Osborn, 'Tendencies in Australian Theology', in *Colloquium*, 12 (1979).
7. See Robert Banks, 'Fifty years of Theology in Australia, 1915–1965', Part One, in *Colloquium*, 9/1 (1976): 36–42; Part Two, in *Colloquium*, 9/2 (1977): 7–16.
8. On Hammond and Morris see Geoffrey R Treloar, 'Hammond, Thomas Chatterton', in *Biographical Dictionary of Evangelicals*, edited by Timothy Larsen (Leicester: Inter-Varsity Press, 2003), 286–87 and Treloar, 'Morris, Leon Lamb', 448–89. On Hebert see Alistair Mason, *SSM: History of the Society of Sacred Mission*, (1993), chapter 9.

significant intellects involved in theological education and in the ordering and direction of Anglicanism in Australia. The enclosure of theology has also meant that the variety of imported theological streams in Australian Anglicanism has suffered from lack of genuine dialogue both internally and with other disciplines. To this extent the seminary tradition in theology has lacked creativity and remained essentially infertile.

A concomitant feature of these general trends is the failure to develop a 'home grown' theological tradition that resonates with the particularities of the Australian context. It may be a troubling but nevertheless accurate assessment that 'Anglican culture in Australia encouraged intellectual activity in every area except theology'.[9] An enculturated theological tradition takes time and a sense of responsibility for its work in the local context. Burgmann was one of the few Australian leaders who recognised the need for a truly indigenous theology.[10] The development of such a tradition usually requires significant historical work and in this area Australian Anglicans have only achieved significant results in recent decades.[11]

Banks saw the future work of theology being conducted in a more open ecumenical spirit, particularly in the aftermath of Vatican II. He also envisaged a stronger link between theology and 'general intellectual activity' with closer relations with universities and other educational establishments.[12] Both these developments have occurred over the last four decades and have impacted upon the nature of theology undertaken by Australian Anglicans. One result of partnerships between theological colleges and universities has been a closer ecumenical cooperation in the teaching of theology, development of common curricula and collaboration at the level of research. The university connection has made theology a more public and accountable activity in the academy. Yet increased pressure to research and publish within a higher profile academic environment has to be negotiated amidst increased workloads, Church expectations and decreasing funding from Church bodies.

It is also unmistakable that the above developments have resulted in a remarkable increase in participation rates among laity, in particular

9. David Hilliard, 'Anglicanism', in *Australian Cultural History*, edited by SL Goldberg and F Smith (Cambridge, 1988), 28.

10. See Peter Hempenstall, *The Meddlesome Priest: A life of Ernest Burgmann* (Sydney: Allen and Unwin, 1993).

11. This shines through the recent publication, *Anglicanism in Australia: A History*, edited by Bruce Kaye et al (Melbourne: Melbourne University Press, 2002), on which see further below.

12. Banks, 'Fifty Years of Theology', Part One, 39.

women. The proportion of Anglican women studying theology compared to men would be an interesting statistic. My experience over the last sixteen years in theological education suggests that women are making an increasingly significant contribution to theological work locally. This is yet to be recognised in the Anglican Church in Australia where there are only a few women in fulltime positions on theological faculties.[13] But the times are changing and there is an emerging community of women scholars of theology.[14] A more public, lay and ecumenical spirit has changed the shape and character of theological work in Australia. Anglicans have been a part of this emergent frame of reference for theology.

What these developments mean is that the notion of a professional theological elite is something of a misnomer in Australian Anglicanism. There are theologians beavering away within evolving institutional settings where time for reading and writing is sparse and the demands great. Increased participation from the lay people of the church has meant there is a great deal of invisible theological work being undertaken by people from other disciplines who connect with theology at some level and are required to think through their faith, work and life beyond the confines of church and academy. Not surprisingly these developments are difficult to track. Often such work re-emerges through membership of diocesan, national and international commissions and working groups on such matters as the environment and ethics. This means that the theological concerns and themes that occupy Anglicans in Australia are increasingly diverse. It suggests a curious parallel track theological existence for Australian Anglicans: one track conforming more to the traditional seminary loci and designed for clergy in training (though even here the changes are significant); another track far more disparate and wide ranging reflecting the rich patterns of engagements of theologically astute lay people.

13. When I returned to Australia in 1990 and began teaching at United Theological College in Sydney one of my colleagues was the Rev Dr Colleen O'Reilly, a lecturer in Pastoral Theology and now a priest in the Diocese of Melbourne. But this was the Uniting Church! Dr Heather Thomson was a fulltime Lecturer in Theology at St Mark's National Theological Centre, Canberra, together with Dr Merilyn Clark, part-time lecturer in Old Testament. Rev Cathy Laufer was a fulltime lecturer at St Francis' College, Brisbane. Around the country there is an increasing number of part-time and sessional lecturers who are women. [In 2011 there are more women in fulltime theological positions in Anglican colleges and of course some changes in the above mix].

14. As just one example, the first five doctorates awarded in the new School of Theology at Charles Sturt University have been to women. The areas range over Old Testament, theology, ecclesiology, the sciences and theology, philosophy and apologetics.

It is also true that in recent years the tradition of Anglicans doing theology in their diverse and challenging contexts has begun to recognise the significance of an Australian Anglican identity as constitutive of the theological task. This is a new development signalling a move from Anglicans who happen to be doing theology to the development of an Australian Anglican theology. These two approaches are not opposed and to some extent stand in dialectical relation to each other. This makes for a healthy theological engagement. However to the extent that the latter approach remains significantly underdeveloped in Australia the theological task is truncated and the particularities of the local context remain on the margins of the Church's reflection on its life and mission.

Interpreting the tradition

How might we understand our tradition? There is little evidence of critical reflection on the Anglican theological tradition in Australia. Perhaps the tradition is not yet sufficiently formed to warrant this. Our strong regional interests and the practical demands of ministry and resourcing the church in a new environment have required significant energies. There has never been much time or recognition of the need for critical reflection on the theological tradition. Engagement with present realities has been the central preoccupation. We await a comprehensive analysis and assessment of Anglican theology in Australia. Provision of a proper historiography has been a critical moment in the process but this is a first step only. How have recent commentators assessed the scene? We briefly consider three contemporary interpreters and observe their emphases and orientations.

Charles Sherlock: recognising diversity

In 1996 the then General Secretary of the General Synod of the Anglican Church, Bruce Kaye, convened a gathering of Anglican theologians in Perth to coincide with the annual Australian and New Zealand Association of Theological Schools conference. This was the inaugural Anglican Theologians Seminar attended by approximately 16 people.[15] The

15. The theme was: 'Where is Anglican Theology Going in Australia?' Subsequently the seminar met in Brisbane in 1997 (ministry and the laity); Melbourne in 1998 (reconciliation in church and society); Morpeth in 1999 (spirituality and society); Canberra in 2000 (the gift of authority); and Melbourne in 2001 (radical orthodoxy); Morpeth 2002 (violence and theology). Over the period approximately 50 people have participated alongside a smaller core group. A forthcoming publication on Anglican

purpose of the seminar was to foster reflection on the tasks of theology for Australian Anglicans. In particular it was hoped to encourage a critical engagement with ecclesiological matters to do with Anglican identity and mission in the Australian context. One of the papers prepared for the seminar was by Charles Sherlock, at the time a lecturer at Ridley College in Melbourne.[16] He noted the diversity and isolation of different theological emphases arising from the development of Australian Anglicanism along strong regional and federal lines. This federal character has impacted upon its 'ability to think theologically about national issues in an Australian context'.[17] As a result it was the various commissions of the General Synod that generated 'most theological thought at national level'.

Sherlock also identified Anglican theological education through its regional colleges and emerging consortia as the 'major vehicle' through which theology has been done in Australia. It was the faculty of such places that undertook the 'bulk of formal theological work among Australian Anglicans'. However due to 'diversity of traditions, and lack of opportunities . . . few encounter one another more than briefly'.[18] Sherlock also discussed the distinctive theological motifs of the colleges. In Sydney Moore's distinctive ecclesiology emphasised the Kingdom of God and hearing the Gospel (through words) and a concomitant eschatology that regarded 'seeing' the rule of Christ 'as exclusively future'. This ecclesiology developed by Broughton Knox—with its emphasis on the local congregation—was set over against society and was focussed on changing individuals rather than society. A broader based Evangelicalism was developed in Melbourne at Ridley where Leon Morris was identified as 'the most prolific Protestant Australian theological author'.[19] Also in Melbourne Trinity's Moorhouse Lectures had generated 'substantial contributions to Australian Anglican theology'.[20] Sherlock did not elaborate but noted the contributions to litur-

theology in Australia represents some of the fruits of the work of the seminar. The theology seminar will be reconstituted in the near future.

16. His short paper was entitled, 'Anglican Theology in Australia'. Unfortunately Sherlock was unable to attend because of illness but the paper was discussed. To my knowledge, the paper has never been published.
17. Sherlock, 'Anglican Theology in Australia', 1
18. Sherlock, 'Anglican Theology in Australia', 3
19. Sherlock, 'Anglican Theology in Australia', 4
20. For a discussion of Melbourne Anglican theology see David Hilliard, 'Intellectual Life in the Diocese of Melbourne', in *Melbourne Anglicans: The Diocese of Melbourne 1847–1997*, edited by Brian Porter (Melbourne: Joint Board of Christian Education, 1997), chapter 2.

gical studies by theologians at St Michael's House, Crafers in Adelaide.[21] The Burgmann tradition at St Mark's, Canberra, did not feature. Sherlock also noted the emerging role of women in Australian colleges and a 'growing concern with theology in and for Australian contexts since the 1970s covering themes such as land, fate, success and failure, and the desert. He further identified liturgical revision and innovation as an important contribution from Australia to the wider Communion and the emerging importance of ethics. The paper offered an important post 1970 update on Anglicanism following Banks' more general survey which had closed with 1965. Sherlock saw a promising future especially 'as the number and quality of those taking part in theological work grows'.[22] The paper offered an initial map of the theological territory and some hints at reasons for its particular character but did not develop an interpretation of Australian Anglicanism. This was a matter taken up with more zeal by Bill Lawton.

Bill Lawton: Christology and social justice

In his contribution to *Anglicanism in Australia: A History*, former Moore College lecturer and Rector of St John's, Darlinghurst, Bill Lawton offered an unusual and provocative account of 'Anglican Theology in Australia'.[23] In Trevor Hogan's review of the book his assessment of Lawton's account captures the flavour well:

> Bill Lawton's chapter is worth the price of this book alone. It is an eccentric account that combines with some alacrity and admixture of the personal, the gossipy, the discursive and the performative dimensions of Anglican theologies in Australia. It is therefore an admirably (because quite unselfconsciously) Anglican historiography, a tradition of scholarship that has a long Oxbridge pedigree. Lawton chooses, as his two exemplary, controversial and articulate figures, the radical evangelical theology of Moore College's Broughton Knox, and the radical liberal theology of the former Archbishop of Perth and Primate, Peter Carnley. He is able to explain the difference of Sydney to the rest of the Anglican Communion and its compelling power to attract and repel in equal mea-

21. In particular, Father Gabriel Hebert and Brother Gilbert Sinden.
22. Sherlock, 'Anglican Theology in Australia', 5
23. Bill Lawton, 'Australian Anglican Theology', in *Anglicanism in Australia*,

> sure. Lawton also shows the representative status of Carnley's thinking for contemporary Anglican communities who seek to combine the pre-eminently cosmological and world-affirming and inclusive Orthodox and Catholic doctrines of the Trinity, Creation, and Incarnation yet without sacrificing a more anthropological and rationalist Protestant emphasis on personal responsibility and autonomy as expressed in the doctrines of Atonement and the Cross.[24]

Lawton's own preoccupations emerge: the necessity for justice and justification to be 'linked as a basis of an atonement theology';[25] revelation that transcends propositional rationalist accounts and incorporates experience and imagination; the priority of Christology over ecclesiology as theological focus. It is this latter issue that deserves further consideration. Lawton argues that Christology and Scripture 'are fundamental for an Australian Anglican self-understanding'.[26] Indeed they 'are much more critical than disputes about theology of the church (or ecclesiology) and the shape of ministry'. [27]For Lawton matters to do with 'church and epsicopate' are secondary, divisive and a distraction and will not become primary issues until 'they are lifted out of ecclesiology and are seen to be about the way justice flows from the revelation of God'. [28]Lawton is thus clear that for 'these questions, and for every issue of social conscience, it is Christology rather than ecclesiology that must be the mainstay'.[29] This is foundational for Lawton's account of the failure and successes of Anglican theology and it is clear where his sympathies lie. The health or otherwise of Anglican theology in Australia will be judged by its capacity to connect Gospel, theology and the requirements for a just society. It was a theme that had occupied Lawton on earlier occasions.[30]

Lawton's approach has all the hallmarks of the Burgmann tradition. What of course is curious about Lawton's approach is that his account of Anglican theology in Australia is, if nothing else, a thoroughly ecclesial

24. Trevor Hogan, review of *Anglicanism in Australia: A History*, in *Journal of Anglican Studies*, 3/1 (June 2005): 123.
25. Lawton, 'Anglicanism in Australia', 191.
26. Lawton, 'Anglicanism in Australia', 179.
27. Lawton, 'Anglicanism in Australia', 179.
28. Lawton, 'Anglicanism in Australia', 179.
29. Lawton, 'Anglicanism in Australia', 179.
30. William Lawton, *Being Christian, Being Australian: Contemporary Christianity Down Under* (Sydney: Lancer Press, 1988).

affair undergirded by Christology. His essential focus turns out to be God in society. His Christology and ecclesiology are deeply connected and resonate with Bonhoeffer's doctrine of the Church as 'Christ existing as community'.[31] His relegation of ecclesiology to a secondary position in the theological loci represents more of an apologetical and political decision as much as a theological one. Why is this so? Part of the answer arises out of the controversial context in which so much theological debate has occurred in Australian Anglicanism. The derivative nature of Australian Anglicanism has meant that the controversies of nineteenth-century English Anglicanism (the ascendency of the Tractarian movement, the Evangelical stream and Maurician Broad Church) became firmly embedded in the regional development of Australian Anglicanism. Ideological commitments to these imported ecclesial positions have been related historically to the exercise of power and dominance in the fledgling colonial Church. Questions of authority, Scripture, Christology and revelation have operated to bolster predetermined ecclesial positions. This gives the quite false appearance of an ongoing preoccupation with ecclesiology as the driver for Anglican theology. In fact a critical and contextual ecclesiology is precisely what has been lacking in Anglicanism since the nineteenth-century controversies which made ecclesiology such a contested matter for Anglicans. Entrenched ecclesial positions are not the environment in which a positive and enculturated ecclesiology can be developed. Lawton is in part correct in displacing a false ecclesiological consciousness with a christological approach. But his intent is clear: the development of an ecclesiology in which God and society are integrally related. It is the work of Bruce Kaye that most clearly embodies a self-conscious and critical engagement with the Anglican doctrine of the Church in Australia.

Bruce Kaye: an emerging ecclesial consciousness

Bruce Kaye holds an important place within the Anglican theological community over the last two decades. His contributions herald the first signs of a self-conscious engagement with Anglican ecclesiology in an Australian context. His 1990 article on 'The Anglican Tradition in Australia' set the agenda in highlighting the imported and essentially conservative nature of Anglican theology in Australia.[32] He called for something more—an engagement with God and society in the interests of a 'public

31. Dietrich Bonhoeffer, *Sanctorum Communio* (London: Collins, 1963) 84 f.
32. Kaye, 'The Anglican Tradition in Australia', 24–33 (see note 6 above).

theology'. To focus on the dynamic interaction between church, academy and society as the coordinates for an incarnational theology seemed to Kaye to embody a 'genuinely Anglican' way in theology in Australia.

With Kaye ecclesiology has become the centre of the theological program. The complaint of Stephen Sykes more than a quarter of a century ago about the paucity of contemporary Anglican reflection on the doctrine of the Church is here responded to with vigour and determination.[33] Over the past fifteen years Kaye has pursued the question of Anglican identity with an intentional Australian focus. 'Being Anglican in Australia', the subtitle of his 1995 *Church without Walls*,[34] brought ecclesiology into relation with the discipleship tradition of Bonhoeffer. At the heart of this project was a search for an authentic ecclesial identity for Anglicans in Australia, one that was orientated to the wider society and the mission of God. What kind of theological framework was required for such a project? Kaye proposed a trinitarian paradigm which generated a rich network of relations and engagements for being church in Australia. This included, but went beyond, the baptismal paradigm of Paul Avis which could not 'adequately deal with the question of Anglicanism's relationship with society and the tradition of natural law, or God's providence in society'.[35] The liturgical paradigm of Stephen Sykes was susceptible to an enclosed and sectarian bias. A trinitarian paradigm provided a richer framework for the baptismal and liturgical emphases. The strength of this model is its orientation to 'existence in society'.[36] 'This is the model of Anglican faith as a "church in society" type of Christianity', a church 'without walls'.[37] This ecclesiology of engagement embodies the tradition of FD Maurice and Ernest Burgmann.

Church without Walls was followed by a full-scale inquiry into the nature of Anglicanism in Australia in the 2002 publication *Anglicanism in Australia: A History* produced under Kaye's general editorship. The publication emerged out of the Anglican History Seminar established by Kaye some years earlier. The identity question and the challenge of being church required a more careful assessment of those forces shaping the development of Anglicanism in Australia. The book represented a seminal stage

33. See Stephen Sykes, *The Integrity of Anglicanism* (London: SPCK, 1978).
34. Bruce N Kaye, A *Church without Walls: Being Anglican in Australia* (North Blackburn, Vic: Dove, 1995).
35. Kaye, *Church without Walls*, 186.
36. Kaye, *Church without Walls*, 188.
37. Kaye, *Church without Walls*, 188.

in such an inquiry. Kaye's own essay on 'The Emergence and Character of Australian Anglican Identity' brought together in succinct form his own assessment of the situation. He noted the 'two underlying forces at work in the emerging self-definition of Australian Anglicans'—'the need to effect a transition into the Australian environment of their English heritage from the Church of England and the tension between the regionalism of the separate colonies and the emerging national sentiment'.[38] These two forces 'have shaped Australian Anglican identity and influenced the way in which issues of church life have been viewed'.[39] The characteristic emphases of Australian Anglicanism are: dispersed authority compared to the more centralist ideology of Anglicanism in England and Canada; plurality institutionalised in diocesan structures and 'socially enmeshed' in ways quite distinct from the 'establishment status' of the Church of England and the separation between church and state in the American Episcopal church; a dynamic and emerging transition 'from a faith pedigree to which Anglicans in Australia are still committed in its essential relations'; and an 'adjustment to the regionalism of Australian society' which remains powerful as a Church shaping force. Kaye argued that the distinctives of Australian Anglicanism sat 'very comfortably with the broader Anglican theological tradition'.[40]

Kaye's historical mode of theological inquiry entered a more programmatic phase in his 2003 publication, *Reinventing Anglicanism*.[41] The very title indicates the agenda. The doctrine of the church has to be reconstituted afresh for a new context. For Kaye this implies a series of engagements with society in its multiple dimensions—political, social, institutional, and religious. This also requires a critical stance towards the past. In this respect Kaye is in his own understated way quite scathing of the way in which the English Reformation is appealed to in support of visions of a purified church. The centralist agendas of Tudor political life have proved inimical to the development of an open, incarnational and contextual Anglicanism. By contrast the ecclesial vision of a Richard Hooker provides a vision for a church which requires a critique of sedimented political/ecclesiastical structures. Australian Anglicans have struggled with the tensions embedded in their own heritage. Reinvention requires critique

38. Kaye, 'The Emergence and Character of Australian Anglican Identity', 170.
39. Kaye, 'The Emergence and Character of Australian Anglican Identity', 170.
40. Kaye, 'The Emergence and Character of Australian Anglican Identity', 175.
41. Bruce N Kaye, *Reinventing Anglicanism: A Vision of Confidence, Community and Engagement in Anglican Christianity* (Adelaide: Openbook Publishers, 2003).

and openness to the world. But it also requires faithfulness to the deeper current in Anglicanism that has given it a resilience and fruitfulness from the earliest centuries. Kaye seems to be searching for the lineaments of a critical contextual ecclesiology. His work represents the most sustained theological interpretation of Anglicanism from an Australian perspective to date. It shows how careful examination of Anglicanism from a particular context can inform an understanding of global Anglicanism. Finally his work indicates that beyond Anglicans doing *theology* and Anglicans engaged in an *Anglican* theology there is a critical task that requires Australian Anglicans to develop a theology of Anglicanism. Ecclesiology may not be the first cab off the rank but a church that does not know how to enter into critical reflection on its own life will remain bound by past ideologies and oblivious to present cultural and political powers. This will have disastrous effects on its mission and engagements in the wider society. With Kaye theology has begun to emerge as a genuine third power in the life of the Church.

This brief consideration of some contemporary interpreters of the Anglican tradition in Australia reminds us that the question of Anglican theology in Australia is a multi-layered idea deserving careful and sophisticated treatment. There are continuing strands to the question and emerging voices displaying the rich texture that constitutes the theological tasks for Australian Anglicans.

Continuing strands and emerging voices: theological modes, themes and directions

What counts as theology? Part of the answer depends on who is responding to the question. The biblical scholar, historian, philosopher, systematician, ethicist and public controversialist might give quite different answers. The diversity of responses would no doubt reflect the different emphases and methods of engagement with faith, sacred text and world. Indeed the question of what constitutes theology is a contested matter. But the tensions and variety within the general discipline of theology also generate creative exchange and fresh insights within the discipline and in relation to other ways of knowledge, such as the social sciences and 'hard' sciences. Australian Anglicans exhibit this remarkable range of approaches to the theological task.

How we answer the question, 'what counts as theology?, determines who we identify as representative of the theological tradition. Hence the contested nature of theology expresses itself both in what theological weight is given to the different sub-disciplines in theology and who is identified as belonging to the theological tradition.[42] As we begin to answer the questions, 'what counts as theology?' and 'who are the representative figures?, we also become aware of another intriguing aspect of Anglican theology in Australia. This emerges when we ask, 'where is theology undertaken in Australia by Anglicans?'. Here the strength of regionalism becomes apparent. Historically the metropolitan centres have been the focus of theological work.[43] The reason is not difficult to identify. Resources for clergy training were concentrated in the regional centres. Hence we are not surprised that the question, 'where is theology done?, has usually been answered in terms of theological colleges in major urban centres. But given the lack of resources from which such places have suffered, the fact that there has been time for any substantive theological output is remarkable, to say the least. It also accounts for the differing emphases in theology emanating from seminary environments reflecting particular traditions in Anglicanism. The 'where' question also begins to answer the 'what' question. Questions of scripture interpretation and authority, ecclesiology, Christology and culture have been the central preoccupations.[44] Of course as theology has moved into closer relationship with the disciplines of modern university life in Australia the range of themes and their interdisciplinary focus has become increasingly important.

There are continuing strands in the history of Anglican theology in Australia representing different levels of engagement. There are also emerging voices and traditions. It is a complex enterprise and a compre-

---

42. Of course there will probably be argument, for example, as to whether some areas are properly theological. For example, in what sense is religious biography part of theology? How does biblical studies or philosophy contribute to the theological task? In what sense can the relatively modern idea of systematic theology claim to be the central and determinative work of theology?
43. We lack a history of Anglican theology in Australia. At present there are only overviews of particular metropolitan centres. For example, see Hilliard, 'Intellectual Life in the Diocese of Melbourne'. Key figures in theology in the Diocese of Sydney appear in Stephen Judd and Kenneth Cable, *Sydney Anglicans: A History of the Diocese* (Sydney: Anglican Information Office, 2000).
44. Some of these matters have been alluded to in earlier parts of this chapter. The work of the Doctrine Commission established under the General Synod would make for an interesting case study of the central themes and preoccupations of Australian Anglicans. Though this commission's work probably reveals as much about the political context of Australian Anglicanism as it does about the agenda for theological work per se.

hensive account remains a major undertaking for the future. The following analysis identifies continuing theological strands. It is selective and representative rather than exhaustive. For illustrative purposes it identifies some examples (mostly recent) of work within the different kinds of theological engagements of Australian Anglicans. However, it does intend to clarify both the *modes* through which theology has been done, dominant themes of the tradition and the *direction* in which it is moving. Minimally what this brief overview and classification does is to show clearly that Australian Anglicans are participants in the theological tasks of the Church in company with their colleagues in other parts of the world. But they engage in this activity from a particular place with its own characteristics, history and challenges.

Australian Anglicans doing theology: modes of theological engagement

Theology through history

There is a strong tradition in Australia of Anglicans engaged in theology through historical inquiry. In this area Australian Anglicans have achieved significant results in recent decades. Theology through history represents a powerful theological stream in Anglicanism generally.[45] Underlying this theological method is a strongly incarnational approach that discerns God's presence in the inter-weave of Gospel, faith and culture. Theology on this account is a thoroughly contingent activity of the Church and it covers a wide range of pursuits.

A characteristic emphasis for Australian Anglicans in the historical mode of theology is historiography. In this approach key figures, movements and themes are pursued. Recent examples of this are found in the essays in *Australian Anglicanism: A History*.[46] Some of the contributors have also explored, from different perspectives, aspects of the character and identity of Australian Anglicanism.[47] At the same time Australian

45. See the essay by Stephen Sykes, 'Theology Through History', in *The Modern Theologians*, edited by David Ford, volume 2 (Oxford: Blackwell, 1989), chapter 1.
46. Contributors include: Brian Dickey, Brian Fletcher, Ruth Frappell, Tom Frame, David Hilliard, Colin Holden, and Stuart Piggin.
47. For example see: Tom Frame, *Church for a Nation: The History of the Anglican Diocese of Canberra and Goulburn* (Sydney: Hale and Iremonger, 2000); Colin Holden, *Church in a Landscape: A History of the Diocese of Wangaratta* (Armadale: Circa Books, 2002); Stuart Piggin, *Evangelical Christianity in Australia: Spirit, Word and World* (Melbourne:

Anglicans are involved in the interpretation of Anglicanism beyond our shores. Some examples of this orientation are Geoff Treloar's examination of the life and work of JB Lightfoot, Rowan Strong on Scottish episcopacy, and David Hilliard on mission in the Pacific.[48] The historian Edwin Judge is a good example of a student of antiquity and early Christianity operating historiographically as an Anglican Christian.[49]

The insights of the historian are significant for understanding the particular colour and shape of theological traditions in Anglicanism in Australia.[50] Indeed the history of an ecclesial tradition is a vital way by which Australian Anglicans appropriate their own heritage and achieve a mature assessment of their own identity and possible future.

Yet the challenge in this mode of inquiry is how to give due regard to the central preoccupation of theology as concern for the particular mode of God's presence in the world in Jesus Christ.[51] Attention to this dynamic is more explicit in the familiar engagements of historical theology. This approach to theology through history traces ideas and themes through different periods and persons in the tradition. It is the familiar way in which most theologians operate, whether Protestant, Catholic, Evangelical, or liberal. This approach makes sense for a church like the Anglican that values its historical roots and inherited traditions. Ordinands would have been taught in this way at Anglican theological colleges in Australia with different emphases and focuses on particular periods and figures

---

Oxford University Press, 1996).

48. See: Geoffrey R Treloar, *Lightfoot the Historian: The Nature and Role of History in the Life and Thought of JB Lightfoot (1828–1889) as Churchman and Scholar* (Tübingen: Mohr Siebeck, 1998); Rowan Strong, *Episcopalianism in Nineteenth-century Scotland: Religious Responses to a Modernising Society* (Oxford: Oxford University Press, 2002); David Hilliard, *God's Gentlemen: A History of the Melanesian Mission, 1849–1942* (Brisbane: University of Queensland Press, 1978).
49. Judge's publications are extensive. His collected works are in the process of being prepared for publication. For an appreciation of his contribution see Stuart Piggin, 'Surprised by Judge: An Anglican History Professor and Australian Public Life', paper given at the Australian Anglican History Seminar on Anglicans and Public Life, Perth, 16–18 September 2005.
50. As an example see the insightful study of the Evangelical minority tradition in Newcastle Diocese by Paul Robertson, *Proclaiming Unsearchable Riches: Newcastle and the Minority Evangelical Anglicans 1788–1900* (Herefordshire: Gracewing Fowler Wright Books, 1996).
51. See Daniel Hardy, 'The English Tradition of Interpretation and the Reception of Schleiermacher and Barth in England', in *Barth and Schleiermacher: Beyond the Impasse?*, edited by JO Duke and RF Streetman (Minneapolis: Fortress Press, 1988), 159 f.

(for example, Patristic, Reformation, nineteenth century Tractarian). This would have been as true for Moore College, Ridley, Trinity, St Barnabas', St Michael's, Wollaston, St Francis', and St Mark's.

The background to this approach can also be linked to the development of theology from the Reformation and the emergence of the theological curriculum in the nineteenth century into the four basic areas: biblical studies, church history, systematics and pastoral theology. Accordingly, until the twentieth century it was customary for Anglican ordinands to undertake a three-year study program structured around the Thirty-nine Articles (first year: scripture and patristic, articles 1–8; second year: reformation doctrines, articles 9–18: third year: church, ministry sacraments, articles 19–39). The collapse of this coherent system of study has presented serious challenges for theological education. These days most colleges have developed a more contemporary curriculum catering for clerical and lay alike. This has generally meant a diminution of historical theology in the traditional pattern but it has not meant a departure from an historical mode of teaching theology. The difference is in the particular focus. For example, newer courses on feminism, radical discipleship, evangelism and mission, and creation and ecology will still generally be taught with a strong historical orientation. A survey of theological curricula in Anglican centres of theology would reveal the tensions between traditional and contemporary approaches to theological work and highlight the variety of mediums through which theology is done.

But this approach can fail to reach a genuine theological engagement in the rehearsing and analysing of ideas and traditions. In this approach theological success requires careful attention to history and ideas, and a keen grasp of the dynamics of divine action through time and space.

Theology through philosophy

A complementary tradition in Anglicanism looks to a more systematic statement of the work of God in the world. This impulse generates a 'theology through philosophy' approach which attends to ideas and conceptual analysis in its rational account of the inner logic of faith.[52] It remains seriously underdeveloped within Anglicanism and not surprisingly in its Australian expression. In Australia this approach is more eclectic, combining particular historical and doctrinal commitments with a more sys-

52. See Daniel Hardy, 'Theology Through Philosophy', in *The Modern Theologians*, volume 2, chapter 2.

tematic bent. TC Hammond's work is an example. So too is Broughton Knox and his theology of revelation,[53] and, more recently, former Principal of Moore College and now Archbishop of Sydney, Peter Jensen.[54] Jensen continues the long line of Moore College scholars writing out of an Evangelical Calvinist tradition. The approach appeals to an historical period but this arises out of a certain confessional theology undergirded by strong doctrinal and philosophical commitments. For this reason it is less historical theology than it might seem and more philosophically driven than is immediately apparent. In this particular case a seventeenth-century Lockean empiricist philosophy is significant.[55] The annual Moore College lectures would be an interesting read on this tradition. However, the danger in this approach is that it can become skewed by ideological and ecclesial interests. Of course there are no value-free positions but there are more open and dynamic ways of construing the theological task.

Some theology moves more freely through history, systematic philosophical analysis and contemporary culture. Duncan Reid, formerly on the faculty of St Barnabas', and until recently Dean of the United Theological Faculty in Melbourne, is an example of the ancient lineage of systematicians who find resources for their work in patristic sources[56] but deploy this in dealing with contemporary issues such as Australian culture and the Spirit.[57]

---

53. In Knox's case his confessional theology also included a scholarly attention to the Thirty-nine Articles, Canon Law and polity. See for example Broughton Knox, *Propositional Revelation, the only Revelation* (Newtown, NSW: Committee for External Studies of Moore Theological College, 196?); also available in his *Selected Works* (Kingsford, NSW: Matthias Media, 2000-2006); *The Lord's Supper from Wycliffe to Cranmer* (Exeter: Paternoster Press, 1983); *Thirty-nine Articles: The Historic Basis of the Anglican Faith*, (London: Hodder and Stoughton, 1967); *Sent by Jesus: Some Aspects of Christian Ministry Today* (Edinburgh: Banner of Truth Trust, 1992). For an appreciation of Knox's range of scholarship see Robert Banks, 'The Theology of D B Knox: A Preliminary Estimate', in *God Who is Rich in Mercy: Essays Presented to D B Knox*, edited by Peter T O'Brien and David G Peterson (Homebush West: Lancer Books, 1986), 377–403.

54. See most recently Peter Jensen, *The Revelation of God* (Leicester: Inter-Varsity Press, 2002).

55. Locke's theory of clear and simple ideas, almost fact-like and propositional in form, has important resonances with a biblical and theological tradition that appeals to a propositional form of revelation. This appeal can be focussed on either biblical 'data' or more complex propositions of revelation closely associated with the data. For further see chapter 4 of this present volume of essays.

56. Duncan Reid, *Energies of the Spirit* (Atlanta USA: Atlanta Press, 1997).

57. Duncan Reid, '"Some Spirit which Escapes": Starting with the Spirit in the Southern

It is not uncommon for Australian Anglicans to traverse a number of sub-disciplines within theology. This is indicative of the way much theology has to be done under pressure and in response to the practical needs of the church and academy. Charles Sherlock is a well-known interpreter of the theological tradition and an example of a scholar who moves freely between biblical studies, theology and liturgy in the interests of a practical theology.[58] This flexibility is also evident in the work of the former Primate, Peter Carnley. He has written on New Testament theology[59] and continued to publish in ecclesial and cultural areas through a heavy ecclesiastical schedule as archbishop and primate.[60] Alan Cadwallader from St Barnabas', Adelaide, is another example of a scholar moving across a variety of fields including New Testament, theology, ethics and spirituality.[61]

On the other hand some theology is more intentionally focussed on the relevance of the faith for the contemporary world. An example of this is Graeme Garrett whose work embodies the Burgmann tradition of mak-

---

Land', in *Starting with the Spirit*, edited by Gordon Preece and Stephen Pickard (Hindmarsh, SA: ATF Press, 2001), chapter 8.

58. For example see Charles Sherlock, *God on the Outside: Trinitarian Spirituality* (Canberra: Acorn Press, 1991); *The God Who Fights: the War Tradition in Holy Scripture* (Lewiston, NY: Edwin Mellen Press, 1993); *The Doctrine of Humanity* (Downers Grove: IVP, 1996); Charles Sherlock and Peta Sherlock, 'What Are We Doing With Words: Five Studies in Liturgy and Language' 1991 [unpublished paper]; and *An Anglican Pastoral Handbook: Guidelines for the Administration of Baptism and Pastoral Services in the Diocese of Melbourne*, edited by Charles Sherlock (Canberra: Acorn Press, 2001.
59. Peter Carnley, *The Structure of Resurrection Belief* (Oxford: Clarendon Press, 1987).
60. Peter Carnley, *Reflections in Glass: Trends and Tensions in the Contemporary Anglican Church* (Pymble, NSW: HarperCollins, 2004).
61. See for example Alan Cadwallader, 'When a Woman is a Dog: Ancient and Modern Ethology Meet the Syrophoenician Woman', in *Bible and Critical Theory*, 3 (2005); 'The Fall, the Samaritan and the Wounded Man: An Example of Multiple Readings of Scripture (Luke 10:25–37)', in *Lost in Translation?: Anglicans, Controversy and the Bible*, edited by Scott Cowdell & Muriel Porter (Thorbury: Desbooks, 2004), 155–84; '"And the Earth Shook"—Mortality and Ecological Diversity: Jesus' Death in Matthew's Gospel', in *Theology and Biodiversity*, edited by Mark Worthing and Denis Edwards (Adelaide: ATF Press, 2004); 'Towards a Living Spirituality', in *St Mark's Review*, 157 (1994): 11–18; and *Aids, the Church as Enemy and Friend: Ambiguities in the Church's Response to Aids*, edited by Alan Cadwallader (North Blackburn, Vic: Collins Dove, 1992); *Episcopacy: Views From the Antipodes*, edited by Alan Cadwallader (Adelaide: Australian Board of Christian Education, 1994). Also *Beyond the Word of a Woman: The Syrophoenician Critique of Ethology* (Hindmarsh, SA: ATF Press, 2010). Cadwallader is also engaged in a critically annotated edition of newly discovered notebooks of BF Westcott on Matthew's gospel.

ing connections between God and society.[62] His editorship of *St Mark's Review* over many years has been a critical factor in the circulation of a distinctly Anglican preoccupation with God, society and the life of discipleship.[63] In the same faculty Scott Cowdell has turned his attention to questions of ecclesiology, faith and discipleship.[64] Through the lens of a renewed Catholic sacramentalism Cowdell is representative of a genuine systematic engagement of post-liberal theology with public culture.[65]

Theology through biblical scholarship

What about 'biblical' theology? This has been a significant preoccupation of Australian Anglican scholars. The relationship between Scripture and theology constitutes the soul of Christian thought.[66] Yet the ancient way of theology as a wisdom tradition in dialogue with the sacred text has fragmented from the Enlightenment period. Sub-disciplines within theology have arisen often disconnected from each other. Biblical studies traces its modern development from the late seventeenth century. In the English tradition it was influenced by the empiricist philosophy of John Locke. Here the speculative and systematic impulse of theology was eclipsed by a concentration upon textual analysis.[67] In this development a Scripture informed theology characteristic of an earlier tradition was transposed into critical analysis and commentary on Scripture which prescinds from

---

62. Graeme Garrett, *God Matters: Conversations in Theology* (Collegeville, Minneapolis: Liturgical Press, 1999) and *Dodging Angels on Saturday: Or Why Being a Theologian in the Twentieth Century Seemed like a Good Idea at the Time* (Adelaide: ATF Press, 2005).
63. A published volume of a representative sample of the *Review* over its fifty-year history will appear in 2007.
64. Following an early doctoral publication on Christology—*Is Jesus Unique? A Study of Recent Christology* (New York: Paulist Press, 1996)—see Scott Cowdell, *A God for This World* (New York: Mowbray, 2000) and *God's Next Big Thing: Discovering the Future Church* (Mulgrave, Vic: John Garratt Publishing, 2004).
65. The background to this approach can be mapped in relation to George Lindbeck's programmatic essay, *The Nature of Doctrine: Religion and Theology in a Post-Liberal Age* (London: SPCK, 1984), and the radical orthodoxy approach represented in the work of the English Anglican John Milbank in, for example, *Radical Orthodoxy: A New Theology*, edited by J Milbank, C Pickstock and G Ward (London: Routledge, 1999). Cowdell embodies elements of both these approaches though his orientation is not backward (as in radical orthodoxy) but innovative and forward looking.
66. See the discussion in William M Thompson, *The Struggle for Theology's Soul: Contesting Scripture in Christology* (New York: Crossroad Herder, 1996), chapter 1.
67. See footnote 49 above.

theological exposition as such.[68] This has had a significant impact upon biblical studies and perceptions of what constitutes theology. It has meant that Anglican theologians have displayed a tenacious commitment to biblical studies. Whilst at one level theological and ecclesial commitments have been sublimated, at another level they have a habit of re-emerging through the medium of biblical studies. It is not surprising therefore that theology through biblical studies has remained a powerful means for the shaping of ecclesial identity and therefore controversial in Anglicanism.

The real issue for Anglican biblical scholars is how to engage in critical reflection on their own discipline in relation to their ecclesial and doctrinal 'interests'. The idea of value-free critical scholarship is a myth. In other words, it is perfectly possible for a strong tradition of biblical studies to be supported by doctrinal commitments which are inevitably woven into or underlie commentary. In this way arguments over interpretation and authority of the sacred text become the arena for deeper doctrinal and faith commitments.[69] Australian Anglicanism displays these characteristics in recent debates over, for example, the ordination of women, lay presidency, and human sexuality.

The other feature of biblical studies is the diversity of approaches and preoccupations among the guild of scholars. For example, there is a discernible attention to 'micro exegesis' in the work of Leon Morris—perhaps the most well-known and prolific of Australian Anglican biblical scholars in the twentieth century—and the Moore College scholar, Peter O'Brien.[70]

---

68. This has begun to break down in contemporary scholarship with the advent of closer cooperation between biblical studies and systematic theology. See for example *Between Two Horizons: Spanning New Testament Studies and Systematic Theology*, edited by Joel B Green and Max Turner (Grand Rapids, MI: Eerdmans, 2000).
69. It is also true that while there are pockets of resistance there has been a trend in recent years for biblical and theological concerns to work in a more integrated manner. For further see the discussion of NT Wright, *The New Testament and the People of God* (Minneapolis: Fortress Press, 1992), chapter one, 'Christian Origins and the New Testament', wherein Wright shows how texts admit of a multi-layered analysis—pre-critical, historical, theological and post-modern. More recently Brazos Press and Eerdmans have initiated a new series of biblical commentaries written by theologians and ethicists. For example see the *Brazos Theological Commentary on the Bible* series, 14 volumes with 2 forthcoming in 2011; and Eerdmans *The Two Horizons New Testament Commentary*, 4 volumes.
70. Morris' writings on the New Testament are extensive. See for example his *The First Epistle of Paul to the Corinthians* (Grand Rapids, MI: Eerdmans 1958); *The Revelation of St John: An Introduction and Commentary* (Grand Rapids, MI: Eerdmans, 1969); *Studies in the Fourth Gospel* (Devon: Paternoster Press, 1969); *The Gospel According to John: the English text with introduction, exposition notes* (Grand Rapids, MI: Eerdmans,

But it is associated with an Evangelical conservatism that has a greater affinity with an interdenominational conservative community than with the Anglican tradition. In Morris' case his contribution ranges across a range of themes in biblical theology.[71]

Other biblical theologians, whilst attentive to text, operate beyond the boundaries of 'micro exegesis'. For example in the Evangelical tradition a scholar such as Donald Robinson embodies a more discernible concern for an Anglican ethos.[72] Robinson's commitments stretch across biblical studies into theology and Anglican liturgy. In similar manner Paul Barnett's biblical scholarship moves between closely argued commentary and wider ranging theological concerns.[73] Other scholars from the Evangelical tradition who write out of an Anglican sensibility, such as Kevin Giles, evidence an engagement with the sacred text, Patristic and contemporary issues.[74] The covenantal theology of the Moore College Old Testament scholar, William Dumbrell,[75] like Giles, Barnett and Robinson, represents a broad-based biblical theology.

1971); *The Gospel According to Luke: An Introduction and Commentary* (Grand Rapids, MI: Eerdmans, 1974). For O'Brien see for example, *The Epistle to the Philippians: A Commentary on the Greek Text*, The New International Greek Testament Commentary (Grand Rapids, MI: Eerdmans, 1991); *The Letter to the Ephesians*, Pillar New Testament Commentary (Grand Rapids, MI: Eerdmans, 1999).

71. See for example Leon Morris, *The Apostolic Preaching of the Cross* (Grand Rapids, MI: Eerdmans, 1965); *The Cross in the New Testament* (Exeter: Paternoster Press, 1967); *The Atonement: its Meaning and Significance* (Leicester: IVP, 1983); *New Testament Theology*, (Grand Rapids, MI: Academie Books, 1986). O'Brien has also written in the area of missiology, for example: *Salvation to the Ends of the Earth: A Biblical Theology of Mission*, co-authored with AJ Kostenberger (Leicester: Apollos, 2001).
72. For example: Donald WB Robinson, *The Meaning of Baptism*, second edition (Beecroft, NSW: Evangelical Tracts and Publications, 1958); *Faith's Framework: The Structure of New Testament Theology* (Sutherland, NSW: Albatros, 1985); *Ordination for What?* (Sydney: Anglican Information Office, 1992); *The Church of God: Its Form and its Unity* (Punchbowl, NSW: Jordan Books, 1965). See also *In the Fullness of Time: Biblical Studies in Honour of Archbishop Donald Robinson*, edited by David Peterson and John Pryor (Homebush West, NSW: Anzea Publishers, 1992).
73. See Paul Barnett, *Is the New Testament History?* (Sydney: Hodder & Stoughton, 1986); *Bethlehem to Patmos: The New Testament Story* (Sydney: Hodder & Stoughton, 1989); *The Second Epistle to the Corinthians* (Grand Rapids, MI: Eerdmans, 1997); *Jesus and the Logic of History* (Leicester: Apollos, 1997).
74. See for example Kevin Giles, *The Trinity and Subordinationism: God and the Contemporary Gender Debate* (Downers Grove, IL: IVP, 2002).
75. William J Dumbrell, *Covenant and Creation: An Old Testament Covenantal Theology* (Exeter: Paternoster Press, 1984). An example of a scholar from the more liberal Catholic tradition is the biblical scholar at Murdoch University, John Dunnill; see his

In more recent decades John Painter is an example of a scholar whose research and publications on the New Testament—in particular his exegetical work on the Johannine corpus—is recognised and respected in the international biblical scholarly community.[76] Painter illustrates an Anglican biblical method embodying critical-historical engagement with the sacred text, and ongoing interpretation and assessment of the tradition for contemporary faith. It is an example followed by a range of Anglican scholars of the New Testament and early Christianity, although with differing emphases and ecclesial commitments.[77] For some, like the United Kingdom based scholar Stephen Barton, this involves an interdisciplinary approach that engages with the social sciences in the interests of a richer and contemporary biblical theology.[78]

Theology through interdisciplinary and public engagements

In more recent theology there has emerged a focus on theology through ethics, and socio-cultural and political engagements. It is a multi-perspectival approach which crosses disciplines and seeks a public engagement

---

Covenant and Sacrifice in the Letter to the Hebrews (Cambridge: Cambridge University Press, 1992).

76. His publications include more than sixty journal articles and seven books. See for example John Painter, *John: Witness and Theologian* (London: SPCK, 1985); *The Quest for the Messiah: The History, Literature and Theology of the Johannine Community* (Edinburgh: T&T Clark, 1991); *Mark's Gospel: Worlds in Conflict* (Abingdon: Routledge, 1997); *Just James: The Brother of Jesus in History and Tradition* (Edinburgh: T&T Clark, 1999); *1, 2 and 3 John* (The Liturgical Press, 2002). Painter's theological studies began at Moore College, followed by doctoral studies in Durham under CK Barrett and appointments in South Africa, La Trobe University and over the last decade at St Mark's National Theological Centre as the foundation Professor of Theology in the School of Theology of Charles Sturt University. Painter has generated a significant body of studies in the New Testament, early Christianity and its background in Judaism. He represents a strong tradition in biblical studies that takes its cue from Lightfoot, Westcott and Hort in the late nineteenth century but owes a significant debt to the Bultmann school of New Testament theology. This dual emphasis grounds his scholarship and offers a critical lever in relation to conservative and liberal forces.
77. For example Andrew McGowan and Dorothy Lee (Melbourne), Mark Harding (Sydney), Ray Barraclough and Greg Jenks (Brisbane; Barraclough now retired), Alan Cadwallader (Adelaide till 2009 then Canberra ACU) and the late John Roffey (Adelaide), John Dunnill (Wollaston, Perth).
78. See for example Barton's use of sociological categories in: *Discipleship and Family Ties in Mark and Matthew* (Cambridge: Cambridge University Press, 1994) and *Life Together: Family Sexuality and Community in the New Testament and Today* (Edinburgh: T&T Clark, 2001). An interdisciplinary approach to biblical studies is also present in the work of Cadwallader, Barraclough, and McGowan.

for theology. Early examples of this approach are Farnham E Maynard and Ernest Burgmann, both of whom did their theology through engagement with the social and political realities of their day. Maynard, the Anglo-Catholic Vicar of St Peter's Eastern Hill, Melbourne (1926–1964), was a controversialist who spoke and wrote on a myriad of topics including economics and the kingdom of God, and religion and revolution.[79] In Canberra Burgmann, through the 1950s and 1960s, was an outspoken commentator and 'meddlesome priest' as far as the political world was concerned and had a particular interest in the relationship between religion and psychology, long before it was considered a topic for theology.[80] His Christian socialism from a Broad Church tradition offered, like Maynard, a more public and prophetic theological voice in their day. They were harbingers of the public theology tradition emerging within the theological scene of today.

In the latter decades of the twentieth century Robert Banks is an example of a theologian whose biblical studies and roots in Anglicanism have been developed into an engagement with the public domain in relation to such issues as work, vocation, time, and a range of ethical matters.[81] His commitments to 'everyday Christianity' beyond the confines of the eccle-

---

79. For a brief introduction to Maynard, his writings and the tradition of St Peter's Eastern Hill see Colin Holden, 'A Not So Respectable Church in a Very Respectable City', paper delivered at the onhundred and fiftieth anniversary of the Church, 1996. See website: <http://web.stpeters.org.au/history/history.shtml>. Accessed 2 February 2011. Holden also notes that Maynard's 'commitment to radical political and social theories was accompanied by doctrinal conservatism'; see 'Gothic Foundations and Rising Damp, or Prophets and Rebels: the Contributions of the Liberal Intellectual Tradition in Australian Anglicanism to National Culture', The Barry Marshall Memorial Lecture, Trinity Papers Number 15 (Trinity College: University of Melbourne, 2000), 21. Copies held at Trinity College. See also Colin Holden, *From Tories at Prayer to Socialists at Mass. A History of St Peter's Eastern Hill* (Melbourne: Melbourne University Press, 1996).
80. See Hempenstall, *The Meddlesome Priest*.
81. Banks began his Christian life as an Anglican, trained at Moore College and then served a curacy at Holy Trinity, Adelaide, before going to Cambridge for his doctorate. While in Cambridge he resigned from the ministry on the grounds that so much of the teaching and practice of the Anglican Church was at variance with Scripture. Technically he remains an Anglican priest but without licence. He has always worked with Anglicans and Anglican churches and his later writings and preoccupations with theology in the public domain embody that strong tradition of God in society so much a feature of his roots in Anglicanism. See Geoffrey Treloar, 'Three Contemporary Christian Radicals in Australia: Robert Banks, Stuart Piggin and Bruce Kaye', in *Agendas for Australian Anglicans: Essays in Honour of Bruce Kaye*, edited by T Frame and G Treloar (Adelaide: ATF Press, 2006), 195–230.

siastical world are illustrative of a fundamental Anglican commitment to God in society. His successor at Macquarie Christian Studies Institute, Gordon Preece, is an example of an Australian Anglican scholar whose theological ethics highlights the importance of maintaining the dialectic between identity—the inheritance and traditions of the faith—with the demands of relevance and connection to the social and cultural realities of the day.[82]

This mode of interaction between the theological tradition and contemporary life is more significant than standard approaches to theology in Australia recognise. There is in fact a long tradition in Australia of Anglican theological work being undertaken in connection with other disciplines. One might say Anglicans, precisely because of their basic commitments to God in society and the search for an intelligent grasp of the faith have, perhaps unintentionally, fostered a certain habit of engagement. Their theological interests bump into their interests in the world—social, political, religious and cultural. However, such an Anglican form of engagement inevitably means that their contributions are highly dispersed and publications that emerge from such interactions do not always occupy central place in the consciousness of the Church.[83] This mode of theological enquiry comes into the category of 'theology and', with a great variety of subjects following, and is an approach that keeps it outwardly focussed and concrete. It is an underrated yet highly significant mode through which Australian Anglicans do theology. And historically it has been done beyond the seminary through professional and vocational work in the world.

82. See for example Gordon Preece, *The Viability of the Vocation Tradition in Trinitarian, Credal and Reformed Perspective: the Threefold Call* (Lewiston, NY: Edwin Mellen Press, 1998). His writings cover a range of areas: ecology, work values, republic, entrepreneurship, education, drug and alcohol, sexuality, stem cells and refugees.

83. The writing of Elizabeth McKinlay, Director of the Centre for Ageing and Pastoral Studies, St Mark's Canberra, illustrates this point. Her work connects theology, spirituality, health care and literature on ageing. See for example Elizabeth McKinlay, *The Spiritual Dimension of Ageing* (London: Jessica Kingsley, 2001). On a personal note, recently I had an experience of an interdisciplinary engagement—in a symposium at the Australian National University on the theme of uncertainty—with scholars from all over Australia across the disciplines and governmental agencies (for example, art, philosophy, medical science, emergency services, music) where a representative of religion was but one of the invited participants. The forthcoming publication will not figure in theological circles; indeed it will probably be lost to the Church.

Theology through aesthetics: poetry, song, sermon, art and liturgy

Anglicanism has a long heritage of poetry, hymnody and liturgical sensibility embodying an implicit (if not at times explicit) appeal to a theological aesthetic.[84] This dimension can be also discerned in the sermon tradition in Anglicanism.[85] Although often obscured or ignored in contemporary Christianity the aesthetic tradition in theology has operated as a powerful strand through which the fundamental realities of Christian existence have been expressed.[86] This is an immensely important and potentially vast area and I can but flag it here as deserving a proper account at some stage in the future.[87]

Australians have been a part of this larger and rich tradition in Anglican aesthetics. Generally its significance has been more keenly felt and expressed through more Catholic and sacramental streams in our tradition. I was reminded of this current in theology when attending the installation of the new Archbishop of Adelaide, Jeffrey Driver, in October 2005. The liturgy was rich and immensely engaging through word and sacrament, spoken and sung. The music traversed old and new; traditional, blues jazz, rock and Sudanese style. There was colour, pageantry, and gravitas. The contemporary hymns from *Together in Song* were by two Australian Anglican poets and hymn composers, Michael Thwaites and Elizabeth Smith.

The hymns of Smith illustrate the potential for the development of an Australian religious aesthetic as a mode through which a fine tradition in theology can exercise an influence and power in shaping the identity and vision for discipleship in this country.[88] Her work has a remarkable resonance with the Anglican tradition stretching back to George Herbert and the seventeenth-century metaphysical poets and composers and connecting with the hymnody and poetry of the American Episcopalian composers, Rosalind Brown and Thomas Troeger. Theologically Smith offers a

---

84. For example see the insightful book by William Countryman, *The Poetic Imagination: An Anglican Spiritual Tradition* (New York: Orbis, 1991).
85. For example, *Imagination Shaped: Old Testament Preaching in the Anglican Tradition*, edited by Ellen Davis (Valley Forge, PA: Trinity Press International, 1995).
86. The eclipse of aesthetics in theology has both a Protestant and Catholic form; see Hans Ur von Balthasar, *Seeing the Form*, in *The Glory of the Lord: A Theological Aesthetics*, volume 1 (Edinburgh: T&T Clark, 1982), chapters 1–7.
87. The significance of the visual arts and architecture for Australian Anglicanism has been the subject of a recent discussion in Colin Holden, 'Anglicanism, the Visual Arts and Architecture', in *Anglicanism in Australia: A History*, chapter 13.
88. See the index to *Together in Song: Australian Hymn Book 2* (East Melbourne, Vic: HarperCollins Religious, 1999), for Smith's contributions and Thwaites' hymn.

sophisticated and nuanced account of the ways of God with the world and her work invites a participatory and responsible following of Jesus Christ.

Liturgical scholarship has not been strong in Australia and there have been few appointments in theological faculties in this discipline.[89] However Michael Dudman's composition for the eucharist is an example of a well-established and 'home grown' setting. The fact that Australian Anglicans have produced two Prayer Books (1978 and 1995) indicates that there is an ongoing search in Anglicanism for forms of common ritual and prayer that give expression to an Anglican identity and relevance. This also suggests that theology through the mode of the aesthetic is a powerful framework for a mission shaped church.

Modes of theology: preliminary conclusions

This brief and selective picture of modes through which Australian Anglicans undertake theology with some representative examples points to a complex weave of interests, and a certain intellectual rigour and vibrancy in the tradition at this point in our history. It also draws attention to the fact that the boundaries between these dominant modes of theological engagement are not always sharp. Indeed, as we have observed, it is not unusual for Australian scholars to display a remarkable theological agility in moving through a variety of modes.

Some of the forms of engagement evidence a greater maturity than others. For example, an historical mode of theology is clearly the substantive tradition compared to the approach via philosophy. However, the different modes are not particularly well integrated either within their sub-disciplines or across the sub-disciplines. Thus within the history stream there is an interesting question about the way the more overtly historiographical approach contributes to the theological task. On the other hand a dominant historical-theological approach may in fact be a front for a doctrinalism located within a particular confessional tradition. In other words theological ideology may be masked by appeals to a more historical mode of inquiry. Within biblical scholarship there is a variety of approaches to text and world with varying degrees of Anglican self-consciousness in such work.

Overall we might ask what weight or significance should be accorded any of the above forms of theological engagement in relation to the central

89. In recent times William Lawton was lecturer in Liturgy at Moore College and earlier Gilbert Sinden at St Michael's, Crafers.

concern of theology, the account of the dynamic of God's presence in the world. Of course this depiction of the theological task might be contested, but if so a discussion of the matter needs to be on the agenda of Australian Anglican theologians. In turn this points to the desirability of stronger collegial and inter-disciplinary activity among Anglican theologians in Australia. It is required for the ongoing vitality and creative development of the discipline and its contribution to the life of the Church.

Australians doing Anglican theology: method and themes

An Anglican method?

It is one thing to identify Australian Anglicans doing theology in the broadest sense. It is more difficult to identify Australian Anglicans engaged in an *Anglican* theology. Perhaps this is as it should be, or so the argument goes. Theologians ought to do theology and the fact that they do it in a particular context and from within a specific ecclesial environment (or none) is a secondary matter. If such work becomes overly self-conscious the risk of introspection and disconnection becomes greater. When such theology becomes overly self-conscious it ceases to be truly Anglican in spirit.

While this line of reasoning has a great deal of merit, a balance is required in order to develop a properly critical account of theological activity as a first step in uncovering the inchoate and unacknowledged ideological and cultural pressures that skew such theological work. This emphasis—the hermeneutics of suspicion—can be discerned in much that goes under the name of contextual theology. The problem of course is that the context becomes the driver but little advance is made theologically. In any case it seems that a healthy theological tradition will encourage attention to text, tradition and context. As indicated above what makes the enterprise *theological* is an overriding concern for the mode of God's presence in the world.

Are we entitled to say anything in regard to Australian Anglicans doing *Anglican* theology? Perhaps we first should note that the matter has been controversial. It was in the late 1970s that the Anglican theologian, Stephen Sykes, exposed the falsity of a tradition harking back to Maurice in the mid-nineteenth century, which claimed that there was no distinctive Anglican theology.[90] Sykes saw this claim as a way to avoid the chal-

90. Sykes, *The Integrity of Anglicanism*.

lenge of critical reflection on Anglican theology and in particular the doctrine of the Church. The 'no special doctrines' theory of Anglicanism was associated with a claim that Anglicanism enshrined an ethos and method rather than particular doctrines.[91] Here it is a question of a method of engagement—respect for sacred texts, attention to traditions in history, interconnections. Thus when biblical scholars apply the best insights of critical scholarship to the understanding of the sacred text and allow this to be informed by the rich traditions of interpretation they bear witness to a very Anglican way of doing theology. This stream is both historical and critical. When these features are present in the way Australian Anglicans undertake their theology, they are not merely doing theology but doing it in some characteristic Anglican ways.

Recurring theological themes

A strong correlation between method and content might not be assured but it is entirely consonant with Anglican method that characteristic themes also emerge: Scripture, authority, Christology, ecclesiology and society. They are concerns that arise out of fundamental commitments to texts, history, communities of faith and traditions of interpretation. Such commitments are undergirded by a conviction that the divine has acted in history, decisively in the Word made flesh, and continues to work through the Spirit in the world witnessed to in the community of Christ. The history of Anglican theology is in fact a history of a rich weave between method and recurring themes. Thus it comes as no surprise that Richard Hooker should be held up—not least by Bruce Kaye—as such an important exemplar of a characteristic way in theology which is scriptural and focussed on the dynamic of God in society.

The weave has not always been harmonious. Indeed conflict has never been absent from Anglican theology. Again this ought not be surprising given an Anglican concern for what is believed together. In other words, the concentration upon sociality as the arena upon which the life of faith has to be grasped and expressed means conflict, and attempts to find consensus and creative engagements will be recurring features of Anglican theology.[92] This Anglican way in theology is well captured by Bruce Kaye:

91. For an example see the former Archbishop of Ireland, Henry McAdoo, *The Spirit of Anglicanism: A Survey of Anglican Theological Method in the Seventeenth Century* (London: Adam & Charles Black, 1965).

92. These are hardly the conditions for the development of a rigid or overly precise doctrinalism, though this temptation has haunted the tradition in times of stress and

> The tradition of theology in Anglicanism may not be capable of such precise definition as Roman Catholic Thomism, or German Lutheranism, or Reformed Calvinism, but it would be marked by certain general characteristics: a focus on the incarnation, respect for human reason, an integration of theology and the worship life of the church, and a continuing interaction with the society in which it operates.[93]

For Kaye this signalled an engagement in the theological task that 'may very well turn out to be more lay than clerical'.[94]

The preoccupations of Anglican theology in this country are understandable given the strong regionalism and imported tensions between the different ecclesial traditions within the Church of England of the nineteenth century. One result is that ecclesiology has been a highly conflictual affair and that matters of authority, Scripture and polity have dominated much of the agenda. In turn this reflected the interest of the Evangelical and more conservative wings of the Church. This has been balanced (to some extent) by the Broad Church tradition's incarnational focus on issues of God in society. Hence the recurring themes of theology have covered both internal and external concerns but in a rather restricted manner. It is also the case that form and content usually go together. Accordingly a concern for history, texts and theology has expressed itself in a focus on authority, polity, Scripture and incarnation.

Towards a theology of Australian Anglicanism: ecclesiological directions

From theology in a general sense to a more intentional focus on theology that is Anglican in spirit and execution, we move to the distinctly ecclesiological task. Does it make sense to pursue a theology of Anglicanism for Australia? Such a venture becomes an exercise in contextual ecclesiology. Australian Anglicans have barely begun to traverse the terrain. The historians have certainly provided material for this particular vocation of

---

anxiety for politico-ecclesial power. When this dominates, biblical and theological work can become skewed to the establishment of structures for control and management of the church. This not only confirms Newman's view of theology as a power but in doing so it also highlights the need for responsible use of such a wisdom tradition.

93. Kaye, 'The Anglican Tradition', 33.

94. Kaye, 'The Anglican Tradition', 33.

Anglican theology.[95] But a question arises: can theologians deploy the insights of these historians and bring them into creative dialogue with the sacred texts of the tradition and contemporary realities of life in Australia? This is the ecclesiological task that still awaits us.

Bruce Kaye has given a lead. He has been a consistent advocate for re-conceiving the Anglican communion. But in his case the task has been undertaken from within his own Australian context and has consistently drawn upon the experience of being Anglican in Australia as a springboard for his critical reflections and constructive proposals for the way ahead for the Anglican Communion.

What shines through from this perspective is the power of regionalism to shape a local ecclesial variety of Anglicanism. Unfortunately the power of the local has not always been positive, for it has also meant that the inherited Anglican forms and ways have too often been imported into our Australian context where they have become embedded even more firmly. The problem of being disconnected from each other has mitigated against a genuine national Church, but it has also resulted in Australian Anglicans having a long history of dealing with regional conflicts, fragmentation and diversity. What this means is that an Australian Anglican theology will require careful attention to the nature of the place in which the church has had to take root and develop.[96] A theology of place may be the way in which Australian Anglicans find a new theological maturity in the twenty-first century. Such a theology would have to take account of the strong incarnational theme in Anglicanism, its concomitant attention to challenges of enculturation and its critical perspective on society and church in relation to the Gospel.

Future agenda

Enculturating the Gospel within the Australian environment and its cultures remains a project on the ecclesial drawing board and a major task for Australian theologians. The challenges here can be discerned in a number of areas: theology, interfaith and indigenous relations, social and political engagements, liturgy, worship and church architecture. Underlying the above is the deeper issue for theology and church of finding an orientation and sympathy with the realities of Australian life at the

95. In *Anglicanism in Australia: A History.*

96. For example see Stephen Pickard, 'Many Verandahs: Same House? Ecclesiological Challenges for Australian Anglicanism', in *Journal of Anglican Studies*, 4/2 (2006):179–200.

intersections of continent, ocean and sky. The specific task is to nurture a theological outlook that attends to our local context and draws upon the givens of our existence.[97] Such an undertaking would be funded by a doctrine of creation interlaced with insights from those disciplines that have begun to recover the importance of place (Cultural Studies, Geography, Psychology). However, idealisation of place as a kind of paradise cannot be sustained in a country with two hundred years of mistreatment of its indigenous peoples. The pain and violence of particular places points to the fuller dynamic of creation in the process of transformation. The restorative and redemptive work of God through Word and Spirit bringing all places to their fulfilment is ongoing and this too belongs to the history (past, present and future) of our places. The task then for church and theology is profound. Key questions emerge. What might a full-orbed theology for Christian discipleship in Australia entail? How can it be done in a manner that honours the place of our habitation? How might Anglicans from indigenous communities be enabled to play their part in the story of theology in Australia? How might Australian Anglicans contribute to a scripture informed local theology?

This challenge is being taken up in a variety of ways at present. There is a developing tradition of public theology, pointed to by Kaye a decade and a half ago, practised in a prophetic way by Ernest Burgmann in the middle decades of the twentieth century, and now emerging through creative collaborations between church, university and Australian society.[98] Where such developments occur they point to a profoundly Anglican way of engagement with the intellectual and social currents of the time. They also feed back into the church offering new horizons, opportunities and critical perspectives.

As noted earlier in this chapter the other remarkable development over the last decade has been the emergence of women scholars of theology. There is a change occurring and in the years to come it will have a profound impact on the temper and direction of Anglican theology in Australia, who does it and to what purpose. Increasingly theology as a

97. See my proposal in this regard: Stephen Pickard, 'The View From the Verandah: Gospel and Spirituality in an Australian Setting', in *St Mark's Review* (1998): 7–11.

98. One such example is the Public and Contextual Theology Research Centre through Charles Sturt University in association with St Mark's National Theological Centre and United Theological College, Parramatta. The Adelaide College of Divinity had, until 2008, an important research centre at Flinders University in the area of Theology, the Sciences and Culture. The Brisbane College of Theology has an emerging research group at Griffith University. Anglicans are actively involved in all these.

discipline of the church will be placed within a wider context both in the academy and society. This points to an emerging mission shaped theology for a twenty first-century church. It also points to the potential of theology to recover a genuine prophetic voice as envisaged by Newman in an earlier time. The advent of the international *Journal of Anglican Studies* from an Australian base and a new monograph series devoted to Australian Anglicanism are signs of this renewal.[99] In this way theology in its many forms and through its great diversity of themes will exercise a salutary power in ecclesial life and discipleship. A future mission-shaped church may require new forms of collaborative leadership that recognise the episcope of the theologian. Such a development would be evidence of a new level of maturity for the church and also recover a strand vital in the history of Anglicanism.

What the above developments signify is a slow but sure appropriation of the Gospel to the Australian context. Anglican theologians, both men and women, are a part of this. In the coming decades a distinctly public, ecumenical, gender balanced, lay and missional theology is likely to emerge within Australian Anglicanism. This will occur beyond the confines of traditional seminary and clerical education. It will signal a move from a hitherto derivative and ideologically driven theological tradition to one which is more open and locally engaged. This will be a far healthier engagement of theology with God and society than so much that has gone before and masqueraded as sacred doctrine but in reality been little more than a shop front for ecclesio-political positioning. The upward call of Christ includes the theologians! As this happens the dynamics of theology within the life of the people of God—their worship and political engagements—will assume its important and critical function. It will find its true place as a power for good—a wisdom tradition for the deepening and enlivening of faith and action in the world, and a witness to the coming Kingdom of God.

99. Both these initiatives came from Bruce Kaye.

Chapter Six
Evangelism and Theology in Dialogue[1]

From the Centre to the World

This essay had it origins in a lecture I gave when I first began my teaching career in theology at United Theological Faculty in Sydney. I had been appointed to a post as lecturer in evangelism and theology. It was a creative intersection. Theologians have been wary of delving into the domain of evangelism—'it's just not for them'—while evangelists have shown little interest or regard for the task of theology, indeed they have often viewed it as disconnected from 'the realities on the ground' and a hindrance to the furtherance of the gospel. For seven years I taught in both areas always trying to help students and anyone who would listen see how complementary and important both evangelism and theology were. The essay sketched out the fundamental relation and it later became a small book, Liberating Evangelism: Gospel, Theology and the Dynamics of Communication, (Harrisburg, PA: Trinity Press International, 1999). More recently the essay was republished in an Eerdman collection of essays.

Introduction

Evangelism and theology have not proved to be very compatible partners, at least in the modern period of the Christian tradition. The relationship perhaps has more the character of a stormy courtship ending in separation rather than a well-established marriage. The nature of their partnership was nicely symbolised in the meeting in August, 1960 of Billy Graham and Karl Barth—arguably the two greatest figures in evangelism and theology respectively in the twentieth century. The Barthian interpretation of the meeting is recorded by Barth's biographer, Eberhard Busch:

1. Originally published as 'Evangelism and the Character of Christian Theology', *Missionalia* 1993.

> His [Barth's] son Markus brought them together in the Valais. However, this meeting was also a friendly one. 'He's a "jolly good fellow", with whom one can talk easily and openly; one has the impression that he is even capable of listening, which is not always the case with such trumpeters of the gospel'. Two weeks later Barth had the same good impression after a second meeting with Graham, this time at home in Basle. But, 'it was very different when we went to hear him let loose in the St. Jacob stadium that same evening and witnessed his influence on the masses. I was quite horrified. He acted like a madman and what he presented was certainly not the gospel. 'It was the gospel at gunpoint . . . He preached the law, not a message to make one happy. He wanted to terrify people. Threats—they always make an impression. People would much rather be terrified than be pleased. The more one heats up hell for them, the more they come running'. But even this success did not justify such preaching. It was illegitimate to make the gospel law or to 'push' it like an article for sale . . . We must leave the good God freedom to do his own work.[2]

It would of course, be interesting to hear Graham's side of the meetings and his version of what happened at the St Jacob stadium. At any rate the story symbolises something of the growing rift between theology and evangelism in the modern period.[3] Lamenting the steady decline in the theological competence of evangelists over the generations and the problems associated with much modern mass evangelism William Abraham concludes that 'it is not surprising if theologians prefer to pass by on the

2. E Busch, *Karl Barth: His Life from Letters and Autobiographical Texts* (London: SCM, 1976), 446.
3. Thus William Abraham, in his recent book *The Logic of Evangelism* (London: Hodder & Stoughton, 1989), 8–9, notes the decline in theological competence of the better know evangelists over the generations. John Wesley was steeped in the classical Anglican theological tradition. Jonathan Edwards was not only pastor and preacher involved in the 'Great Awakening' of his time—he was only alos one of the great theologians of the modern Christian tradition. Charles Finney, though able intellectually, was less patient with the academy and the theological tradition and more pragmatic in outlook. In later evangelists, such as DL Moody and Billy Sunday, there is little theological substance left. Billy Graham, while sympathetic to the task of theology in the work of evangelism, has contributed little. The new generation of television-evangelists have shown, in Abraham's view, little 'serious attempt to reflect deeply about the work in which they engaged', 10.

other side and leave the whole mess to whatever Samaritan may have mercy upon it'.[4] Of course, given the fortunes of theology in the wake of critical enlightenment thought, evangelists may well have felt justified in adopting similar strategy in regard to modern theology.

Clearly there is a need for a fresh approach in which is developed 'a fresh universe of discourse that will open up a critical conversation on the complex issues that relate to evangelism'.[5] However, what this fresh approach might entail remains as yet undetermined. At one level there does not seem to be any shortage of published material on evangelism as such, particularly from the late 1960s. Generally speaking much of this material is preoccupied with questions of biblical foundations and principals, discussions concerned with apologetics and the developing of effective programmes for evangelism.[6] In more recent material greater attention to questions of culture and context can be discerned.[7]

Two dominant strands run through the material. One strand is associated with a strong focus on verbal proclamation and is characteristic of Protestant evangelicalism.[8] Another strand has a strong emphasis on communicating the gospel through social action. This perspective has traditionally been an important plank in the World Council of Churches understanding of evangelism.[9] However, these two strands are increasingly difficult to disentangle, if recent statements from the Lausanne Congress and the WCC are to be taken with the seriousness they deserve.[10] It seems

4. Abraham, *Logic of Evangelism*, 10.
5. Abraham, *Logic of Evangelism*, 10.
6. The bibliographies of most books on evangelism will quickly bear this out. See, for example, bibliographies in *Evangelism in the Twenty-First Century*, edited by TS Rainer (Wheaton, IL: Harold Shaw, 1989); DJ Kennedy, *Evangelism Explosion* (London: Coverdale House, 1972); Michael Green, *Evangelism in the Local Church* (London: Hodder & Stoughton, 1990).
7. See for example, O Costas, *Liberating News: A Theology of Contextual Evangelism* (Grand Rapids, MI: Eerdmans, 1989); Leslie Newbiggin, *The Gospel in a Pluralistic Society* (London: SPCK, 1989).
8. See for example, Kennedy, *Evangelism Explosion*.
9. For a useful discussion see for example, Paulos Mar Gregorios, 'The Witness of the Churches: Ecumenical Statements on Mission and Evangelism', The Ecumenical Review, 40/3–4 (July–October 1984): 359–66.
10. The relevant documents are: *The Manila Manifesto an Elaboration of the Lausanne Covenant Fifteen Years Later* (Pasadena, CA: Castle Press, 1989) and *Mission and Evangelism: An Ecumenical Affirmation* (Geneva: WCC, 1982). Both documents evidence important attempts to develop an understanding of evangelism that includes both words and deeds. The traditional emphases remain but clearly reflect the influence of each others ecclesial orientations.

that with the approach of the end of the second millennium the evangelism spectrum is becoming increasingly complex and controversial. The rise of Pentecostalism in the twentieth century has played no small part in this emerging diversity.[11] Important statements from the Roman Catholic and Orthodox Churches have enriched and stimulated discussion of evangelism.[12] Consequently the old boundaries are not so easy to maintain. Evangelism is moving in new directions. What is required is a fresh willingness to listen and learn from each other, particularly those who see things differently from us but with whom is shared a common bond in communicating the mystery of the gospel. But to what extent do evangelists and theologians listen and learn from each other?

Evangelism and theology: a tale of two ships

One thing absent from the wealth of material on evangelism is any well developed contemporary theology of evangelism that might inform the Church's practice of it.[13]

---

11. Any discussion of the recent history of evangelism is incomplete to the extent that it ignores the growth and impact of Pentecostalism in the twentieth century. This is well documented in the well-known authoritative work by Walter J Hollenwegar, *The Pentecostals* (London: SCM, 1972). The point was well made some years ago by FD Brunner, 'Pentecostalism and Mission are almost synonymous', in *A Theology of the Holy Spirit* (Grand Rapids, MI: Eerdmans, 1970), 32.
12. See *Evangeli Nuntiandi: Apostolic Exhortation of Paul VI On Evangelisation in the Modern World* 1975 (Sydney: St Paul Publications, 1989); *Redemptoris Missio: Encyclical Letter of John Paul II On the Permanent Validity of the Church's Missionary Mandate* (Sydney: St Paul Pub, 1991); I Bria editor, *Go Forth in Peace: Orthodox Perspectives on Mission* (Geneva: WCC, 1986).
13. Abraham's *The Logic of Evangelism* is an important recent effort to articulate a contemporary theology of evangelism with a strong ecclesiological orientation. Costas' *Liberating News* is vigorous in its approach to 'contextual evangelisation'. The strength of both books is that they identify important issues and provide a useful frame of reference for future thinking. Abraham is well aware of the difficulties of overcoming the divide between evangelism and theological concerns. Ben Johnson in *Rethinking Evangelism: A Theological Approach* (Philadelphia: Westminster, 1987) writes out of a concern that evangelism in the mainline churches be done 'with integrity' and for 'the right reasons'. 'The starting place for this important task is theology'. Accordingly his book, born of the fruit of his own experience in evangelism and teaching of theology, is an attempt to 'examine the central theological categories from an evangelistic perspective'. However, he seems somewhat apologetic for this approach stressing that his real concern is that the book will enable the development of 'fresh models and strategies' and the setting forth of plans to get on with the task! The pragmatic thrust is understandable but begs many questions about the relationship between theology

In this respect, at least, the old boundaries between evangelism and theology are still firmly in place. It might be said that the good ship *Evangelism* has a lot of crew members all of course busy at important tasks. But the ship is short of theological fuel. This fact remains hidden, at least to the upper deck crew members. They do not know there is a shortage of fuel, they are not even aware that fuel of that kind is necessary. When they are not asleep, you can see them on deck painting, polishing rearranging and reorganising.

Meanwhile, down in the engine room are to be found the engineers. They meet regularly, that is, have conferences to discuss the machinery of the ship. The question of fuel is an important topic on the agenda below deck. The problem is that the fuel supplied in the past no longer provides the energy the ship requires. What of course is desperately needed is new fuel, but where is it to come from?

So the good ship *Evangelism* is afloat, its crew are highly activated, though if you look closely some appear a little worn. The really pressing issues about where the ship is headed, or rather how it is managing to head in a number of different directions remain high on the agenda. But alas these matters do not seem to be any clearer for the many rounds of discussions held among engineers with occasional inputs from the above deck crew. In fact, some crew members and a couple of engineers became so frustrated that they lowered a life-raft and quietly paddled off to a desert island where they could learn again about building ships, ocean currents and how to tread water over 70,000 fathoms.

One day the crew on deck of the good ship *Evangelism* noticed a very large ship passing by, *The Charismatic Queen*. The top decks seem filled with people throwing streamers, waving and beckoning the *Evangelism* crew to join them. It looked so inviting even if, on closer inspection, the ship appeared to be going around in ever decreasing circles.

It is as well to note that there are other ships sailing upon this ecclesial ocean. The most impressive of these are the bulk oil tankers, in particular the 500,000 tonne bulk carrier *Theological Tradition*. Oddly enough when

---

and the evangelistic task. A more traditional reformed theological approach to evangelism is offered by R Kolb, *Speaking The Gospel Today: A Theology for Evangelism* (Saint Louis: Concordia, 1984). Again, the burden of the book is to allow evangelists and theologians to listen to each other (preface 8). Green's magnum opens *Evangelism Through The Local Church* has a strong apologetical and practical bias. What is missing is a more theologically informed discussion of evangelism. He is more concerned with getting on with the job. But the task he envisages looks quite different from those proposed by Abraham and Costas.

you inspect the various containers on such carriers you cannot find any that would seem, on first inspection at least, to provide the right kind of high octane fuel required for the good ship *Evangelism*. This, at least, was the opinion of some of the crew of the Evangelism ship when, upon sighting the bulk carrier *Theological Tradition* (a rare occurrence), rowed over to seek help with their fuel problem. Perhaps not surprisingly the crew were not well received.

Captain Dogmatic was clearly embarrassed at the prospect of having to welcome the *Evangelism* crew. Following a clumsy and rather condescending greeting the crew were allowed to sniff around. But not being at all sure of what they were looking for, they soon became discouraged and left. The Captain and crew of the tanker had tried to tell them that such carriers no longer serviced evangelism-class ships. In fact, it soon became apparent in the short exchange between the two crews, that the tanker crew were no longer certain who they supplied with fuel. But they were deeply committed to steaming around the ecclesial ocean, if only to meet up with other such tankers for cordial exchanges and perhaps the exchange of a container or two.

To be truthful the tanker fleet were not in good shape. More ominously there were moves afloat to remove the enormous tanker fleet to a safe harbour just off Cape Irrelevant. This would solve the immediate problem of oil spills which did nobody any good. In the last few decades a number of dangerous ones had occurred which had caused a great deal of damage to the evangelism-class ships. As a result the tanker *Bultmann* had already been towed away to join the *Patristic Fleet*. The tanker *Continental Calvin* and alas, the giant tanker *Judicious Hooker*, much beloved of the tribe Anglicanus Classicus had met a similar fate. Needless to say the HMS. *Higher Criticism* had long since rusted.

Exploring the connections: the priority of communication

Evangelism and theology often seem poles apart, unable and unwilling to come close, let alone join forces. The fear is loss of purity, of being contaminated by the other. Theology is frightened that in the interchange it will forfeit its academic and scholarly reputation. Evangelism might find itself being led up a dead end. But evangelism and theology need each other and more importantly their life-source is a shared one. The church's practice of evangelism and theology arises out of its life in Christ. The one-in-Christ bond is the presupposition for all ecclesial communication.

The argument that follows presupposes an interwoveness between evangelism and theology. What of course is critical is to clarify how the inter-dependence of evangelism and theology, which arises out their common life in Christ, actually works. This points to the importance of clarifying some of the interconnections between evangelism and theology in the church for it is in the process of exploring the interconnections that a more adequate understanding of evangelism and theology can emerge. For this reason tight definitions are inappropriate at this stage. However, what is important is that evangelism and theology are understood to belong to the more general theme of communication. In particular, it is the dynamics of communication as it relates to evangelism and theology that emerges as critical. The paper is thus about the character of communication that is 'worded'. From another point of view what is offered here is a rather extended comment on Ephesians 6:19: 'And in particular pray for me that utterance may be given to me as I open my mouth that I may boldly and freely make known the mystery of the gospel'.

The communicative life

Communications is a massive area in modern life and thought. There is good reason for this: 'every act, every pause, every movement in living and social systems is also a message; silence is communication; short of death it is impossible for an organism or a person not to communicate'.[14]

It would seem that communication is both a condition of and essential to our humanity. Communication has been referred to as 'the transmission of energy in a form'.[15] This is a highly compressed definition that needs more time than can be given here. It is clear from this definition, however, that communication cannot be restricted to language. All language is communication but very little communication is language.[16]

Touch is a rich medium for communication. Visual communication is perhaps the richest of all. A traditional Chinese proverb states, 'One hundred tellings are not as good as one seeing'.[17] It is true that

14. Amos Wilder, *The Rules Are No Game: The Strategy of Communication* (London: Routledge & Kegan Paul, 1987), 124.
15. Daniel Hardy and David Ford, *Jubilate: Theology in Praise* (London: DLT, 1984), 157.
16. Wilder in *The Rules Are No Game*, 137, notes that the 'non-linguistic modes of communication in society include music, the visual arts, the visual aspects of film and television; kinship, status, money, sex and power, accent, height, shape and beauty; much mathematics, dreams, and fantasy; images, ideals, emotions, and desires; the production and exchange of commodities; and class, caste, race, and sex'.
17. Wilder, *Rules Are No Game*, 122.

> we often fail to recognise the importance and influence of other modes of communication, especially those associated with popular culture. It is also true that 'since the scientific revolution of the seventeenth century, language has been commonly identified with 'thought' or 'reason', and assumed to be more important or more significant than other modes of communication, such as the environment of non-verbal communication that makes thought and language possible.'[18]

However, it is also the case that 'there is no communication system between animals, insects, or computers that remotely approaches the complexity flexibility, and capacities of language.'[19] We are more intimately involved in communication through language than in any other activity besides love and work—and both of these are modes of communication that usually require language. Communication is thus a general category within which language appears as a special case. An important conclusion from these brief and unsurprising comments is that language is not simply a means to another end, an instrument for other purposes. Rather language is a medium through which the communicative life occurs. In this sense it is constitutive of human life. Human social life is formed and shaped through language. As such language is a part of human reality rather than a copy or misrepresentation of it.[20]

Communication and language: some ecclesiological perspectives

These general remarks about communication and language are important in considering evangelism and theology in the church. Both these themes can be treated as tasks of the church. However, as a particular task of the church communication can be done well or poorly. What then becomes important is the improvement of communication. This involves strengthening techniques and devising more appropriate strategies. In this context those interested in evangelism might allude to the character of God's communication and spend a good deal of energy analysing the strategies and principles that informed Jesus' evangelism.[21] This is all well and good but

18. Wilder, *Rules Are No Game*, 138.
19. Wilder, *Rules Are No Game*, 136.
20. Wilder, *Rules Are No Game*, 130.
21. A popular and important book in this regard is RE Coleman, *The Master Plan of Evangelism* (Grand Rapids, MI: Spire Books, 1987). This book was originally published in 1963 and is now in its forty-fith print.

it does not push the discussion very far. The main problem is that in this context communication is quickly reduced to a question of method, strategy and style. Communication is here what the church does to and for others who are unchurched. It is what the church does to achieve another end. Language is reduced to an 'instrumentalist' function. A lot of modern evangelism operates within this instrumentalist framework. Evangelism in this context can too easily operate in a 'tool-like' way, and become excessively manipulative.

Not surprisingly some people find this pragmatic approach reductive and distortive of the gospel. There is, it is claimed, more to the task of communication than simply 'wording truths', as if the gospel could be reduced to the delivery of certain information in a neat and pure form. Accordingly, advocates of the alternative view argue that good communication involves a self-giving which is more than merely information requiring a response. Rather, communication has the character of an open exchange in which the distance between hearer and speaker is bridged in a fullsome way which includes but goes beyond mere words. This approach has its ecclesiastical form in the history of the WCC with its stress on social action as a necessary part of spreading the good news.

What is easily overlooked is that both the above approaches see communication as a task to be performed by the church. In other words both end up operating with an instrumentalist view of communication whether it is in evangelism through word and/or deed. This does not have to be the case but it often is.

Communication moves to a different level when it is no longer considered as simply one task among many but rather becomes a way of understanding the whole life of the church. Communication is here no longer one church practice but concerns its very existence. The focus is the church as a communicative system. What is important in this view is the quality of interactions that occur between texts, traditions persons and institutions. This approach can illuminate how communicative life is disturbed or disrupted by ideological elements. This perspective on communications can offer important insights into the structuring and activities of ecclesial life. It can provide the basis for an understanding of the church as a 'sacrament of non-dominative communication'.[22]

22. See *Communication In The Church*, edited by G Baum and A Greely, in *Concilium* CX1 (1978): 92, 98ff.

These comments link up with the earlier discussion of language and communication as constitutive of human community. Communication is not, on this basis something the church does, but is. The critical factor is the quality of the church's communicative life. It is of high quality to the extent that it mirrors the character of God. This means it is called to be a sacrament of non-dominative communication. This essential note of the church ought ideally to be present in all its communicative tasks. Thus the wording of truth in evangelism and theological discourse ought to occur in a non-dominative way. Of course, to speak about non-dominative communication is to speak about power relations. To communicate through language is to be implicitly involved in certain power relations. The apostle Paul was acutely aware of this:

> For I resolved to know nothing while I was with you except Jesus Christ and him crucified. I came to you in weakness and fear, and with much trembling. My message and preaching were not with wise and persuasive words, but with a demonstration of the Spirits' power, so that your faith might not rest on men's wisdom, but on God's power (1 Corinthians 2:2-5).

If then, we are to be communicators of the gospel then the content and form of our language ought to be informed by the non-dominative ideal, through which we, as well as others, are continually surprised that through weakness God's power is manifest.

A question arises as to how this ideal feature of the church's communicative life might be reflected in the evangelistic and theological tasks of the church. Quite clearly at this level the concern is primarily with communication through language with 'wording' the truth of God. This is the domain of logos communication. There is a long tradition in Christianity of 'wording' truth. It has to do with the character of God whose word is creative of light and life, whose word takes the form of Torah for the people of Israel, whose word is spoken by the prophets. Logos reality comes to its most concentrated form in Jesus Christ: 'In the beginning was the word and the word was with God and the word was God . . . and the word became flesh and dwelt among us' (Prologue of St John's Gospel). It is the word of God that is preached in the early church and the word of God expands (Acts 6:7; 12:24). The subsequent Christian theological tradition is a tradition of 'wording' the truth. So in one sense it is not surprising that the Western theological tradition has been so dominated by logos theology.

The crisis in word communication

There is, however, a crisis in logos communication. It has been around for some time and it will remain. People generally are suspicious of mere words. And perhaps with good reason. Lies are told with words. In many walks of life it seems that the more uncertain and insecure people become the more words are used to cover up inadequacies.

Within theology the crisis of logos communication is well established. It may be symptomatic of a deeper loss of confidence that God is really present in the community of faith.[23] Furthermore, there is at present a strong reaction against the long dominance of the word tradition in Christianity. This is evident when language is given a secondary significance, a medium for expressing something more primal.[24] Language on this account operates as a means to another end. This instrumentalist view of language and thus of theology is a natural reaction to a type of word communication that presupposes a tight or rigid one-to-one correspondence between human word and Divine Word. This is exemplified in modern theology by a form of docrinalism that codifies truth in particular and fixed language forms. This form of propositional objectivity ends up codifying God; a point well appreciated by Karl Barth.[25] Human words are, on this view, no

23. See the discussion in Edward Farley, *Ecclesian Man: A Social Phenomenology of Faith and Reality* (Philadelphia: Fortress Press, 1975), chapter 1.
24. This view of religious language is implicit in what has been referred to in recent theology as the 'experiential-expressive' dimension of religion. In this view attention is focussed on feelings, attitudes, existential orientations and practices rather than what happens at the level of 'symbolic objectifications', for example, at the level of language which expresses experience. This powerful trend in religious understanding stands in the tradition of Schleiermacher. For further discussion see G Lindbeck, *The Nature of Doctrine: Religion and Theology in a Post-Liberal Age* (London: SPCK, 1984), chapter 1.
25. A good example of the rigid doctrinalism against which Barth so vigorously contended can be found in Barth's critique of the tradition of fundamental articles of faith. Barth linked the emergence of this notion of articulating the faith with seventeeth century Protestant Scholasticism. Barth argued that the codification of faith into certain articles of faith which were then raised to the status of a 'classic text' involved 'a definition, limitation and restriction of the Word of God' (865). When the expression in doctrine of the Church's encounter with 'God in His Word' became the pretext for 'the establishment of specific, irrevocable, fundamental articles' (864), then the way was blocked, in Barth's view, for the free operation of the Word of God and the Church. For page references see Karl Barth, *Church Dogmatics* volume 1, part 2, (Edinburgh: T&T Clark, 1956–1978), 863–66.

longer fed or capacitated by God's Word but effectively block the full and free flowing Divine Word. Of course the more unstable and fragmented life seems to become the tighter become the institutional controls upon the language of faith. The result is 'orthodox reductionism'. Full and free speech is thwarted in the interests of a false notion of purity which requires a tight one-to-one correspondence between the reality which faith witnesses to and its form in language. Naturally, logos communication of this kind will set up a counter reaction which seeks a freer communicative life. Unfortunately this option, already mentioned above, can easily get caught in the trap of human subjectivity. It becomes unclear how human words mirror or refer to the truth of God. Evangelism might end up being merely the good news of my life rather than the good news of the life of God in which I live. Theological discourse might end up being just what I think. Ironically anxiety over the wording of truth has contributed to a massive reductionism in evangelism and theology. This reductionism is evident both in a tight formalised 'orthodox reductionism' and in an undisciplined subjectivising of faith. What has been sacrificed in both developments is joyful praise of God through language. What has been forgotten is that the logos of God authorises and legitimates free flowing abundant discourse directed by praise of the God of Jesus Christ.

What is being suggested here is that God is logos—language. Language is not merely instrumental, a means to another end. Language is a medium of God's presence and power energising and directing all things to their truth in God. Human response to the presence and activity of God is to praise God. This praising occurs in language as it is informed by the truth of God. Such language, if it is to be the language of true praise, can be neither overformalised nor undisciplined but within the community of Jesus Christ it is constrained by the love of Christ (2 Corinthians 5:14).

Dynamics of full and free speech in the church

But the critical issue now concerns the nature of that inner constraint by which the language of faith is not held back but released in order to praise God. What is thus urgently required in the Church is an improved understanding of the dynamics of full and free communication. In other words, what is happening in good communication of the truth?

There are perhaps at least three dimensions to full and free speech in evangelism and theology that ideally inform and direct the church's praise of Jesus Christ. First, full and free speech involves an implicit appeal to *simplicity*. Second, such communication operates with a bias towards *repetition*. Third, it witnesses to the presence of *wisdom*.

It is not just any kind of simplicity, repetition and wisdom in mind here but simplicity, repetition and wisdom understood in quite particular ways. Our task now is to develop an understanding of how good communication occurs under or with the guidance of the above three parameters. The suggestion is that speech in the church which is constrained by the love of Christ will be speech that involves an appeal to simplicity, a bias towards repetition and a witness to the presence of wisdom. Within each of these three dimensions of communication evangelism and theology operate in different but complimentary ways.

The appeal to simplicity

The first mark of full and free communication is simplicity. The contemporary Protestant theologian, Jürgen Moltmann has said,

> What cannot be said simply does not need to be written at all. Simplicity is the highest challenge to Christian theology. Theology stands under the demand to speak simply because, as Christian theology, it stands or falls with the church.[26]

In the context, Moltmann clearly has in mind the issue of communication in the church. His sentiments would, no doubt, find joyful approval among those involved in evangelism. Though before we go any further it is also as well to note that for every difficult and complex problem there is always a perfectly reasonable and simple answer that is wrong.

Nevertheless, the good news is never confusing or complicated. Neither is it simplistic. There is, it seems, a way of wording the faith—seeding the word—which communicates with a profound simplicity the mystery of the gospel. Such simplicity is not that which 'boils' truth down to the bare essentials. That is a popular strategy but that is all it is; a useful strategy of questionable worth. It can easily lead to a 'check list' gospel, in which certain propositions are offered for assent. But there is a way of communicating with simplicity that has more of the character of a concentration of profundity. This might take the form of a 'word in season'—that word for which Paul prays when he opens his mouth: 'Pray also for me, that whenever I open my mouth, words may be given me so that I will fear-

26. Jürgen Moltmann, *The Open Church* (London: SCM, 1978), 9.

lessly make known the mystery of the gospel' (Ephesians 6:19 (NIV)). His prayer is not for 'the bare essentials' but a compelling snapshot of the faith of Jesus Christ; a rich compression of the truth. It is precisely because the Gospel is not simple but profound that he prays for the wisdom to put the mystery with simplicity. On this account evangelism might be understood as communicating the gospel in microcosmic form.

There are no blueprints for achieving this simple profundity in the truth. It is Spirit led, and informed by the love of Christ. Sharpness, clarity and depth of insight are not merely well-honed skills but capacities bestowed by God for his praise. Furthermore, in the body of Christ it should not be presumed that all these qualities will be present in the same person to the same degree. What is critical is an openness to God in order that, like Paul, utterance may be given the evangelist as he or she opens their mouth, that they may be freely released to open up the secrets of the good news of God. There is no appeal here to a ready made plan. Rather what we find is a reliance upon God as one speaks freely and flowingly of the love of God in Christ Jesus.

I have suggested that simplicity properly understood has more of the character of concentrated abundance. It has to be like this to be the truth of God. However, precisely because the evangel is this kind of simplicity it is capable of significant expansion. In fact the compression of truth is not only capable of being 'strung-out', so to speak, it has an inbuilt drive for extension. This movement to concentration points and extension in a very free-flowing and fullsome way belongs to the dynamic of truth itself.

In this compression/extension dynamic inherent in communication of the Gospel evangelism represents a recurring moment. It belongs to a process of communication. Evangelism is not a full stop, but a comma. Theological discourse participates in this communications process as it moves beyond the comma. Theology unravels the truth further, bringing fresh illumination and sharpness to it. In this sense theological discourse is called to playfully and joyfully 'string-out' the truth. The snapshot offered in evangelism now becomes the video of theology, though the analogy ought not to be pressed too far.

A good example of this dynamic between compression and systematic extension of faith is provided by the work of the American Paul Tillich. Tillich recognised the concentrated abundance of the gospel in relation to his own highly developed systematic enterprise: 'The statement that Jesus is the Christ contains in some way the whole theological system, as the telling of a parable of Jesus contains all artistic potentialities of Christianity'.[27]

Given the above formulation of simplicity as concentrated abundance in the truth it is clear that evangelism and theology are, properly speaking, complementary forms of gospel communication. Evangelism represents a concentration point—the comma in the sentence—theology represents the extended form of communication. Good communication requires both compression and extension of the truth. Evangelism and theology act as catalysts for each other in the process of communication. Precisely because such communication is dynamic what in fact we find is a multiplicity of concentration points en route to fuller communication. Free-flowing communication actually requires continual re-focusing or reconcentration. Compression of the truth in a concentrated form—as in evangelism—is in fact a recurring moment in communication of the truth. This is important. It suggests a second feature of gospel communication which might be termed the bias towards repetition.

The bias towards repetition

Repetition is not usually treated as a theme in modern theology though it is important in everyday life and thought, and certainly warrants serious theological consideration. Good evangelism evidences certain recurring patterns or references to God's ways with this world and human life. The history of the Christian tradition is informed by a recurring focus on the creative, redemptive and life giving character of the Triune God. This is the God who is praised in Jesus Christ. On this account evangelism might be understood 'as the horizontal dimension of praise *repeated* and *explained* to others so they can join the community of praise'.[28]

From this perspective it is not the fact of repetition per se but its quality that is of critical importance. Repetition in evangelism and in everyday life has both healthy energising forms as well as more disturbed, barren and ultimately destructive forms. Modern society is highly repetitive in its structure and routine. Negative forms of repetition abound. For many heavy industry is a world of repetitive and unfulfilling work practices where human beings often function in a machine-like manner. In the area of mental health the compulsion to endlessly repeat certain behav-

27. Paul Tillich, *Systematic Theology*, volume 3 (New York: James Nisbet & Co Ltd, 1964), 215.
28. Hardy and Ford, *Jubilate*, 19 (my italics).

iour patterns is well known. Again, in Altzimer's disease there is a loss of the power of recall. This loss of the capacity to remember means that those who love and care for such people are themselves locked into repetitive communication patterns. There is the constant re-presenting of one's identity and love as well as more routine tasks.

More generally, repetition is viewed in a negative light in our society. Repetition is often associated with inauthenticity.[29] What society seems to demand is constant change which involves discarding the past and present in the search for the totally new. Advertising is a good example of this search to overcome repetition. It is, of course, a self-defeating exercise. What becomes paramount is maximum exposure of the consumer public to the new product. Such exposure requires repetition and so the cycle is perpetuated.

The negative aspects of repetition ought not to blind us to the fact that repetition is an important and necessary feature of our everyday life. If the toothbrush and soap as well as a regular and balanced food intake are to count it is obvious that the repetition of the daily rituals associated with these things gives vitality and freshness to human life. The dream of every golfer is to develop a swing that repeats itself. Definite recurring patterns of behaviour, communication and exchange (for example, greetings, farewells) seem to be a necessary part of the healthy ordering of human society. Not surprisingly the positive and negative aspects of repetition can be discerned in religious life, for example in worship.[30]

---

29. In this respect Stephen Sykes quotes Lionel Trilling: 'In an increasingly urban and technological society, the natural processes of human existence have acquired a moral status in the degree that they are thwarted' (Lionel Trilling, *Sincerity and Authenticity* (London, 1974), 128), and comments, 'Anything resembling a mechanical process, and that would include the order and repetition of a liturgy, is felt to be inimical to the authenticity of experience and being' (Stephen Sykes, *The Identity of Christianity* (London: SPCK, 1984), 325).

30. In my own tradition of Anglicanism worship was patterned liturgically around the *Book of Common Prayer.* As the title indicates it was prayer that was common to the congregation and repeated Sunday by Sunday and daily for those who said the Daily Offices. At the opposite end of the spectrum is Pentecostalism. This church life is self-consciously non-liturgical, seeking freedom and spontaneity. In between are a whole range of differing ecclesial traditions. How is repetition relevant here? It is relatively common place to view Anglican liturgy as unhelpfully repetitive over against more free-flowing charismatic worship. However, highly structured liturgical worship does have the capacity to generate freedom. One is mercifully relieved from what has been termed 'the introspective conscience of the West'. Freshness from without becomes a real possibility. But of course it is also true; such worship can prove sleep inducing. At the other end of the spectrum Pentecostal worship can assume a highly predict-

Accordingly, there is an expectation in evangelism that what is proclaimed today is the same good news that brought redemption yesterday and will do so tomorrow. Minimally, we are right to expect a recurring pattern in the proclamation of the 'evangel'. Furthermore, earlier it was suggested that this recurring pattern will have a Trinitarian form if it is to do justice to God's relation with creation. In this sense certain components or dimensions in the evangel will recur; creation, redemption, fulfillment. The challenge is to repeat the 'evangel' in its fullness—its rich simplicity—rather than some mutilated form. There is, at this level, good and bad evangelism.

Theological discourse participates in the dynamic of creative repetition. Here the aim is comprehensive communication of the truth of Christianity. So what ought to emerge in good theology is a fullsome opening of the gospel as it is woven into myriad of themes and life situations. Furthermore, what we ought to observe and in fact can discern in the Christian tradition is a recurring engagement with a Trinitarian understanding of God. Why Trinitarian? Because this is the form of the God who has generated Christian worship, mission and service in history. A recurring Trinitarian pattern in theology can, of course, be linked to the very nature of the being of God. This was articulated most powerfully in the twentieth century by Karl Barth who referred to God's threefold repetition of himself. Some notion of repetition belongs, it seems, to the structure of the being of God.[31]

---

able and structured form in which the weekly repetition of certain activities is eagerly sought for among the gathered worshippers. Music in worship is undergoing a renaissance right now. One feature of the newer forms of music is repetition. This has the capacity to completely kill the spirit or alternatively take it to new heights. It is not repetition per se that is the problem but its quality, that is, whether or not it mediates freshness.

31. Barth's treatment of the threefold, 'repetition in God' (366) is highly sophisticated and programatic for his theological enterprise. What is revealed and witnessed to in Scripture is a threefold differentiation in God in his unimpaired unity (299). God repeats himself three times, in three quite 'inexchangeable' modes of being. 'God reveals Himself. He reveals Himself through Himself. He reveals Himself—this subject, God, the Revealer, is identical with his act in revelation and also identical with its effect' (296). For this reason the doctrine of revelation begins with the doctrine of the triune God. For page references see *Church Dogmatics*, volume1 Part 1, 295–383. In Barth's theory of the repetition of God priority tends to be given to the unity rather than the threefoldness within God. This incipient modalism is succinctly put by a recent commentator, 'God's triple restoration of himself is much more prominent than his relation to himself' (Alistair C Heron, *The Holy Spirit* (Westminster Press, 1983), 167).

However, it is precisely at this point that the problem of repetition becomes acute. Good repetition requires *freshness through sameness.*[32] What is required in good evangelism and theology is creative repetition. What this amounts to is that there can be no such thing as simple or pure repetition. It is impossible.

Creative repetition is required by the very character of God whose threefold repetition—of Father, Son and Spirit—is the ideal of 'freshness through sameness'. Creative repetition is required by the intimedness of human experience. Life goes on, and demands new responses. The world is becoming increasingly complex, it is not the same as it was 2000 years ago. Good repetition is not achieved by simply imprinting what was said yesterday upon a new context; that is the way of domination. Good repetition emerges through attentiveness and discernment in the contingencies of life, that is, the context. Context is, after all, the weaving together of different textures. There are no short cuts.

One such short cut is implicit in the notion that the gospel is 'substance-like'. In this case the substance is equated with propositions of truth that are to be worded in precisely the same manner. Pure repetition is, on this view, a sign of faithfulness. Such repetition offers the illusion of security but the price is high; the truth of God is reduced to a form of doctrinal legalism. However, the real problems are transferred elsewhere, that is, into the practical sphere concerned with the application of truth. This gives the illusion of secure foundations but such theology has forfeited freshness for a kind of sameness. Or perhaps the element of freshness is transferred to the question of application and practice of the truth. Is it any wonder that theology soon loses its vigour and appeal? It no longer witnesses to the freshness and creativity of God.

Another equally dangerous short cut is to discard the past altogether. Creativity and freshness are sought but this is thought to require severing links with the tradition. Often this amounts to newness for newness sake. This approach strikes a deep cord in Protestantism and produces an 'occasionalism' of the Spirit. God comes and goes, continuity is hard to discern. It seems here that the idol of pure repetition has been firmly rejected. No sameness, only freshness. However, there quickly emerges another kind of repetition via the back door so to speak. What is repeated is often nothing

32. This, of course, was the burden of Barth's development of the threefold repetition in God: 'Although, in keeping with God's riches, revelation is never the same but always new, nevertheless, as such it is always in all circumstances the promulgation of the logos, of the Lordship of God', *Church Dogmatics*, volume 1, part 1, 306.

more than the profundities of human subjectivity. This is characterised by a fairly directionless, free floating Christianity which becomes curved-in on the human subject and simply repeats a range of human thoughts uninformed by God's presence. To end up communicating 'just what I think', is to end up with sameness without freshness.

To conclude, what is repeated in evangelism and theology is the content of praise, repeated in such a way that others will want to join the community of Jesus Christ. We ought not to be frightened of repetition but welcome it, seek to understand what we are doing, and allow our repeating of the good news to be informed by our praise of God.

With simplicity we have identified the basic complementarity between evangelism and theology, the former representing a concentrated expression of the latter's more extended discourse. This gave rise to repetition as a feature of both modes of communication. It should not go unnoticed that the challenge of repetition—of freshness through sameness—provides a useful theological heuristic through which to reconsider context as constitutive of good communication in evangelism and theology.

However, it might fairly be asked, simplicity of what, repetition of what? Has not the discussion skirted around the main issue of the 'content' of evangelism and theology? The issue of content has been implicit in what has already been said and has occasionally surfaced. It is time to treat this explicitly as an issue in communication.

The presence of wisdom

The question of content might be more fruitfully and adequately understood as a question of the presence and nature of wisdom. This requires some further teasing out. Earlier it was suggested that in evangelism and theology the content of praise is repeated in such a way that others join the community of Jesus Christ. What is repeated here is 'the content of praise'. Now 'content of praise' is a fundamentally dynamic understanding of content. It can't be reduced to a static substance-like thing. What is praised in Christian worship and discipleship is not a set of propositions or certain truths. Of course, no one would actually want to say this. It is the living God. However, there is a form of doctrinalism in the church that quickly codifies the truth of the living God in such a way that the language of faith is set in certain fixed and tight forms. This is not to suggest that any language will do. But unfortunately, the inevitable tendency to doctrinalise the truth in the above way eventually has the affect of solidifying the truth of God's dynamic presence. Belief becomes law-like, God is legalised as the law-giver. A good test of this tendency is the prevalence of the language of 'substance' in relation to the gospel. The language suggests physicality, concreteness and fixity. More generally, this approach to content often gives the impression that the good news is 'information-like'—a unique assemblage of facts. Christianity as an obediential religion fits well within this framework. The purpose of evangelism is thus reduced to the communication of certain information that will generate obedience to God.

It is true that we live in an information culture where power is vested in the holders and disseminators of information. But the 'content of praise' cannot be too readily reduced to certain information now available to the world.[33] If, however, the 'content of praise' is to be information then it will have to be information of a particular kind, that is, it will have to be such that it is capable of forming and reforming humankind in the way of godliness. What is critical here is attention to the dynamics of the presence of God forming and transforming created life. This suggests a patterning of God's life in human life. This is not merely a case of delivering information and then invoking some added on doctrine of the Holy Spirit to do something with the information.

What we are dealing with in 'the content of praise' may be information-like or knowledge-like but it is never *just* knowledge or information. Rather it is knowledge which is properly directed. It is goal seeking. Now in the Christian Tradition such 'content of praise' used to be referred to as wisdom. Theology was originally wisdom that bestowed illumination and salvation.[34] Such wisdom was not substance-like nor codified propositions. Rather it concerned the en-wisening of human life with the life of God. This wisdom came to its concentration in Jesus Christ.[35] Furthermore, it was the wisdom of God in Christ crucified and risen that has been witnessed to in the 'evangel' (1 Corinthians 1:18–2:8).

33. Interestingly, Karl Barth's massive resurrection of the Christian tradition did not entirely escape this problem. There is a lingering sense in this great theologian's work that all that is really required, given the triumph of grace in the world in Jesus Christ, is for humankind to be informed of this event. Passing on the knowledge is what it is all about, or so it might be construed.

34. See, for example Edward Farley, *Theologia: The Fragmentation and Unity of Theological Education* (Philadelphia: Fortress Press, 1983), chapter 2.

35. For a discussion of Jesus Christ as the concentration of the wisdom of God see Daniel Hardy, 'Rationality, the Sciences and Theology', in *Keeping The Faith: Essays to Mark the Centenary of Lux Mundi*, edited by Geoffrey Wainwright (London: SPCK, 1989), 294ff.

It is this wisdom that is praised in the Christian community, repeated in evangelism and meditated upon in theology. The theme of wisdom seems to be enjoying a renaissance in these last few years. But there is always a danger that over-use will lead to shallowness. It can easily become a synonym for well-honed common sense. In Christianity, however, wisdom is that which God bestows and it is that to which all things are to be assimilated, that is, brought into relation with and changed accordingly. Wisdom as such is the dynamic activity of God's presence lifting or raising created life to the fullness of truth. I have referred to this process as the enwisening of life. It is God's Christ-like work in the world. This is what is praised in the Christian community. This is what is repeated in its simplicity in evangelism. This is what is unravelled in its infinite richness in theological discourse.

Transformation: the purpose of communication

The second half of this paper has offered a brief consideration of some of those dimensions of full and free speech relevant to evangelism and theology in the church. The essential structure of the relationship between evangelism and theology was developed through the theme of simplicity. The basic dynamic calling forth and calling for continued communication—what is normally treated as a question of context—was developed under the theme of repetition. The question of content was briefly redeveloped as the presence of wisdom. Simplicity as concentrated abundance of truth, repetition as freshness through sameness and wisdom as properly directed knowledge are the three key parameters that guide good communication in evangelism and theology. These three parameters, understood in particular ways, are present and operating as speech in the church is 'constrained by the love of Christ'.

What happens within this communicative framework? In the Christian tradition the answer has been transformation through conversion. This points to the fact that communication involves exchange, in this case an exchange of lives. The communicative life is always a life of bestowing and receiving, that is, a life of exchange. When this is done well human life is built up; life is raised to its full truth in God.

This points, however, to the fundamentally expansive nature of human life. It is capable of being added to quantitatively and qualitatively. Human life is raised to its full truth. This perfecting occurs in and through communication. Good communication is the condition for fresh expanded life possibilities. This is a process in which the past is transcended without being wasted. The old is taken up into something new (2 Corinthians 5:17). In the resurrection Jesus Christ did not leave his wounds behind (John 20: 19–23). They belonged to his new life but in a new way. When we think of Christian conversion it might be helpful to consider it from the point of view of the potential of godly human communication to expand and build up human life. This happens through the bestowal of fresh understanding, energy and direction. This is what happens when our life is assimilated to the wisdom of God who himself is the energy order knowledge and purpose of all things.

Conclusion

It has been suggested that evangelism and theology are complementary forms of human response to God's communication. The further suggestion is that these forms are informed and directed according to the criteria of simplicity, repetition and wisdom, understood in quite particular ways. These three criteria provide the conditions for faithful 'wording' of the gospel. Why these three criteria? Ultimately to be good criteria they have to be developed in relation to the truth of God. Who is God? In the Christian tradition God is praised as a being of communicative love. There is a simplicity to such a God; an abundance of richness in a highly concentrated form. This simplicity of God's being is repeated in self-differentiation as creator, redeemer and fulfiller. In this repetition of God's simplicity wisdom is bestowed and created life is transformed. The communicative structure of the being of God is concentrated in Jesus Christ and overflows in the presence of the Spirit of the Father's Son. This is the God who evokes human praise. When this is repeated in evangelism and theology the outflow of God's communicative love expands and manifests itself through more open free and wise communicative life in human society.

Full and free communication in human life is thus a response to God's own self communication. Evangelism and theology occur under the constraint of God's own simplicity, repeated in Jesus Christ that wisdom might be realised in human life. As evangelism and theology realise in language God's wisdom they praise the truth of God. So ultimately, to engage in such activities is itself a praise of God. In this context it is appropriate to refer to evangelism and theology which is praise centred. Praise which honours the truth of God in communication is the way through which

God's presence is realised and human life is built up and expanded by the truth. This is God's converting work. As such it is salvific.

This essay has invited readers to leave their ecclesial boats, don scuba-diving gear and explore the life of the ocean upon which so much ecclesiastical sailing takes place. Without the ocean there would be no ships. And without God's overflowing love in Jesus Christ there would be dead silence. As it is we are compelled to echo St Paul: 'And pray for us that we may be given utterance when we open our mouths that we might freely and fully communicate the mystery of the gospel'.

Part Two

Church: Finding Community in a Disturbed World

Chapter Seven
Recovering an Ecclesial Sense of Place Down-under[1]

Finding Our Place

This essay examines the theme of place in theology drawing upon insights from the discipline of geography. I am interested to explore the nature of the church as God's ecclesial place. I do this through examining features of the Australian context (geography and culture) and I connect this to the way the search for spiritual life expresses itself. The church is called to live in the place in-between. This accent on liminality is risky but ultimately bears witness to the character of the in-between God. The essay had its genesis in my inaugural lecture as Director of St Mark's National Theological Centre in 1998. In that address I appealed to the idea of the verandah as the in-between place where God is to be found. This God of the intersection is the God of the Holy Saturday tradition. There are clues here for the form of the church and Christian discipleship for our times to which I return in Part Three.

Introduction: ecclesiology in focus

Some years ago the well-known Lutheran theologian, Jaroslav Pelikan, stated that 'the doctrine of the church became, as it had never quite been before, the bearer of the whole of the Christian message for the twentieth century, as well as the recapitulation of the entire doctrinal tradition from preceding centuries'.[2] Pelikan was pointing to the emergence of ecclesiology as the principle of coherence for the central themes of Christianity. Was this a sign of the failure of Christianity—a retreat into its religious

1. Originally published as 'Church of the In-between God: Recovering an Ecclesial Sense of Place Down-under', in *Journal of Anglican Studies*, 7/1, May (2009).
2. Jaroslav Pelikan, *The Christian Tradition, A History of the Development of Doctrine*, volume 5, *Christian Doctrine and Modern Culture (since 1700)*, (University of Chicago Press, Chicago, 1989), 282.

'enclave'[3]—at least in the West? Or was it indicative of an intuition about community and sociality, something quite central and creative in the life of faith in the world?

Pelikan pointed to a mediating role that ecclesiology might have within the framework of Christian theology. His perspective resonated with my own longstanding concern for ecclesiology, mission and culture. In my own case this has increasingly focused on the nature of place as a concept critical for ecclesial reflection and this in turn has led me to an earlier interest in the discipline of geography. The reason for this is simple. To talk about ecclesiology is to talk about place: about God's place; about our placement in the world; about how and why our social life operates as it does; about what engenders optimal life-enhancing community. Within the modern disciplines it is geography where such matters are particularly in focus.

My concern in recent years is to see how theology might meditate upon the significance of place. In terms of Anglicanism it has seemed sensible to me to ask about our place down-under: about what it means to be Christian disciples in this place; about how our place has been constructed and how we might understand the transformation of place by the presence of Christ in the Spirit. As a result place has become a central mediating concept through which theology, ecclesiology, mission and ministry can be organised and better understood. This is more than an academic pursuit, as the deliberations of many Church Synods would testify.[4]

To focus on place is inherently controversial. It leads into considerations of our colonial past and post-colonialism. This present paper had its genesis in such a discussion at a conference May 2008.[5] This article unfolds in the following manner. In the next section I consider the theme of place as it is discussed in professional geography and briefly examine

3. Robert Bellah et al, *Habits of the Heart: Individualism and Commitment in American Life* (New York: Harper & Row, 1985), 71–75 refers to 'lifestyle enclaves' signalling retreat from the public to the private domains of life.

4. An example from my own context is pertinent. At the Adelaide Diocesan Synod (October 2008) the consideration of place proved to be quite central on a number of fronts: to sell or not to sell Bishop's Court: whether parish boundaries made any sense in regard to church planting in various places in the diocese; whether the diocese could envisage itself as a place within which all manner of Anglican species might happily co-exist or whether our places were quite sharply delineated; in other words whether place is an strongly bounded matter or is it osmotic in form and function. It has to do with how we organise our life and behave towards others, about ethics and finally our understanding of the God of all places.

5. Conference on Post-colonialism and Anglicanism, Manchester May 2008.

some implications for being church and the Anglican Church in particular. This consideration of place leads into a second section in which I tackle more directly the issue of place within an Australian context. In doing so I examine the motif of verandah as a depiction of ecclesial place down-under. The key concept of 'in-between place' to depict a postcolonial way of being church is deployed in order to recover an ecclesial sense of place down-under.

Such an enquiry is of particular relevance to my own context of Australia. Anglicanism in Australia cannot be understood apart from the location of a colonial church twelve thousand miles on the other side of the known world on the largest and driest island continent on earth. The place and its associated tyranny of distance[6] has been, and continues to be, the major driver in the development and shape of Anglican ecclesiology in Australia. For example, it has significantly increased imported tensions between an Anglican conformist culture and dissenting and rebellious traditions. Place continues to shape the way Australian Anglicans conduct themselves nationally and see themselves in relation to the storm and tempests of contemporary Anglicanism.

The colonial yearning to create a 'home away from home' in a far away place has made creative adaptation difficult. As a result the most fundamental challenge is the development of an inculturated form of Anglican Christianity on Australian soil.[7] It is the ecclesial project on the drawing board. It has to be undertaken whilst remaining attentive to the dangers of ideological and other interests taking over. The task can be conceived in terms of recovering a sense of ecclesial place beyond the conquests of colonial space.[8] However, this has to be negotiated in such a manner that

6. Geoffrey Blainey, *The Tyranny of Distance: How Distance Shaped Australia's History*, revised edition (Sydney: Sun Books, 1991).

7. See the perceptive discussion of inculturation in relation to enculturation and acculturation by Steve Clarke, 'A Sociology of Theology and the Australian Context: The Challenge of Inculturation', in *The Gospel and Cultures: Initial Exploration in the Australian Context*, edited by Randall Prior (Melbourne: Victorian Council of Churches, 1997), 76–96.

8. This necessarily entails a move from competitive and violent dynamics in ecclesial life to a pacific ecclesiology. Such an ecclesiology of peace may be one of the fruits of the remarkable insights of Rene Girard on the scapegoat mechanism and social life. For an assessment of Girad's work in relation to the doctrine of the atonement see Raymund Schwager, *Must There Be Scapegoats? Violence and Redemption in the Bible*, translated by Maria L Assad (New York: Harper and Row, 1987). Transcending a colonial ecclesiology is a case study of the possibilities that arise when an atonement theology based on breaking the cycle of violence is translated into an ecclesial form.

(a) it does not succumb to new forms of tribalism when priority is given to the local and (b) it is alive to the danger of importing new patterns of dominance associated with neo-colonial webs of power. Both these dangers can be observed in the Australian context and both dangers rely on contested notions of place in contemporary discourse.[9] I now want to move to a consideration of the concept of place and consider what insight it might offer the distinctly ecclesial project.

The fate of place in a global world

Colonialism and the fate of place

The concept of place and related ideas concerning 'home' have been subject to significant scrutiny in recent years by professional geographers.[10] Cresswell identifies at least three approaches to place. The descriptive approach is typical of regional geographers where the concern is with the distinctiveness and particularity of places. A social constructionist approach remains interested in the particularity of places but the concern is uncovering the underlying social processes 'by showing how places are instances of wider processes of the construction of place in general under

---

What is required is a pacific ecclesiology.

9. The fact is that Australian Anglicanism has been and continues to be most appropriately depicted as 'tribal diocesanism'. See David Hilliard, 'Diocese, Tribes and Factions: Disunity and Unity in Australian Anglicanism', in *Agendas for Australian Anglicans: Essays in Honour of Bruce Kaye*, edited by T Frame and G Treloar (Adelaide: ATF Press, 2006), 57–81. The reasons for this are complex and I have addressed them in part in my article, 'Many Verandahs: Same House? Ecclesiological Challenges for Australian Anglicanism', in *Journal of Anglican Studies*, 4/2 (2006): 179–200. A more recent phenomenon that highlights the dangers of a neo-colonial impulse facilitated by contemporary globalism is apparent in the Anglican Diocese of Sydney *Affiliated Churches Ordinance*, 2007. Under this Ordinance Independent evangelical congregations of like-minded biblical Christians are linked up through a series of Sydney Church plants in other Anglican Dioceses. Administrative matters including, for example, superannuation payments are handled through the Diocese of Sydney and usually clergy from Sydney Diocese are in charge of the congregations. The process is undergirded by new conceptions of territory which do not recognise traditional boundaries. The only thing that has not happened is for these congregations to be badged 'Anglican'. In 2008 a Brisbane group of disaffected Anglicans broke away and formed a new congregation to operate under the Sydney Ordinance. The trans-territorial global ecclesial world provides the new environment for parallel 'Anglican' congregations and quasi jurisdictions. It is Separatism from within. Such a place, divided against itself cannot stand for much longer; or can it?
10. Tim Cresswell, *Place: A Short Introduction* (Oxford: Blackwell Publishing, 2004), 53.

conditions of capitalism, patriarchy, heterosexism, post-colonialism . . .'[11] This second approach is clearly indebted to Marxist, feminist and post-structuralist forms of interrogation. A third phenomenological approach is less interested in 'places' and more interested in 'place' as a fundamental feature of human existence.

The three approaches are interconnected and all contribute to our understanding of place. Place remains a contested concept. Post-colonial critiques of religion are clearly indebted to the social constructivist approach to place. On this account place appears as a dangerous and imperialist site of conquest and assimilation. This arises where enlightenment and colonial assumptions about space as an infinite expanse available for occupation dominate. The result is the collapse of place into space. Place as such vanishes. The philosopher Edward Casey has stated it succinctly, 'For an entire epoch, place has been regarded as an impoverished second cousin of Time and Space, those two colossal cosmic partners towering over modernity'.[12] As a child of this colonial spirit it was axiomatic that the Church of England in Australia would leave a distinctive footprint on antipodean soil, a footprint necessarily encoded with a colonial tread. Australia was essentially a colonial space to be tamed and inhabited, however benevolent the fashion. The doctrine of Australia as *Terra Nullius*—empty place—relies on such conceptuality. It belongs to the dynamic of conquest and assimilation of foreign places as 'non-place' or as a place in the process of construction. Yet even this is construed as an issue of transplantation rather than inculturation.

Place and globalisation

In the shrinking world of globalism, what happens to place? It seems that ideas of place sit uncomfortably alongside notions of fluidity, networks, and interconnecting flows associated with globalisation. This development has contributed to the loss of a sense of place. This has been associated with new forms of colonialism operating covertly on the back of a highly mobile and self-consciously global world where market dominance is the fundamental paradigm. In this context place disappears or rather, place becomes ubiquitous. Particularity of places is always under threat of dissolution or assimilation. Rapid networks of communication generate a sense of immediacy and feedback. In terms of the Anglican global com-

11. Cresswell, *Place*, 51.
12. John Inge, *A Christian Theology of Place* (Farnham, UK: Ashgate, 2003), 11.

munion it may mean that we are able to misunderstand each other more quickly than ever, that perceptions of each other as fundamentally similar—because of shared liturgical, doctrinal and governance provisions—in fact proves to be a chimera. The global world might be a story less about being pulled apart but of deeper and problematic connections. Is this a blessing or a curse? Minimally it points to the ambiguous nature of the shrinking global Anglican Communion. It can generate a new appreciation of 'diversity communion' and it can also become the basis for new forms of neo-colonial alliances. What it does mean is that place and any particular place can become the site for creative recovery of local identity because at one level all places are invested with a new significance in the wake of an anti-imperial global connectivity. On the other hand all places are susceptible to alliances that threaten to dissolve local identity. Place emerges as an ambiguous concept and highly vulnerable.

Diversity globalism and the retreat to place

A positive reading of 'diversity globalism' invests all places with renewed significance. Ian Douglas thus counters Phillip Jenkins' *Next Christianity* globalist vision with an alternative vision:

> If there is a crisis in world Christianity, it is not between an old Christendom of the West and a new Christendom of the South but rather between an hegemonic, monocultural expression of Western Christianity and an emerging, multicultural global Christian community embodying radical differences. The emergence of the diverse voices of Christianity in the Third World is not 'the next Christendom' but rather a new Pentecost . . . God's ongoing intervention in the world is being made real in the many tongues and cultural realities of a new Pentecost.[13]

This radical diversity globalism invests places with renewed significance. It offers a positive rationale for continued enculturation of the gospel. How does it fit with the realities of the Anglican Communion? The matter is complex for whilst some liberals and moderates view the years since Lambeth 1998 as an era of Anglican neo-colonialism undermining the

13. Cited in M Hassett, *Anglican Communion in Crisis: How Episcopal Dissidents and their African Allies are Reshaping Anglicanism* (Princeton: Princeton University Press, 2007), 258.

diversity globalist vision other of a more conservative persuasion view the same period as a new decolonised era opening up new possibilities for liberation and respect for minorities.[14]

The danger of the new diversity globalism is that it might promote a retreat into place as a protected space which runs counter to the new Pentecost spoken of by Douglas. Here place is construed as a retreat from alien forces with a concomitant tendency to create new exclusions and tight borders. On this scenario globalisation can be generative of new tribalism as well as neo-colonialism.[15]

It seems that our need for roots persists amidst the homogenisation of place. But it can lead to new assertions of homeland and territory where place becomes a heavily bounded concept. It is not surprising that such conceptions are subject to critique and reformulation in postcolonial theology and new notions of boundaries and home have emerged.[16] Such approaches give priority to life at the boundary as the location at which new and creative opportunities for life together exist. In the Gospels it is remarkable how often Jesus walked the boundary and in doing so reconnected people with each other and God.[17] When the accent is on life at the boundary or intersection, traditional notions of territory are reformulated to take account of the fact that it is both *at* and *across* boundaries that new home places are constructed and new patterns of human interaction arise. This leads to notion of 'in-between spaces' as a counter to more sedimented conceptions of place which involve 'parcelling out a closed space to people'. By contrast a 'nomadic spaciality' 'distributes people (or animals) in an open space'.[18] It is associated with an affirmation of cultural hybridity as preferable to cultural hegemony.[19] The notion of the place 'in-

---

14. Hassett, *Anglican Communion*, 216.
15. Indeed the two are not mutually exclusive, for a new imperial model of relationship with the rest of the world may also involve strong protective boundaries for a local power base.
16. M Nausner, 'Homeland as Borderland: Territories of Christian Subjectivity', in *Postcolonial Theologies: Divinity and Empire*, edited by C Keller, M Nausner and M Rivera (St Louis, USA: Chalice Press, 2004), 118–132.
17. Exactly why Jesus has to go via Samaria in John chapter 4 is a puzzle and is most easily explained by his desire to walk the boundary and touch 'enemy' territory. His subsequent encounter with the Samarian woman at the well is a classic example of ministry at the in-between place where conversion happens and new bonds are forged.
18. Nausner, *Postcolonial Theologies*, 127.
19. K Pui-lan, 'The Legacy of Cultural Hegemony in the Anglican Church' in *Beyond Colonial Anglicanism: The Anglican Communion in the Twenty-First Century*, edited by Ian Douglas and K Pui-lan (New York: Church Publishing, 2001), 47–70.

between' is an important ingredient for a reformulated ecclesial sense of place down-under which I will return to in the next section of the article.

A global sense of place?

This raises a fundamental question. Is it possible to have a global sense of place whilst remaining rooted in the local? This is pertinent to the life of the body of Christ, which is both a universal and a local phenomenon. Such an approach endeavours to mediate between the 'whole history of place as a centre of meaning connected to a rooted and "authentic" sense of identity forever challenged by mobility' and the 'erosion of place through globalisation and time-space compression'.[20] Is there then a third way that (a) retains the importance of rootedness but is not bound by colonial attitudes to place as site of conquest and (b) is not overwhelmed by global movements that appear as threat to all places and seem at first sight to represent new forms of colonial conquest of the market? This has led one geographer to develop an 'extroverted notion of place' as 'open and hybrid—a product of interconnecting flows—of routes rather than roots'.[21] On this account place is marked more as process, defined by the outside, a site of multiple identities and histories, a uniqueness marked by the quality of interactions, of 'routes' rather than 'roots'. What some had earlier argued generated 'non-places'[22] this more positive assessment of place as dynamic interconnected flows of people in relation to places accentuates routes but only in relation to specific locales.

Recognition of the global emphasis on mobility and routes does not necessarily displace the need for roots. Rather there exists a 'dialogical relationship' between the two with 'roots' 'signifying identity based on stable cores and continuities' and 'routes suggesting identity based on travel, change and disruption'.[23] A sense of place is constituted through such a dialogical relationship. It is associated with boundaries as 'permeable borderlands of exchange, blending and transformation'.[24] Might this be sufficient to overcome the subtle and not so subtle influence of neo-colonial conquests of economy, social life and even the form of the Christian community? This seem to me to be a fundamental issue for the Anglican Communion. On the one hand we cannot wind the clock back—there is no

20. Cresswell, *Place*, 53.
21. Cresswell, *Place*, 53.
22. Cresswell, *Place*, 74.
23. Nausner, *Homeland as Borderland*, 129.
24. Nausner, *Homeland as Borderland*, 129.

protected place as such, but on the other hand, to do justice to God's ways with the world, a recognition and acknowledgement of particular places is axiomatic to the gospel. These are issues for the Australian context. What would it look like for Anglicanism in Australia to recover a sense of place which was both global in intent and consciousness but at the same time fully embedded in the local place as an incarnate and resurrected ecclesiology might require? How might recognition of 'in-between spaces', open territories and notions of home be deployed in the service of an antipodean ecclesiology that was truly inculturated and indigenous?

Preliminary assessments: the ecclesial potentialities of place

In this section I have briefly examined the concept of place as it has functioned in contemporary geography. Some of the implications of this discussion for ecclesial life and colonial Anglicanism in particular have been flagged. What does appear incontrovertible is that place is an essentially contested concept.[25] A number of themes flow through the discussion.

First, I note the dialectical relationship between place and space. The two terms are not the same but they belong to a similar field of enquiry in geography. The Western preoccupation with special categories to the virtual exclusion of place is in the process of correction. Place and space operate in tension with each other. This means that notions of space as a vacuum to be filled and assimilated to alien presence has to be kept in tension with a concept of place as a rich web of engagement leading to discovery of new ways of being.

This is associated with a second feature of recent reflections on place. This concerns place as a human construct and place as an elemental form of life together. In the former aspect place reveals itself as the result of certain values and ideological impulses; in the latter emphasis, place is recognised as an indispensable feature of being human prior to its constructed quality.

A third matter concerns the relationship between 'roots' and 'routes' reflecting the human need for sites of habitation and the wrestless and

25. WB Gaillie, *Philosophy and the Historical Understanding* (London: Chatto & Windus, 1964). Gaillie discusses 'essentially contested concepts' as those terms which, in the history of discussion about a subject, generate significant and repeated disagreement. For Gaillie the meaning of the term can only be grasped from within the history of the disagreements. In geography the term 'place' seems to qualify as an essentially contested concept.

fluid movement connecting sites. Roots and routes are key elements in a dynamic sense of place that obtains in our contemporary world.

A fourth matter concerns place as 'in-between' existence. In this approach place is a liminal concept and primary emphasis is on boundaries, meeting points and intersection as locations for new possibilities for personal and communal life in God's world.

Each of the above four areas have implications for ecclesial life; how it might be reconceived and what practices this might involve. Minimally our preliminary examination of the concept of place suggests that the recovery of an ecclesial sense of place will lead to a more dynamic and prophetic ecclesiology. The idea of the church of Jesus Christ as a pilgrim people required to engage with new places prior to imposing new forms of church culture—of a community of faith embodying both sacred sites and sacred journeys; of a church that is at home in a liminal in-between existence beyond prevailing forms and structures—all present some profound challenges to the way the Anglican churches of the colonial empire have shaped their presence and engagements. In the next section I pursue the above themes relating to place in relation to the Anglican church of Australia. I am particularly interested to see what value there may be in the idea of the church as in-between place, the resonances it may have with *terra Australis* and the possibilities that arise for a more dynamic Anglican ecclesiology down-under.

Church as in-between place: verandah as a form of God's ecclesia

Place, space and spiritual sensibilities

In the Christian tradition in Australia the theme of land has become important in recent years, usually in relation to indigenous spirituality.[26] Yet the significance of place for the development of the church in Australia is in its infancy.[27] The recent examination of a Christian theology of place by John Inge provides some important markers for such an exploration. Inge develops a relational understanding of place as 'the seat of relations or the place of meeting and activity in the interaction between God and the

26. Tony Kelly, *A New Imagining: Towards an Australian Spirituality* (Melbourne: CollinsDove, 1990), 103–117; Rainbow Spirit Elders, *Rainbow Spirit Theology: Towards an Australian Aboriginal Theology* (Blackburn: HarperCollins, 1997).
27. D Hannah, 'Experience of Place in Australian Identity and Theology', *Pacifica*, 17, (2004):297–310; Geoffrey Lilburne, *A Sense of Place: A Christian Theology of the Land* (Nashville, TN: Abingdon Press, 1989).

world'.[28] He explores the way in which place attains a sacramental character through the particular interactions that involve people, place and God. It leads him to consider the conditions necessary for the emergence of holy places and shrines, which maintain continuity through time. At the heart of this recovery of place is a reading of the Scriptures that point to the significance of place both in the life of the people of Israel and radically through the incarnation of the divine Word made flesh. Inge maps out a way forward for a positive appreciation of the significance of place in religious experience and as a factor in theological understanding.

Inge's approach connects with the reflections of the Australian architect, Philip Drew.[29] Drew argued that Anglo-Saxon Australian cultural identity has been formed largely in relation to the experience of living on the fringes of the continent. This explains why Australians look outward rather than inward and why our spaces are linear rather than centripetal. This outward and lineal orientation for Australian identity was linked by Drew to the verandah in the Australian experience. For a variety of social and environmental reasons the first Europeans in Australia sought what Drew referred to as a 'safe openness', a 'balance between looking out—a measure of openness—and shelter, or refuge, whose solution was the verandah'.[30] Thus, for Drew, the verandah is a 'primary metaphor' and he used it to explore the 'characteristic Australian expression of edges and open boundaries'.[31]

Drew argued against what he called the 'centric myth', which he associated both architecturally and culturally with the dominant European cultural tradition. This was the tradition of 'centralised space, the conception of a closed centric world'. In Drew's view this European attitude 'distorted perceptions of Australia at the same time as it failed to match the geographic reality'.[32] Drew proposed that Australians were pre-eminently verandah people, looking outward, not into the centre of *Terra Australis Incognitio*.[33] This was certainly reflected in the development of architec-

28. Inge, *A Christian Theology of Place*, 52.
29. Phillip Drew, *The Coast Dweller: Australians Living on the Edge* (Ringwood, Vic: Penguin, 1994).
30. Drew, *Coast Dweller*, 11.
31. Drew, *Coast Dweller*, 13.
32. Drew, *Coast Dweller*, 11.
33. W Lines, *Taming The Great South Land: A History of the Conquest of Nature in Australia* (London & Athens: University of Georgia Press, 1991), 14–26.

ture in Australia in housing, shop fronts, pubs and grander colonial buildings—in all except churches.

Drew's analysis has been an important catalyst for my own explorations of place and ecclesiology.[34] It offers a way through two often-competing approaches to fundamental religious experience. One the one hand there is a strong and dominant approach which focuses on spiritual authenticity being gained through the way of purgation, associated with a return to the centre and a companion desert spirituality. This has been a theme in the Australian writers Manning Clarke (history), Patrick White (literature) and more recently David Tracey (cultural studies). On the other hand there are more recent counter-proposals from a feminist perspective that draw attention to the importance of divine interaction at home in the everyday, on the fringes or at the margins.[35] Both these approaches to religious experience draw upon significant streams in the Christian tradition. The centric orientation has been a feature of Christian asceticism (with a strong focus on denial and purgation and a tendency to undervalue materiality and bodily life in its conception of holiness). It has been associated with a theology of transcendence—the Divine is the mystery beyond the horizon of present existence. The spirituality of the everyday is funded by a theology of immanence and finds the Divine erupting in ever new and surprising ways in the ordinary—the tradition of Brother Lawrence springs to mind.

However, without wishing to dismiss these two spiritual traditions it seems to me that neither takes seriously the sense of place referred to by Drew and characteristic of those who inhabit the continent of Australia. The majority of Australians to this day have their cultural and social identities shaped not by one fundamental reality, that is, the land, but by three—land (continent), ocean (we inhabit the largest *island* continent) and sky (with its infinite extension into space). Furthermore, since the majority who live on this continent live on the costal fringes the fundamental experience for such people is not one of living on the edge or at the margins in relation to a mysterious centre. Rather, the fundamental experience is one of living at the point of intersection, the intersection of three great realities of our physical environment. This constitutes one of the givens of our sense of place. The companion language to intersections is intervals and corridors. The geography of the eastern seaboard,

34. Stephen Pickard, 'The View from the Verandah: Gospel and Spirituality in an Australian Setting', in *St Mark's Review*, Winter (1998): 4–11.

35. Elaine Lindsay, 'Divining', in *Eremos*, 51, May (1995): 25–29.

where 80% of Australians live, is an extensive land corridor from the tip of northern Australia to Melbourne in the South, a distance of over three thousand kilometres. This corridor is bounded by ocean to the east and the Great Dividing Range to the west, a distance usually no wider than sixty kilometres. This is the matrix within which our spiritual identity and life has to be crafted. The impact of this particular place on the shape and texture of our spiritual lives has yet to be uncovered.

What has this to do with Anglican ecclesiology in Australia? First, the regionalism that afflicts Australian Anglicanism and has been a major factor in the development of an independent diocesanism may be significantly influenced by place as much as any imported ecclesiastical party spirit. The Church of England developed where the centres of population were established. These places were strung out along the coast at the estuaries of magnificent harbours. The colonial church was in fact a church in many quite different colonies. Regionalism was a matter of survival. Second, the orientation of the coastal dwellers was outwards to the ocean, to home base, to England on another shore. Again, the strong links to the mother country were a matter of survival and comfort in a strange place. Significant links between these different regions were more difficult to sustain compared to perceived connections to origins abroad. Third, the continent itself was perceived as alien and strange by comparison with the place of origin. Under conditions of extreme isolation and alienated from home base[36] the quasi-established church found that its most pressing need was to transplant as much as possible of the Church of England within the confines of the separated colonial settlements. Such a transplant could not involve creative adaptation, for the place itself was fundamentally alien and in need of charting, taming, and ordering. Not only would this inevitably happen on a regional basis, it would also occur with as little disruption as possible to the inherited forms and patterns of worship, belief and practice.[37]

The fundamental need was reassurance and comfort in an alien environment. The church was shaped by a sense of social, cultural and religious dis-placement. Its sense of place was construed negatively in the interests of creating a home away from home. Accordingly the space was filled with

36. The relationship between 'home base' and 'reach' is an important one in geography. Where 'reach' (distance from home base) extends to the point of rupture of the relation, significant anxiety and alienation can be generated.

37. Rowan Strong, 'An Antipodean Establishment. Institutional Anglicanism in Australia, 1788–c1934', in *Journal of Anglican Studies*, 1/1 (2003): 61–90.

European exotics; local indigenous forms were largely ignored.[38] This was certainly the case with the development of the Church of England in Australia. In this colonial expansion of the church engagement with the place was determined by underlying beliefs that here was a space that required European impress and assimilation. Given the dialectic between place and space, between listening and discovery of what was present, any creative engagement leading to a new synthesis was muted at best. The sense of dis-placement was profound; the need to recreate in the colonial space a cultural form that closely mirrored home base was paramount. This certainly meant that the spiritual rhythms of the new place could not easily emerge in the ecclesial consciousness. An implication of this was that place as an elemental form of life gave way to place as a social construct. In an alien environment this was indeed an urgent matter. The experience of dis-placement meant that the transplanted Church of England was distinctly out of place in the new environment.

Not surprisingly the architecture of the Church of England was also transplanted and exhibited the signs of an established and secure church in a tough colonial world. Generally ecclesiastical architecture followed international trends in neo-gothic revival. In this context accommodation to local conditions (for example, climate and landscape) was not prominent.[39] The failure of local adaptation, architecturally, was of a piece with a general failure of the Church of England to transcend its establishment social and cultural European world. What the church has been manifestly unable to do is develop an orientation and outlook more in keeping with the nature of the place. For example, whereas the inherited Georgian geometric box architecture was modified by the development of the verandah, this was not a significant feature of holy places of worship.

Retrieving verandah as ecclesial place

Perhaps a verandah ecclesiology is precisely what is required for a truly inculturated form of Christianity in Australia. Something of this sense is captured by the Australian theologian Bruce Kaye in his reference to a 'church without walls'.[40] In Kaye's view the basic challenge for Australian

---

38. John Harris, *One Blood: 200 Years of Aboriginal Encounter with Christianity*, (Sutherland: Albatross, 1990).
39. Colin Holden, 'Anglicanism, the Visual Arts and Architecture', in *Anglicanism in Australia: A History*, edited by Bruce Kaye (Melbourne: Melbourne University Press, 2002): 265–66.
40. Bruce Kaye, *A Church without Walls: Being Anglican in Australia* (Melbourne: Dove

Anglicans is to become an outward-looking and open community, actively engaged with society and its concerns. The verandah is a place without walls and barricades but offers posts and railings to lean upon.[41] It does not dissolve the importance of boundaries and the dynamics that occur across bounded spaces. The verandah motif may provide an imaginative construal for the kind of ecclesial place Australian Anglicans occupy. The verandah, like the place of our habitation, is a place of intersection between outer world and inner house. It is a corridor or interval, which catches the breeze; a safe and hospitable place, orientated outwards but mindful of the deeper recesses from within and from which it draws life. An ecclesiology shaped in relation to this image feeds a notion of the church as an open sanctuary offering safety, nourishment and energy for work.

Certainly the key element here is our placement at the interstices of life, in the middle, in-between. The notion of the land down under is relative to those who are on top. But the particularity of our place is otherwise. We have to take stock of our place amidst the great cosmic realities, land, sea and sky, inhabiting a corridor bounded by salt water and the driest continent upon earth. This in-between place was well understood by the aboriginal peoples of Australia for over 50,000 years. Europeans are relative latecomers and our degree of integration with our place is in the early stages. This fact alone makes the dialogue between indigenous and recent arrivals imperative.

Can the verandah motif provide a rich enough idea for a properly inculturated church? Perhaps we have to move beyond a verandah ecclesiology in order to respond to the need for reconciliation with indigenous Australians.[42] From this perspective the verandah metaphor is vulnerable on two points. First, the verandah is derivative from the main body of the dwelling. The pre-existing structure is aligned with the colonial home. As a result, to invoke the verandah metaphor is to maintain a certain ideological dominance of prevailing European values and attitudes that are no longer appropriate for genuine meeting and reconciliation. Second, to occupy the space of the verandah is to assume the stance of one who gazes

Publications, 1995).

41. The word verandah seems to have a Spanish/Portuguese origin, a sixteenth-century lexicon referring to 'varanda' as 'rails to lean the breast on'.

42. Tracey Spencer, 'Contextual Australian Theology beyond the Verandah', in *South Pacific Journal of Mission Studies*, September (2006): 12–18; Tracey Spencer, 'Getting Off the Verandah: Contextual Australian Theology In-Land and In Story', in *Pacifica* 19 (2006): 323–341.

upon another at a distance.[43] Thus the verandah motif appears problematic as a metaphor for renewed ecclesial life in Australia because of its associations with colonial power and detachment from indigenous Australia. On this reading the attempt to create a home away from home has resulted in an Anglicanism still welded to the mother-house and at some distance from the local cultures. What seems to be required is a 'contact zone', a 'neutral zone' that is free from 'traces of colonial discourse',[44] though such zones may function as a 'detached verandah, detached from colonial centres and colonial power and even from hard boundaries'.[45] However, I remain unconvinced by the notion of 'contact zones'. The phrase has its own baggage associated with militarism and sporting prowess as well as privileging the idea of space rather than concrete place.

In response to such a critique it may be sufficient to draw attention to the remarkable variety of verandahs in Australian culture and the manner in which they actually draw people together rather than maintain distance. Indigenous people too have their own versions of verandahs. This is not to ignore the fact that increasingly in Australia the verandah of private dwellings has been relocated from the front to the back of the house. This retreat from public to private place has a variety of names, such as patio, entertainment area, sundeck, courtyard. It is a feature of suburban life.[46] Yet the matter is more complex. Beyond the domestic verandah there are numerous other structures and places that function in a verandah-like way in contemporary culture, for example, places of meeting where race, ethnicity, class, gender, social status are no longer barriers to social encounter. Sports ovals, beach, esplanades, pathways and shopping malls come to mind.[47] The migration of the verandah to the public places of our life may constitute 'the great good place' that creates the possibilities for encounter and communal sensibilities beyond the enclosure of our private worlds.[48] In this sense the verandah depicts a third place beyond work

43. Spencer, 'Contextual Australian Theology', 14.
44. Spencer, 'Contextual Australian Theology', 17.
45. Spencer, 'Contextual Australian Theology', 17.
46. See Simon Holt, *God Next Door: Spirituality & Mission in the Neighbourhood* (Melbourne: Acorn Press, 2007).
47. See J Fiske, B Hodge and G Turner, *Myths of Oz: Reading Australian Popular Culture*, Australian Cultural Series (Sydney: Allen & Unwin, 1987) for an interesting discussion of the way the pub and the beach function as gathering places. They have an 'in-between' character for social interactions.
48. See Ray Oldenburg, *The Great Good Place: Cafes, Coffee Shops, Bookstores, Bars, Hair Salons, and Other Hangouts at the Heart of Community* (New York: Paragon House,

or home where new forms of interpersonal life might arise. The metaphor may yet offer some rich possibilities that move us beyond the constraints of colonial ideology. How the church might respond to such in-between public places and attempt to re-envisage its own life within such liminal existence is a project that awaits us. The emergence of new forms of religious fundamentalism and enclaves of spiritual life hermetically sealed from the wider culture may look attractive but in terms of our discussion such features of religious life constitute resistances to an ecclesiology of the in-between as developed here. Appeal to 'emerging church' and so-called 'fresh expressions' may not in fact break through such resistances but embody them in new forms of tribalism.

It is also the case that verandahs are inevitably tied to homes and such places are freighted with meanings and established relations. And home itself is a powerful and complex biblical image for salvation.[49] By contrast the quest for neutral places where relationships are less clear and consequently open to new possibilities are manifestly not home, and people do not live there but pass through them. In the biblical tradition they are analogous to roads and are implicated in journey motifs. The Emmaus road is one such well-known neutral contact zone. There exists an inevitable tension between home base (albeit of a more open and inviting kind) and the neutral space beyond the 'fence line', between, as we have already observed, roots and routes. A verandah ecclesiology makes some modest moves towards a more open engagement from the home. This will necessarily involve a creative move beyond the verandah and/or the reconstitution of the church as in-between existence. But the dialectic between fence-line and home base; between routes and roots is critical and the verandah as liminal place will play its part. When the fence line or frontier becomes the space occupied by our verandahs then a new home is in construction at the point of intersection.[50] The dynamism inherent in this reconfiguring of church is consonant with the migration of the sacred in

1989).

49. J Martis, 'Living Away From Home—and Loving It: Tweaking a Christian Metaphor', in *Pacifica*, 15/2, June (2002): 123–37.

50. The language of boundaries, albeit dynamic interpretations developed by Nausner ('Homeland as Borderland', 124–29), function to rehabilitate binary categories. The language of intersections, corridors and intervals has the twin advantages of first not being so easily trapped in binary categories and second gives stronger reference to the idea of place as location amidst intersections of life.

contemporary society beyond the established ecclesial walls into new and unchartered places that await careful engagement by the churches.[51]

However, it is at this point we need to recall the limitations of metaphor. Metaphors cannot stand alone; they require a conceptual framework within which to operate. It is the choice of an appropriate framework that is critical and it is precisely at this point that deeper engagement with the theological tradition is required.

My own deployment of the verandah motif as a place in-between connects with a postcolonial sensibility[52] and can be fruitfully linked with a minor yet clear theme in the Christian tradition. The place of the in-between has been developed in relation to pneumatology and more recently in relation to Holy Saturday.[53] The breeze-way of the verandah church with its obvious appeal to the activity of the Spirit may find a creative correlation to the Holy Saturday tradition of existence between old life and new, under threat of extinction and anticipation of new possibilities. For in this tradition the possibility of Jesus' resurrection from the dead lies within the gift of the Father through the agency of the life-giving Spirit. The mode of God's presence in the Holy Saturday tradition is one of vulnerability and openness to an as yet unfulfilled future. There are resources here for the development of a trinitarian dynamic woven into church, discipleship and the particularities of place in Australia. Such an interweaving seems to be precisely what a grounded trinitarian ecclesiology requires. It will require nothing less than 'the long days journey of the Saturday'[54] of the Church of the in-between God. It requires an ecclesial ethic that embodies resilience, patience, respect and resolve.[55]

The project for Australian Anglicans depends upon the discovery of a richer sense of place and a commitment to the theological task in that place. Clearly such an account of 'place' is not to be equated with land

---

51. For discussion of the idea of the migration of the sacred see Richard Roberts, 'Ruling the Body: the care of souls in a managerial church', in *Religion, Theology and the Human Sciences* (Cambridge: CUP, 2002), 178.
52. Pui-lan, 'The Legacy of Cultural Hegemony', 53–54.
53. Hans Ur Von Balthasar, *Mysterium Paschal* (Edinburgh: T&T Clark, 1990); A Lewis, *Between Cross and Resurrection: A Theology of Holy Saturday* (Grand Rapids, MI: Eerdmans, 2001); D Lauber, *Barth on the Descent into Hell: God Atonement and the Christian Life* (Aldershot: Ashgate Publishers, 2004).
54. George Steiner, *Real Presences* (Chicago: Chicago University Press, 1989), 231.
55. Inter Anglican Doctrinal and Theological Commission (IATDC), *Communion, Conflict and Hope: The Kuala Lumpur Report of the Third IATDC*, 2008 (London: Anglican Communion Office, 2008), para 52.

as such. Minimally it includes the entirety of the physical environment. This is necessary but not sufficient, for the dynamic of place can only be uncovered theologically as it includes environment, human interaction and a construal of the presence of God.[56] Place is thus a dynamic concept that grounds reflection in the local but is orientated towards more universal categories. A Christian theology of place necessarily strains towards the universal; it is freighted with universal intent. The value of a focus on place is that it facilitates a critical deconstruction of inherited identities and opens up new possibilities for re-conceiving the nature of ecclesial existence.

Conclusion

Church of the in-between: an Anglican possibility?

Australian Anglicanism has a long history of struggle trying to make a 'home away from home'. But this enterprise is driven by a colonial conception of space where homemaking equates to transplantation. Yet even this project has proven a conflictual and difficult task. A colonial church always generates modifications whether intended or not. Furthermore it is not surprising that eventually more dissident voices and aspirations emerge advocating a more authentic local voice and shape. A good case can be made out for this in the Australian context at least at some levels, for example, synodical government. But the nature of the place, its sheer vastness and the immensity of the spaces in between, as well as the infinite expanse of surrounding oceans and limitless high skies contribute to a certain ecclesial character that is fearful of the new and untamed and more at home with the known from another place. The sheer immensity of this particular colonial space has been at times simply overwhelming.

Conquest of such a space has been both alluring and heartbreaking. This has meant that in many significant respects the ecclesial character is derivative, unformed and immature. It has generated a kind of ecclesial retreat mentality, a certain preoccupation with internal life because it appears, at first sight, as more manageable, which is false. Even notions of mission and mission action plans, as worthwhile as they are, often operate within a culture of anxiety and fundamental enclosed-ness. The church's foray into the world betrays a failure to ground its own life in a doctrine

56. For an intriguing exploration see Simon Schama, *Landscape and Memory* (London: Harper Perennial, 1995).

of creation, an appreciation of the sacredness of place. We lack a sense of holy reciprocity between human life and the environment of our lives. We do not expect to discover God's holy presence in creation. The colonial mentality and its neo-colonial offspring continue to create place in their own image; an idolatrous conception of place repeatedly emerges. Place as formed in God's image is always under threat of erasure. The new heaven and the new earth of Revelation paint a different picture: of the reconstitution of God's place, of the recovery of all places as beloved of the Lord of place. This is clearly not a matter of occupation and domination but of a holy assimilation of all places to the wisdom of God. The form of this wisdom and its dynamic is succinctly expressed in the hymnic theology of Paul's letter to the Philippians 2:5–11. The bended knee is the recognition that beyond the colonial stance is another posture appropriate for human habitation of the place of God's tabernacle.

The recovery of a sense of place has implications for our relation to indigenous culture in Australia. Indigenous peoples neither own nor fill and colonise spaces, but rather they inhabit particular places. A Christian sensibility, fuelled by an incarnational theology, has resources to overcome the latent pressure of colonial conquest and recover a deeper sympathy with indigenous ways of community and gospel. Reconciliation will include a 'kenotic listening' by European diasporia to the first inhabitants.[57] In this process colonial space is subtly transformed into ecclesial place.

Amidst all the challenges for Anglicanism and the particular challenges for those from the Antipodes, perhaps the critical issue is one of becoming dwellers in our own place, no longer merely creating a 'home away from home' but finding a different home with God in our part of the planet. Reconciliation with the place of our habitation as a place loved by God is co-related to reconciliation with indigenous peoples. It requires a new Emmaus journey of recognition and wonder at Christ in our midst.

57. Mark Brett, '*Canto ergo sum*: Indigenous Peoples and Postcolonial Theology', in *Pacifica* 16 (2003): 205.

Chapter Eight
Innovation, Undecidability and Patience[1]

Finding an Ecclesial Patience

This essay explores the twin challenges of innovation and uncertainty. It examines how it is possible to live faithfully amidst the unresolved and ambiguous nature of our world. This gives rise to a reflection on the ecclesial virtues of trust and patience which I touched on in chapter two. It had its origins in a paper I prepared for the Inter Anglican Theological and Doctrinal Commission of which I was a member 2001–2007. The Commission represented a wide diversity of views on a number of contentious topics, not least being the matter of gay and lesbian unions and leadership. The fact is our different voices did not all sing the same song. It seemed that some matters were practically undecideable but yet required concrete action. This required the exercise of a considerable deal of patience.

Innovation

Innovation derives from the Latin *innovare*, meaning to renew or alter; essentially to bring in or introduce something new. Hence we may speak of novel practices and/or doctrines. It is a controversial feature of the life of the Christian church. Innovation is almost endemic to Christianity. The very nature of the gospel suggests that notions of surprise and novelty belong to the life of discipleship because they first inhere in the very character and action of God. The great surprising act of God in the incarnation and resurrection of the Messiah sets the pattern for the emergence of nov

1. Originally published as 'Innovation & Undecidability: Some Implications for the *Koinonia* of the Anglican Church', in *Journal of Anglican Studies*, 2/2 December (2004): 87–116. The themes of innovation and undecideablity were more briefly treated in chapter 2 of the present volume with the result that there is some overlap between the two chapters. Whist not frequent this is unavoidable in such a volume of collected papers.

elty at the heart of Christianity. However, as is well known, novelty and innovation have been, from the outset, highly contentious in the Christian community. The reasons are related to the need and importance felt by the early Christian movement to discover its own particular identity in relation to its roots in Judaism and also as it moved out into the Gentile/Roman world developing its particular apologetic.

The controversial nature of innovation covered both doctrine (for example Christology, Trinity) and practice (ethical domain, organisation/ecclesiastical matters). The controversies that occurred were perfectly understandable. For while, on the one hand, the gospel of Jesus Christ had generated something entirely new in the history of the world and religion, on the other hand the very novelty of this outbreak of God's grace in the world had to be preserved and enabled to endure without deviation and contamination. It is partly for this reason that the Apostle Paul exhorts Timothy to 'guard' [preserve] the deposit of faith entrusted . . .' (2 Timothy 1.14).[2] The emergence of Gnosticism and the encounter with the philosophies of the Roman world all required robust theological responses in order for the novelty of the gospel to be maintained. It also accounted for the importance a church theologian like Irenaeus placed on identifying the authoritative teachers and bearers of the Christian tradition. In an entirely different domain the Apostle Paul attempted to adjudicate regarding meat offered to idols (Romans 14). Faith in Christ gave a certain flexibility regarding this practice, which might not otherwise have been considered possible.

In this context the Arian controversy is an early example of the church's attempt to preserve a theological innovation regarding the doctrine of God. In this case Arius's attribution of a creaturely status to Christ—'there was a time when was not'—and his distinction between Christ as 'creature' and the divine 'Ungenerated One' undermined the consubstantial nature of the second person of the Trinity and inappropriately exalted the status of the Father over the Son.[3] His heresy involved a failure to appropriate the innovation of the incarnation into a doctrine of God founded on a traditional philosophical account of Divine simplicity.[4] Arius's Christology was

2. Note that even here the process of guarding/preserving is not simple. It requires the assistance of the indwelling Holy Spirit, the teacher of truth. Guarding is an inherently dynamic interpretive activity that resists attempts at political and theological short cuts.
3. See Frances Young, *From Nicea to Chalcedon* (London: SCM Press, 1983), 63–64.
4. For a discussion of the influence of the doctrine of divine simplicity from its origins

deficient in so far as it lacked the radical innovative edge expressed in the doctrine of the *homoousion*.[5] Innovation was an implicate of the Christian community's fidelity to the gospel. Yet securing and maintaining this trinitarian innovation was a drawn-out and highly conflictual process that divided Christian communities, fractured relationships between church leaders and altered political alignments for generations.

With the emergence of a 'normative' doctrinal consensus expressed through the great ecumenical creeds of the early Church the question of doctrinal innovation had the appearance of being settled. As a result it was not unusual until relatively recent times for novelty to be considered as essentially antithetical to Christianity. Novelty was thus a feature of heretical movements and a sign of unfaithfulness to the established theological tradition. Tertullian encapsulated the ideal: 'Look, whatsoever was first, that is true; and, whatsoever is latter, that is corrupt'.[6] Constancy and fidelity to the past rather than innovation became the great virtue. This gave particular force to the well-known Anglican appeal to antiquity and the ecumenical creeds. Thus the sixteenth-century apologist, John Jewel (1522–71) argued that the English reform did not constitute an innovation but was in continuity with the primitive ecclesia:

> we have searched out the holy bible which we are sure cannot deceive, one sure form of religion, and have returned again unto the primitive church of the ancient fathers and apostles, that is to say, to the first ground and beginning of things, as unto the foundations and head-springs of Christ's church.[7]

---

in Greek metaphysics see Wolfhart Pannenberg, *Basic Questions in Theology*, volume 2 (London: SCM Press, 1971), 165–73. The Roman Catholic theologian, William Hill, suggests that the early centuries of trinitarian and christological reflection can be understood as an attempt to show how 'neither the Incarnation of the Word nor the real distinction of divine persons is in any way injurious to God's simplicity' ('Simplicity of God' in *New Catholic Encyclopedia of Theology*, volume 13, edited by State Catholic University of America (Washington: McGraw Hill, 1967), 230).

5. See the discussion of *homoousion* by Thomas Torrance, *The Trinitarian Faith* (Edinburgh: T&T Clark, 1988), 132–35.
6. For this translation of Tertullian's *Prescription Against the Heretics*, see John Jewel, *Apologia Ecclesiae Anglicanae: An Apology of the Church of England* and *Defence of the Apology*, edited by J Ayre, in *The Works of John Jewel*, volume 3 (Cambridge: The Parker Society, Cambridge University Press, 1848), 106.
7. Jewel, *Apologia Ecclesiae Anglicanae*, 106.

This approach provided Jewel and his fellow reformers with a rationale for convicting the Church of Rome of having introduced innovations that departed from the purity of the early church. The appeal to antiquity as a means of countering innovations was succinctly stated by the Anglican divine, Lancelot Andrews (1555–1626): 'One canon reduced to writing by God himself, two testaments, three creeds, four general councils, five centuries, and the series of fathers in that period—the centuries that is, before Constantine, and two after, determine the boundary of our faith'.[8]

The appeal of such an approach is security. But it is more imagined than real. The actual history of Christianity is one of constant eruption of new and surprising elements in the community of faith, in both beliefs and practices. What are we to make of the last 1500 years of faith and practice? What response might be possible to novel beliefs and practices? Historically, one option (in line with the appeal to antiquity) has been to charge those who proposed such new things with introducing novelty. The charge itself did not necessarily resolve the matter but it set the framework for the ensuing debate. Thus proponents of alleged novelty exerted a great deal of energy defending their position as something entirely consistent and faithful to the gospel tradition. Thus the innovation might be viewed as a logical implicate of the gospel tradition or necessarily implied. This was not an unfamiliar tack in the Reformation debates about the doctrine of justification by faith. Years later the Anglican Newman, in his *Lecturers on the Prophetical Office of the Church* of 1837 concluded that the baptismal faith may contain many beliefs such as justification by faith, that were not necessarily stated but subsumed within it.[9]

Another option involved making a careful distinction between those parts of Christianity that could admit of change and novelty, and the parts that had to remain constant, not subject to change and innovation. Hence the traditional Anglican appeal to fundamentals in the faith compared to non-fundamentals—and the associated concept of *adiaphora*[10]—became important. Such a distinction was not unique to Anglicanism (for exam-

8. Henry McAdoo, *The Spirit of Anglicanism* (London: A&C Black, 1965), 320. The force of the appeal to antiquity was weakened with the emergence of a more critical and refined historical critical method in the course of the seventeenth century. See BJ Shapiro, *Probability and Certainty in Seventeenth-Century England: A Study in the Relationship between Natural Science, Religion, History, Law and Literature* (Princeton: Princeton University Press, 1983), 109.
9. See 'On the Essentials of the Gospel', in *The Via Media of the Anglican Church*, volume 1 (London: Basil, Montague & Pickering, 1877), 254–55.
10. *Adiaphora*: things neither commanded nor forbidden.

ple, Lutheranism). Indeed, it is an unavoidable distinction in Christianity even in the corpus of belief associated with Roman Catholicism.[11]

The historical nature of Christianity innovation—in response to new contexts in time and space—has been a given. However, the historically contingent character of innovation is a matter that has become more clearly recognised in more recent centuries. It was certainly an important factor for John Henry Newman whose 'hypothesis to account for a difficulty' became the famous *Essay on the Development of Doctrine* of 1845.[12] Newman was all too aware of the remarkable innovations that had been introduced into the church of his choice—Roman Catholicism—and he felt it incumbent to give an account of such novelties (for example, cult of the saints, purgatory). His theory of development posited a doctrinal tradition in which innovations appeared as part of the 'homogenous evolution' of doctrine. This organic conception described a process whereby Christianity became ever more fully itself.[13] His seven tests for authenticity and legitimacy of doctrinal development as opposed to corruptions[14] facilitated Newman's move from Anglicanism into Roman Catholicism with a reasonably clear conscience.

What of course was surprising was how Newman was able to weave everything into a singular organic whole. This was not lost on his critics, especially FD Maurice who was more willing than Newman to recognise the discontinuities in the history and development of Christianity. Newman's smooth organic evolutionary theory for doctrinal innovation took the element of surprise out of the tradition—he had almost explained too much! The debate at least pointed to one thing: the development of criteria to assess the status of novelties was both important and at the same time no insurance against inappropriate assessment of innovative developments. Formal

11. This has been developed in the wake of Vatican 2 through the concept of the 'hierarchy of truths'. See 'The Notion of "Hierarchy of Truths": An Ecumenical Interpretation' (Joint Working Group between the Roman Catholic Church and the World Council of Churches, Sixth Report; Geneva: WCC, 1990), Appendix B, 38–46.
12. *An Essay on the Development of Christian Doctrine* (Harmondsworth: Pelican Books 1974).
13. For further discussion, see Stephen Prickett, *Romanticism and Religion: The Tradition of Coleridge and Wordsworth in the Victorian Church* (Cambridge: Cambridge University Press, 1976), especially 162–63.
14. Preservation of the essential idea; continuity of principles; power of assimilation of true developments; definite anticipation at an early period in the history of the idea to which development belongs; gradual and orderly logical sequence; an addition which is conservative of what has gone before it; chronic continuance.

development of criteria for assessment is necessary but not sufficient when dealing with innovations in the Church.

This fact highlights the importance of the wider faith community as an essential criterion for assessment and judgments regarding innovations in belief and practice. The *consensus fidelium* becomes fundamental in the process.[15] Here the critical factor is the existence of communities of interpretation in which change occurs, is assessed and in turn transforms the ecclesia. Where such communities of interpretation lack coherence and adequate interconnectedness the notion of *consensus fidelium* retracts into ecclesiastical enclaves. This is a feature of our contemporary contexts within Anglicanism. How should one view this? It could mean that innovation becomes a much more unwieldy occurrence and subject to premature decisions in local ecclesial/cultural contexts. An alternative view would suggest that this development offers a measure of local freedom that would not be possible beyond the local/regional level. What capacity does the church now have to decide in matters of innovation? Perhaps genuine communion-wide consensus is impossible: Perhaps some things are essentially undecidable!

Undecidability

It may seem odd, and certainly it may seem to run counter to Christianity, to refer to some things as essentially undecidable in the church. The fact is the church has decided (eventually!) about a myriad of innovations in the course of its history.[16] It is also the case that the decision-making process has been exceedingly conflictual.

The relevance of the notion to our discussion is fairly clear: while some sections of the church may firmly believe that a matter is decidable in a particular way, another section may firmly believe that the matter is decidable, in a manner directly at odds with the former approach. A good example of this is the ordination of women to the priesthood. This issue has been determined in some parts of the Anglican Church in the affirmative and in other parts in the negative. There is no consensus within the international Anglican community. The matter cannot evidently be resolved

15. Paul Avis has commented that '*Consensus fidelium* has now established itself as one of the key concepts of contemporary ecclesiology'. See Paul Avis, *Ecumenical Theology and the Elusiveness of Doctrine* (London: SPCK, 1986), 60.

16. The question of slavery is a relatively modern example and even more recently the issue of racism.

by recourse to Scripture. This necessary and indispensable reference in conflict resolution nevertheless remains insufficient, by itself, to decide the matter. Local context and cultures of interpretation add further layers of complexity. The status of the innovation remains essentially contested and undecidable, particularly if the *consensus fidelium* is important in the determination of decidability. The truth question cannot be resolved apart from and prior to the ecclesial form in which the issue presents itself for determination. Precisely because the ordination of women is a deeply ecclesial matter—as are most innovations in the Church—the manner of resolution cannot be easily separated into prior questions regarding truth and secondary questions concerning ecclesial form. The two are interwoven and the honouring of this symbiotic relation between the truth of things and the ecclesial frame is integral to the decision-making process.[17] Inevitably consensus will be slow, painful and retain a certain provisionality. On this account we can argue that undecidability is related to the eschatological nature of the church. The ecclesia is essentially an open system which admits of innovation but this very openness ensures that many matters cannot finally be decided upon, or even if they are it can never be more than provisional at best. In this context living truthfully as the people of God and making difficult decisions as a church requires the cultivation of a certain habit of life, and an approach to holiness founded upon humility. Yet recognition of this does not dispense with the need to make difficult decisions. A question remains: How then can a church make decisions regarding innovations when many of these innovations appear practically undecidable within the ecclesia, regardless of how theoretically decidable (abstracted from the ecclesia) we might like to think such matters are? Perhaps, in this context, the issue of undecidability deserves further exploration.

The immediate horizon for the discussion of undecidability is the recent philosophical contribution of Jaques Derrida who introduces the notion to highlight the essential disjunction between preparing for a decision and the actual decisions we make.[18] There remains, argues Derrida, an

17. In Anglicanism, at least, the truth we can carry together is the truth that binds us. We have never had the luxury of splitting questions of truth from the social/ecclesiological context—which is always more than mere context but rather the essential condition for the emergence of truth.

18. For a useful overview and discussion of Derrida's scattered references to undecidability in relation to moral decision see John Llewelyn, 'Responsibility with Indecidability', in *Derrida: A Critical Reader*, edited by David Wood (Oxford: Blackwell, 1992), chapter 4. I am grateful to Dr Winifred Lamb, for references and discussion on this issue

elemental risk, requiring a leap of faith. No amount of prior preparation or consideration can provide a guarantee of a hoped-for or anticipated outcome. Derrida invokes Kierkegaard; 'The instant of decision is madness'; the decision is thus 'something one can neither stabilise, establish, grasp [*prendre*], apprehend, or comprehend'.[19] Derrida is reflecting at this moment on the sacrifice of Abraham.

Derrida has been criticised for the way in which his appeal to undecidability avoids the necessity of responsibility in the public sphere.[20] His 'philosophy of hesitation' seems to offer little assistance for facing the practical realities that confront us in our public, political and ethical life. This may or may not be the case though it is hard to deny that the philosopher has identified something quite fundamental for our times. We are unsure of our footing; it is not always, if ever, clear what course of action to follow. More particularly, there exist significant disagreements in our communities regarding the ethical and moral dilemmas we face. Furthermore, the dilemmas actually look quite different depending upon our context. If we hesitate we might not be lost; we might simply be bearing witness to our very humanity. Undecidability may be a given of our existence. If this is the case it points to the importance of a degree of faith and 'courtesy' being extended to others when we make our decisions.[21]From this perspective undecidability points to the impossibility of control over outcomes and scenarios. Innovations generate a variety of responses and the hesitant society may be a natural outcome. Perhaps instinctively we recognise that to decide is an act of madness!

Undecidability may have deeper roots than Derrida supposes. Perhaps there are elements in the nature of Christianity itself—alluded to earlier—that generate a 'natural undecidability' about many matters of faith and morals. Here we are in the region of ontology and specifically that which

---

and a copy of an unpublished paper by Jack Reynolds, Australian National University, 'Habituality and Undecidability: A Comparison of Merleau-Ponty and Derrida on Decision'.

19. Jaques Derrida, *The Gift of Death*, translated by David Wills (Chicago: University of Chicago Press, 1995), 65–66.
20. See the discussion by Simon Critchley, *The Ethics of Deconstruction: Derrida and Levinas* (Oxford: Blackwell, 1992).
21. 'Courtesy is the style of interaction with the "other". It is characterised by thoughtfulness, respect, graceful speech and attentive listening'. George Steiner refers to both the 'yearning' and 'fear' of the other necessarily involved in courtesy. For discussion see Graeme Garrett, 'Open Heaven/Closed Hearts: Theological Reflections on Ecumenical Relations', in *Faith and Freedom, A Journal of Christian Ethics* 6 (1998): 18.

has to do with the being and action of God in the Christian tradition. As Richard Hooker said some years ago, the essential character of the Divine might be identified as 'riches', 'abundance' and 'variety'.[22] When it comes to the Christian doctrine of God we have to do primarily with a theology of divine abundance—for example creativity, grace, forgiveness—that is shaped and substantiated by the life of Jesus and the Spirit in the world and the people of God. The characteristic theme here might be overflow or abundance.[23] Much could be said here but the basis is laid in the Christian tradition for recognition of God's plenitude manifest in the creation.[24]

Minimally this points to a profound creativity that belongs to the Divine life. Few have explored this with such insight as the Orthodox theologian, Nicholas Berdyaev.[25] Such creativity is not necessarily to be equated with 'a cult of the future and of the new'; rather 'true creativeness is concerned neither with the old nor with the new but with the eternal. A creative act directed upon the eternal may, however, have as its product and result something new, that is, something projected in time'.[26] Berdyaev notes that creativeness, always the work of the Holy Spirit, does not necessarily bring 'bliss and happiness' but has its own pain and suffering. His reflections are most apposite for they draw attention to the necessary distinction between creativeness per se and the domain of human innovation. The relation is not one of direct correspondence; innovations as human deeds may simply instance the emergence of something new but without reference to 'the eternal'. The need for practical judgment and discernment arises precisely because human innovations and creativeness do not directly and unambiguously bear witness to the creativeness that flows from divine abundance.

---

22. Richard Hooker, *Of the Laws of Ecclesiastical Polity* [1593] (London: Dent, Everyman edition, 1907), book 1, chapter 1, para 4.
23. See, for example, Colossians. 1:19, 2:9 *pleroma*; John 10:10b *abundance*; 1 Timothy. 1:14 superabundance. In the same vein Ricoeur refers to Paul's letter to the Romans 5.15–21 as 'the "odd" *logic of superabundance*' wherein an 'ordinary "logic" collapses and the "logic" of God . . . blows up'. Paul Ricoeur, 'Paul Ricouer on Biblical Hermeneutics', in *Semeia* 4 (Missoula, MT: SBL, 1975): 138.
24. This of course makes the problem of theodicy fundamental for Christianity. Perhaps the undecidable of all undecidables!
25. See Nicholas Berdyaev, *The Destiny of Man* (New York: Harper, Torchbook edition, 1960), chapter 3. Berdyaev develops a trinitarian approach to Christian ethics moving from the ethics of law to redemption to the ethics of creativeness, the last being the work of the eternal Spirit.
26. Berdyaev, *The Destiny of Man*, 151.

However, the foregoing discussion of the pleroma and creativity of the triune God in the world does provide a foundation for a more peculiarly Christian understanding of the roots and logic of undecidability. It has ontological weight. Diversity of understanding, multi-perspectives, and possibilities for new and surprising responses—all of these things may in fact belong to the character and ways of God in the world. Therefore if the church finds new problems, situations and moral and ethical dilemmas it should not be surprised that this is accompanied by an inability to reach consensus. It may be that the significant differences of interpretation of divine intentions and desires are precisely what one should anticipate in the Christian tradition. This also suggests that the Church urgently requires an ethic of creativeness in order to practise wisdom and discernment in the practical affairs of its life and mission.

Of course there are a variety of other reasons for undecidability connected to issues of cultural mores, social life, different value systems, and human sin. However, it is not so easy to disentangle these and one wonders whether it is ever finally possible or appropriate. What it does mean is that our ecclesial life is often messier than we would wish. This is difficult for us to tolerate and we mostly desire clarity and sharpness of boundaries as a means to preserve and nurture personal and communal identity. Being vague and unsure are hardly virtues that we hear our leaders extol. However, when dealing with the difficult terrain of innovation in the Church and the undecidables that seem to haunt us we are in urgent need of resources that enable us to live with ambiguity and vagueness.[27] This is quite difficult given the strong views increasingly voiced these days by those of the church who call for sharper delineation of moral, ethical and doctrinal boundaries. The legislative impulse is powerful.

The dualisms that prevail in our present culture and church contexts are often quite uncompromising. We are often assailed by the either/or, which leaves little room for positions that occupy what may be termed the excluded middle ground. This in-between place can appear unattractive to many. Voices from this place are significantly silent in many of the de-

27. While we seek plain and clear texts, doctrines and ethical standards, perhaps the reality is quite different. We have difficulty dealing with the 'irremediable vagueness' and indefiniteness that seems to lurk within the plainest of statements and positions. Yet this very 'vagueness' provides the conditions for diverse and new interpretations and responses. Charles Peirce's (1839–1914) notion of 'irremediable vagueness' is interesting in this regard. See Peter Ochs, *Peirce, Pragmatism and the Logic of Scripture* (Cambridge: Cambridge University Press, 1998), chapter 7.

bates of the church today. The error of the 'undecided' is usually identified as their inconsistency. There are rigorists on both sides of the divide who share a common aversion to perceived inconsistency. Their systems and ideologies are tight, consistent and uncompromising. Those unsure and the vacillating display many of the opposite tendencies—divided minds, inconsistent positions, apparent double standards, essentially vague in their habitation of the fast receding middle ground. The virtue of the former position is internal coherence and consistency but the price is high. The system is notoriously incomplete and essentially closed.[28] There seem to be only two options. One can accept the either/or approach and argue for the rejection of all views save the preferred one. Alternatively one can reject the either/or approach and recognise the essential incompleteness of any position and the resultant possibility of various viewpoints. The merit of the latter is that it does give those who occupy the undecided place—the middle liminal space—the opportunity to be recognised and heard in the debates of our times.

Innovation, undecidability and koinonia

'The Church has power to decree Rites or Ceremonies, and authority in Controversies of Faith: And yet it is not lawful for the Church to ordain anything that is contrary to God's Word written . . . '.[29] This article enshrines within the Anglican Church a responsibility to exercise appropriate authority in matters pertaining to faith. Innovations in teaching, doctrine and morals would seem to fall within the ambit of this article. However, part of the problem today (and quite different from the sixteenth and seventeenth centuries) is that Anglicanism in now an international communion spanning the globe. Structurally it is a complex organisation operating at a variety of levels of existence: Diocesan, national, provincial, international—a communion of churches bound by certain moral, theological and ecclesial ties that trace their heritage to certain common origins. When such a church decides in matters of controversy, what does this mean? Who is it that is deciding?

28. If a system is internally consistent it will not be complete: If it aspires to completeness it will invariably contain inconsistencies. This, in essence, is Thomas Torrence's interpretation of Godel's theorum in *Theological Science* (Oxford: Oxford University Press, 1969), 255. Torrance points to the inevitability of open systems containing 'undecidable or extrasystematic propositions'.

29. Article 20 of the *Thirty-Nine Articles*

In matters of innovation affecting fundamental issues of church life—both in doctrine and morals—does it matter at what level or degree of organisational complexity the decisions are made? Is there a case for differentiating between different levels of ecclesial structure in relation to Article 20? For example, innovations that might be inherently difficult or impossible to reach consensus about at a meta-level might be resolvable (at least in a provisional sense) at a less complex level of organisation such as the diocese. This approach accords with the well-known principle of subsidiarity by which 'every "higher" authority ought to encourage the free use of God's gifts at "lower" levels'.[30] The implication is that a central authority should only undertake those tasks that cannot be effectively handled at more local levels. This principle points to a view of authority in the church that is focused in particular bodies at particular levels of national church life (vestry, diocesan synod, general synod). A multi-foci and layered approach is very different from a centralist approach to authority. Within the arena of international Anglicanism the common mind of the church is sought through discussion and consultation. The exercise of authority occurs in informal and powerful but indirect ways through, for example, allocations of funding and representation within committee structures. Whether it is possible and appropriate for the Anglican Communion to develop an international system for decision-making that is binding throughout the communion and thus decisively rule on innovations in a province(s) is a critical issue for contemporary Anglicanism. The attraction of a binding authority at the international level is that it appears to overcome the problem of undecidability in the communion.

However, at present the situation is quite different. Within the communion it is possible to have a variety of innovations that remain undecided upon at higher levels of the ecclesial organisation but are settled for the moment at lower levels of complexity. Their essential (practical) undecidability at one level does not preclude decisions made at other levels. Indeed, it could be argued that some matters ought to be decided precisely in this way. Decisions at one level do not bind the church at higher levels of *koinonia*, nor do they provide grounds for rejection or fragmentation of the *koinonia* at lower levels. Conflicts between ecclesial bodies at similar levels across the globe would undoubtedly persist but this would simply witness to the fact that what might be regarded as essentially undecidable at a meta-level

30. For a discussion of subsidiarity, see *The Virginia Report* (Anglican Consultative Council, 1997), chapter 4 and para 4.10 for present reference.

remains provisional, even at those levels at which decisions have already taken place.

This approach is attractive for a number of reasons. First, it provides a way to ensure oneness with freedom, two basic ecclesiological principles of Anglicanism. This suggests a *koinonia* that has reached a level of ecclesial maturity. It does this by properly differentiating the church, refusing the tendency to create a monolithic entity which cannot respond to the very different cultural and religious contexts in which it exits. In other words, it enables the church to take account of the different communities of interpretation (ecclesially, theologically and culturally) of text and tradition that coexist in the one worldwide Anglican Church.

Second, it endorses a notion of the *consensus fidelium*, which is fundamentally of an emergent quality rather then a top-down process. In truth consensus is usually occurring from both directions at once. However, a ground-up emergent process allows time for decisions over contentious issues to be tested and practised at levels of church life that remain fundamentally open to critique and revision. An expanding and deeper consensus is thus a product of time and requires a certain level of intensity in commitment by all parties to the *koinonia* of the church. Without that commitment the consensus cannot expand nor importantly can it be tested beyond the local. It remains an innovation within an enclave of the church and easily falls prey to a postmodern tribalism. This compromises both the catholicity and the apostolicity of the local church.

A ground-up approach to decision-making seems to be an Anglican way of living out the gospel. It is enshrined in the variety of canon law and constitutions of the communion.[31] Yet such a decentralised approach to the exercise of authority cannot ignore the relationship between the level of decision making and the nature of a proposed innovation. This requires some explanation for it has an important bearing upon some of the disputes and conflicts in the Anglican Church today. On the one hand there are powerful voices that point to the importance of the independence of the provinces of the Anglican Communion. As autonomous provinces each has a certain independence and responsibility to order its own ecclesial life in response to local needs for mission and witness. Thus it is not unusual for strong reaction over perceived interference from the wider communion over local decisions. The recent conflict over homosexuality is a case in point. However, there are a number of matters that signifi-

31. See Norman Doe, *Canon Law in the Anglican Communion* (Oxford: Clarendon Press, 1998).

cantly impact upon the claim of Provincial autonomy. To open this area up is simple enough. For example, no province or local church—within an Anglican ecclesiology—would ever claim that it had the authority to introduce innovation in doctrine or practice that undermined the divinity of Christ. This is a matter that has the widest possible consensus in the Christian tradition and is not open to renegotiation—at least in a manner that denied the ecumenical consensus through time and space. Here the claim for provincial autonomy does not work, if it is meant in the sense of freedom to change something so substantive for Christianity. The example raises the importance of a fundamental relation that is singularly missing in much of our current debate, that is, the relation between the nature of the matter in dispute and the level of ecclesial life at which the dispute is handled and determined. We might posit a fundamental relation here: the level of dispute settling in the church is correlated to the nature of the issue in dispute. This correlation is axiomatic for the life of the Anglican Communion and the appropriate exercise of authority.

This leads to a number of important issues regarding the way Anglicans deal with conflict and make decisions regarding innovations. First, a theological judgment is called for concerning the substantive matter in dispute. This is a fundamental activity of the church. It is a sign of a lack of wisdom to avoid or devalue the need for practical theological judgements in the church.[32] For example, exactly how important is the issue of ordination of openly homosexual persons or the blessing of 'same-sex unions' by the church? Judgments here are notoriously difficult but nonetheless critical. The fact that the church is in dispute about these very matters is a sign that it finds consensus extremely difficult if not impossible. The matter may be practically undecidable. However, as argued above, this fact does not mean that the church can avoid making decisions about such matters

32. In this regard it is worth noting the nature of the questions posed for the Primate's meeting in October 2003 by the *Inter-Anglican Theological and Doctrinal Commission*. The first question asked the Primates to make a theological judgment concerning the significance of the blessing of same-sex unions, the ordination of non-abstinent homosexual persons to the diaconate and priesthood and the appointment of such a person to the office of bishop. This theological question was followed up with two further questions of an ecclesial and pastoral kind. While consensus might not have been possible on the first question nonetheless the Commission was signalling the importance of responsible theological engagement as a primary task of church leaders precisely at a time when emotional, political and ideological tensions were most powerful. The full text of the Commission's paper is available on the web page of the Anglican Communion.

but it does mean that the decisions will have a certain provisionality about them.

The difficulty of coming to a settled view about such matters often generates moves to avoid the theological task by opting for more immediate practical and political outcomes. This is understandable but it has the effect of closing down the numerous conversations and face-to-face engagements required in earnest and passionate theological debate. There are a number of possible scenarios. One familiar approach is to appeal to a traditional authoritarianism. This can occur either through appeal to a top-down leadership that decides on matters without recourse to a wider consensus (typical of the Roman Church) or an appeal to the plain sense of Scripture interpreted by those with authority in the church. Both these options lie within a 'top-down' authoritative mode of action and both marginalise the theological task of the church. The other option appears under a more democratic model of polity and process where the top-down appeal cannot be invoked. This has more of the flavour of a 'bottom-up' approach but the outcome is similar in principle to the former approach. A decision is made by majority—in lieu of the possibility of a consensus—which settles the matter politically.[33] Again the theological task is studiously avoided. In both approaches the accent is on law and its processes and in both cases the substantive matter remains essentially undecided.

Now there may be a good dose of Anglican pragmatism here which recognises the impossibility of a theological consensus (at least in the short term) and seeks solutions to conflict and division through political and constitutional processes. This appears to have occurred at the General Convention of the Episcopal Church in 2003 in relation to the appointment as a bishop of a person in a committed same sex relationship. The emphasis at the Convention was on due process according to the canons of the Episcopal Church rather than debate of a substantive theological report.

As a result the key text was not any considered piece of theology but a legal ruling from the Wrighter case in 1996 when a Church Court had held that, in the absence of any clear rule or canon on the matter, Bishop Wrighter had not been in breach of any core doctrine or discipline in ordaining a homosexually active person. The Convention's decision was entirely logical given the Wrighter judgement: if there is no church

33. Daniel Hardy's unpublished paper, 'Anglicanism in the Twenty-First Century: Scriptural, Local, Global', delivered at the *American Academy of Religion*, Atlanta, 2003, critiqued these two approaches to decision making in relation to the idea of Anglicanism.

policy against homosexually active priests, why should there be against bishops?[34]

In the Wrighter Case a distinction had been made between matters of 'core' doctrine and matters of ethical and moral issues. This somewhat dubious distinction curiously enough simply confirmed the importance of carefully determining the relation between the theological weight of a matter in dispute and the appropriate level of decision-making in the church. The distinction implied that on matters of 'core' doctrine a provincial church would not be able to introduce an innovation without reference to the wider communion. However, the over-simple distinction between matters of core doctrine, and ethical and moral issues, and the assignment of the issue of homosexuality to the latter category, made it simpler for the church to decide on a highly contentious issue through political and legal process.

But who can make such a decision? In Anglicanism the answer might be that such decisions are made at all levels of the communion. This means that the more local the decision is the more provisional it is; the more open to revision, the more open to critic from 'outside', the more fragile the outcome, the more patient and slow to over-determine the innovation. This at least is on the agenda from an ecclesiological point of view and it is curious how little in the disputes of the church in relation to its calling and mission, the specifically ecclesial significance of its life is recognised in the decisions it makes. Provincial autonomy ought not to operate without reference to the wider ecclesia in precisely those areas in which a wider consensus would be appropriate.

This discussion highlights the importance for the church of determining the nature of an innovation in faith and practice; primarily its significance in relation to the gospel. A guide in such matters is Article 6 of the Thirty-nine Articles. It also confirms the principle of subsidiarity: decisions ought not to be taken at higher levels that are properly the province of lower levels. But it also calls attention to the importance within the principle of subsidiarity of the necessity of a theological judgment as to the nature of the subject matter in dispute in deciding at what level provisional decisions ought to be made. A ground-up approach to decision-making, while the natural ecclesial default position in Anglicanism, does not have an absolute claim. This would be most un-Anglican! It is informed by and proceeds on the basis of a recognition of the correla-

34. Comments from an observer at the Convention.

tion that obtains between the level of decision making and the substantive matter under consideration. Determining the weight of any particular matter requires a theological judgment in relation to the nature of Christianity. This points to the crucial importance of an informed and discerning church in which theological education is not only vigorously encouraged but also seen as one of the critical means for the enrichment of the *koinonia* of the communion.

It is clear from the above discussion that *koinonia* is not a simple state of affairs but a dynamic and somewhat restless feature of the life of the Church. Such *koinonia* is fostered and nurtured by constant innovation—new responses in new contexts that seek faithfulness to the tradition and relevance in the modern world (in other words, innovation belongs to the dialectic of the gospel). *Koinonia* is also constantly threatened by innovation. Innovation is thus inherently conflictual and unavoidable. For these reasons innovations appear in the life of the church as undecidable yet at the same time they require determination for the sake of our discipleship in the world. This suggests that a key thing for the Anglican Church might be how it carries itself or is carried through its ecclesial life. Perhaps there is a moral vision of the kind of communion we are called to be which provides the framework and substance of our shared life. It cannot be one that seeks simple default solutions through authoritarian top-down or democratic majority bottom-up approaches. It will necessarily be one that constantly struggles with allowing freedom and space for others yet constantly struggles to include others in decision-making and life practices.

This discussion also highlights the fact that *koinonia* requires patience and long suffering. There are no short cuts for the Anglican Church either through political or legal manoeuvres that do not also include a moral vision of what it means to be a communion that travels, in the words of George Steiner, 'the long days journey of the Saturday'.[35] Steiner's invocation of the Holy Saturday tradition at the end of his remarkable *tour de force* of the cultural and philosophical condition of the twentieth century provided a powerful reminder that we find ourselves in times of immense transition and uncertainty. In such a context of radical innovations and so many undecidables a cultivated waiting that brims full of vigour, life and resilience becomes paramount. Steiner counsels neither the despair of Good Friday nor the triumphalism of Easter Sunday but rather a hopeful waiting. It is a theme picked up by Rowan Williams' meditations in the

35. See George Steiner, *Real Presences* (Chicago: University of Chicago Press, 1989), 231–32.

aftermath of 11 September 2001.[36] In closing, Williams reflects on Jesus' writing in the dust recorded in chapter 8 of John's Gospel. In this strange and enigmatic gesture Williams senses hope:

> He [Jesus] hesitates. He does not draw a line, offer an interpretation, tell the woman who she is and what her fate should be. He allows a moment, a longish moment, in which people are given time to see themselves differently precisely because he refuses to make the sense they want. When he lifts his head, there is both judgement and release. So this is writing in the dust because it tries to hold that moment for a little longer, long enough for some of our demons to walk away.[37]

An Anglican Communion that provides resources for the long day's journey of the Saturday will be a church that fosters a particular fruit of the Holy Spirit; the spiritual discipline of patience (Gal 5.22). It was Tertullian in the third century who considered disharmony and conflict in the ecclesia—the family of siblings—as a sign of impatience.[38] He saw the archetype of this present in the Cain and Abel story wherein Tertullian argued that 'Therefore, since he [Cain] could not commit murder unless he were angry, and could not be angry unless he were impatient, it is to be proved that what he did in anger is to be referred to that which prompted the anger'.[39] Tertullian's exegesis may be unconvincing but his appeal to the sibling metaphor for the ecclesial family and his emphasis upon harmony and discord revolving around the theme of patience may yet prove instructive in our present context. It may be precisely through this ancient discipline that the Church is enabled to find a richer and resilient *koinonia* informed by God's Spirit.[40]

---

36. Rowan Williams, *Writing in the Dust: Reflections on the 11 September and its Aftermath* (London: Hodder & Stoughton, 2002).
37. Williams, *Writing in the Dust*, 81.
38. Joseph Hellerman, *The Ancient Church as Family* (Minneapolis: Fortress Press, 2001), 173–82.
39. Hellerman, *The Ancient Church as Family*, 178.
40. The Holy Spirit as the active divine agent in the emergence of new *koinonia* was a key theme at the World Council of Churches in Canberra in 1991: 'The Holy Spirit as the promoter of *koinonia* (2 Corinthians 13:13) gives to those who are still divided the thirst and hunger for full communion. We remain restless until we grow together according to the wish and prayer of Christ that those who believe in him may be one (John 17:21). In the process of praying, working and struggling for unity, the Holy Spirit comforts us in pain, disturbs us when we are satisfied to remain in our division,

A *koinonia* that emerges out of patient and hopeful waiting in troubled and unsettled times cannot be one that can be artificially manufactured and managed.[41] It comes as gift but requires fundamental trust between people, and across boundaries of cultural and ethnic differences within, as much as beyond, the boundaries of contemporary Anglicanism. Trust is not an easy matter in our present situation, though the giving and receiving of trust is basic to shared lives, and genuine community. Trust has a somewhat troubled history and is difficult to establish and sustain in modern society.[42] However, *koinonia* based on trust and associated mutual respect and recognition is precisely what the gospel invites us to embody in our life together. Such trust includes face-to-face relations, interdependent lives, openness to correction and willingness to offer and receive wisdom. The richest context for such trust and the critical referent in all our disputes is our common worship in which the ultimate Other, who addresses, re-forms and raises creation, can be encountered. Maximal openness to God in the eucharistic life is thus at the heart of all our engagements and the cauldron in which our innovations and undecidables have to be continually placed. In this context we do not capitulate to a happy pluralism nor can we take the road of a rigorist legalism. Rather we are enjoined to find our common life in Christ in the *koinonia* of the Spirit in the 'long day's journey of the Saturday'.

leads us to repentance and grants us joy when our communion flourishes' (The Canberra Statement: 'The Unity of the Church as *Koinonia*: Gift and Calling', in *The Unity of the Church as Koinonia*, edited by Gunther Gassmann and John Radano, Faith and Order Paper No. 163 (Geneva: WCC, 1993), para 4.1).

41. Though this is not a reason for ignoring possibilities to establish ways and means for the communion (at all levels of its life) to seek those things most needful: time, space and peace.

42. For a discussion see Anthony Giddens, *The Consequences of Modernity* (Cambridge: Polity Press, 1990), especially chapter 3.

Chapter Nine
New Monasticism, Theology and the Future Church[1]

Emerging Places of New Community

In the light of our thrown-ness in the world and the experience of being overwhelmed and unable to decide what way forward is best a question arises: How then might we live together? This essay examines the possibilities inherent in new forms of monastic community. Such communities provide locations and forms for engagement with God in an uncertain and often disturbed world. The essay highlights the ecclesial nature of Christianity and the ways in which this might be re-envisioned and lived.

Community *after virtue*

Alasdair MacIntyre ends his important work, *After Virtue*, with an enticing proposal on the future of human community:

> It is always dangerous to draw too precise parallels between one historical period and another; and among the most leading of such parallels are those which have been drawn between our own age and Europe and North America and the epoch in which the Roman Empire declined into the dark ages. Nonetheless certain parallels there are. A crucial turning point in that earlier history occurred when men and women of good will turned aside from the task of shoring up the *Roman imperium* and ceased to identify the continuation of civility and moral community with the maintenance of that *imperium*. What they set themselves to achieve in-

1. Originally published as 'Community *After Virtue*: New Monasticism, Theology and the Future Church', in *'Into the World you Love': Encountering God in Everyday Life*, edited by Graeme Garrett (Adelaide: ATF Press, 2007).

> stead—often not recognising fully what they were doing—was the construction of new forms of community within which the moral life could be sustained so that both morality and civility might survive the coming ages of barbarism and darkness. If my account of our moral condition is correct, we ought also to conclude that for some time now we too have reached the turning point. What matters at this stage is the construction of local forms of community within which the civility and the intellectual and moral life can be sustained through the new dark ages which are already upon us. And if the tradition of the virtues was able to survive the horrors of the last dark ages, we are not entirely without grounds for hope. This time however the barbarians are not waiting beyond the frontiers; they have already been governing us for some time. And it is our lack of consciousness of this that constitutes part of our predicament. We are waiting not for Godot, but for another—doubtless very different—St Benedict.[2]

Within the decaying structures of Western society MacIntyre sees the one hopeful possibility for human life in new forms of community in the spirit of St Benedict. MacIntyre has a quite particular form of community in mind. It is one that lives beyond itself; its character is shaped by reference to the dynamic presence of God in society. Under these conditions the human project of forming and sustaining community within a shared framework of core virtues (justice, truth and courage) might be rekindled for future generations. MacIntyre's proposal for the recovery of a fundamental human practice (growing community) appears urgent and challenging and finds echoes in the theological ethics of Stanley Hauerwas.[3] Whilst some may see in this a radical and innovative move others sound a more critical note under the banner of the 'new traditionalism'?[4]Yet Ma-

2. Alasdair MacIntyre, *After Virtue: A Study in Moral Virtue*, second edition (London: Duckworth, 1987), 263.
3. See, for example, Hauerwas' early work *A Community of Character: Toward a Constructive Christian Social Ethics* (Notre Dame & London: University of Notre Dame Press, 1981).
4. Jeffrey Stout, 'The New Traditionalism', in *Democracy and Tradition* (Princeton: Princeton University Press, 2004), chapter 5. Stout argues that MacIntyre's critique of the Enlightement and the liberal tradition it has spawned is heavily dependent upon a modernity Macintyre has rejected. Stout considers, contrary to Macintyre, that

cIntyre's proposal does raise some critical questions. Can there be 'community' after the disappearance of virtue? How might the virtues and the kind of social life they are designed to sustain survive in a market economy premised upon competition and survival of the most powerful? How might we live together peaceably when the virtues and their preconditions (shared stories and values) no longer operate as the framework for human sociality?

Is MacIntyre's proposal concerning religious community the way forward for life in the twenty-first century? In the fragmenting social world of Western civilisation the search for genuine and sustaining community is persistent and difficult when the forces of individualism are as powerful as ever.[5] Perhaps even more troubling is the fact that we seem to lack understanding of what it is that holds human beings together. No longer is it clear how human community is constituted and sustained.

We not only find the experience of human community elusive and unsatisfying, but we lack a theory that can justify true community. Utilitarian approaches work up to a point; the point being at that stage when certain parts of society become finally expendable. Pragmatic utilitarianism is useful for the powerful and is an important companion to a market economy where human life is more often reduced to the status of a commodity.

Most responses to this are no more than tinkering around the edges. Though perhaps it is precisely around the edges that social tinkering has to take place. Maybe it will be from such locations that new possibilities for human community might be imagined and practised. Community after virtue may have to be crafted at the margins of the twin empires of market and militarism. Alternative community from the margins is not an unfamiliar feature of our times. However, such protests only point to the power of the market economy and its destructive nature. Alternative ways

---

there are far more possibilities *within* the liberal democratic tradition, for the critical reconstruction of the virtues. On this reading new monastic communities are either unnecessary or a distraction.

5. For a discussion of the various options for religious communities within the Christian tradition see, for example, Thomas Rausch, *Radical Christian Communities* (Collegeville, MN: The Liturgical Press, 1990). At a popular level the attraction and significance of new forms of monastic community is receiving attention. See, for example, Jason Byassee, 'Alternative Christian Communities: the New Monastics', in *The Christian Century*, 18 (October 2005): 38–47; Rob Moll, 'The New Monasticism', in *Christianity Today*, September (2005): 39–46. These articles highlight the location of such communities among the poor and the marginalised in the USA.

of human community highlight the fragmentation of human society and raise questions about what kind of theory we need to justify true society, one founded on virtues, vision and hope. Even to name such things invites cynicism and dismissal.

How fares the society of the ecclesia of God? Surely here an alternative way of life together might be evident. If this is not our experience what shall we conclude? That it is a vain hope? Or perhaps the church is hopelessly entwined in the market and simply represents its basic destructive dynamic in a religious garb? Such a proposal ought not be too quickly dismissed. But before we conclude that the church too seems to be going the way of all flesh we do well to remember that if there is a problem of the church mimicking the surrounding culture (which it most certainly does) then this problem arises, at least on a positive reading, from the very fact that the gospel calls the church into the market place. The doctrine of the incarnation is about embodiment of the ways of God with the world. The dangers that lurk within such a project are legion: compromise, sell out, loss of prophetic voice, baptism of the prevailing market values and so on. But throughout human history the gospel call to engage with culture—to make a difference, to be the leaven in the bread, and light upon the hill—has exercised a powerful shaping force on the character and nature of the church in the world.

Yet, as the prologue to John's Gospel makes abundantly clear, the doctrine of the incarnation is never a theory of uncritical engagement. 'He was in the world and the world knew him not . . . he came to his own and his own received him not' has echoes of rejection, misunderstanding and failure. The gospels tell a story of protest, compassion and, particularly in the parables of Jesus, new imagined worlds. Such an incarnational engagement generates conflict and leads to suffering and death. When the church follows in the footsteps of Christ it will travel up a hill to Calvary.

Yet for the most part the church of the West presents a religious echo of the prevailing culture. As a result, for the most part, the church has surrendered its prophetic voice and forgotten the foundations of its common life. The fragmentation of society is reflected in a fragmenting church. It might be possible to say that the church's image is pixellating or breaking up. It is not clear what will emerge. But no amount of technical/ bureaucratic management will save the image. Eventually the pixellation will be so severe that the image will completely decompose.

If a new community is to be imagined and lived it will be one that cannot bypass Calvary. It will live under the shadow of the cross and out of hope for something new emerging from the tomb of modernity. A society in search of the foundations of its own inner life will be a society prepared to undergo a profound *metanoia*, a turning away from its own preoccupations, repenting of its false values, a society willing to undergo a new baptism. Perhaps this is the calling of the church in the twenty-first century. Is this what a new St. Benedict symbolises? If it is then such a community can no longer be one shaped and driven by the market and utilitarian interpretations of the virtues. Rather, it will be a community literally 'after' virtue, seeking ways to embody the virtues of the gospel for the sustaining of new ways of life together.

Theology after community

How might the theological tradition of Christianity conceive its task in relation to the above context? There are at least two levels of response. Where the concern is with practise and is preoccupied with systems, structures, strategies and processes for recovery and sustenance of Christian community, theology will transpose into practical ecclesiology. This is a critical moment in any theological work and requires discernment and courage. A critical reflective ecclesial praxis is one of the fruits of such an approach. The church desperately needs such a practical prophetic ecclesiology to overcome the force of a prevailing unprincipled ecclesial pragmatism.[6]

However, a practical ecclesiology cannot operate in a vacuum. I am not referring here to the need for a concrete context in which church practises are undertaken, critiqued and developed. This too is critical but insufficient to undergird a sound and fruitful prophetic community of faith. A deeper level theological engagement is also required to examine the basis of true community and provide fuel for a well-conceived practical ecclesiology. For example, what might justify MacIntyre's proposal for a new St. Benedict? Is it simply that all the other ideas have been tried and found wanting? Or perhaps the Benedictine Order has historically been a powerful shaper of human society and this is where the church might

6. See Nicholas Healy, *Church, World and the Christian Life: Practical-Prophetic Ecclesiology* (Cambridge: Cambridge University Press, 2000). Healy critiques what he terms 'blueprint ecclesiologies'—ideal models of church—which are less orientated 'to the living, rather messy, confused and confusing body that the church actually is' (3) and 'undervalue the theological significance of the genuine struggles of the church's membership to live as disciples within the less-than-perfect church and within societies that are often unwilling to overlook the church's flaws' 37.

play its part in a new world? Or is it simply the expression of a wistful romantic scholar who pines for a past time when all was settled, clear and religious community had its place in the social world? MacIntyre's proposal requires a deeper level inquiry into the roots of human community. Specifically, it requires a theory to justify the proposal and clarify the direction for a new practical ecclesiology. For example, if there is to be a new monasticism inspired by a new St Benedict, it will have to be a principled experiment in new community with deep theological foundations that go beyond a managed budget and organisational framework.

So the task of theology within a search for community 'after virtue' operates on at least two levels: practical and theoretical. And it is in the latter area that some of the most important work has emerged in the last few decades. I refer here to the explosion of material on trinitarian theology and its link to human society. The volume has grown over the last two decades and theologians such as Zizoulas, Moltmann, and Volf, are common 'household' names when it comes to Trinity and community.[7] In many respects this is a positive development. It points to the fact that there is a perceived need for a deeper level justification for the social nature of Christianity and an implied need for a critique of structure and process that is inimical to true community. The doctrine of the triune God has a natural reciprocity with concerns for personhood and a conviction about the relational nature of human community in the world. Thus we might say that the theological instincts of the Christian community are basically right.

However, we often lack the skill and discernment to figure out how the theological tradition and specifically its central subject, that is, God! might be invoked to come to our aid in the crisis of a fragmented and dysfunctional sociality. The temptation to develop neat and simple blueprints of trinitarian models of society and apply them to cure the ills of contemporary society ought to be resisted.[8] This is necessary for two reasons: first because that is not how good trinitarian theology actually works and second because such a method falsifies how God is actually involved

7. See, for example, Jürgen Moltmann, *The Trinity and the Kingdom of God* (London: SCM, London 1997); Catherine LaCugna, *God For Us: The Trinity and Christian Life* (San Francisco: Harper, 1991); Miroslav Volf, *After Our Likeness: The Church as the Image of the Trinity* (Grand Rapids, MI: Eerdmans, 1998); John Zizioulas, *Being as Communion: Studies in Personhood and the Church* (Crestwood, NY: St Vladimir's Press, 1985).

8. See Healy, *Church, World and Christian Life*, 34f.

in the dynamic of human society. What usually emerges is an idealised vision of human society generated from an abstracted theory of divine operations. Significantly this procedure almost always fails to give an account of conflict and suffering as a feature of human community.[9] What tends to occur is that an idealised doctrine of God is invoked to support a pre-determined ideology for a reformed social world.[10]

What founds human society and more generally the social nature of the created order? How is true religious community rooted in and expressive of the dynamic of God's sociality? These are some of the questions that theological work needs to attend to in the service of a practical ecclesiology for new community. Might we be able to speak of a created sociality before we speak of a redeemed sociality?[11] Is it possible that the basis for a true society is to be located in the creating activity of God, that is, that sociality is a constituent of createdness *per se*? This seems to be supposed in much of the trinitarian discourse in the area of ecclesiology. But for the most part this assumption remains implicit, unexamined and therefore underdeveloped. However if sociality is an axiom of creation this would have far reaching consequences. Such a starting point would signal a departure from the more traditional theological approach that locates the basis for human community in redemption. Where this latter axiom obtains the immediate effect is to privilege the church as the locus of God's activity. One consequence is that it raises serious questions about the status of the rest of the created order, particularly human society. Is this all merely preparatory to the creation of real community? Can human life outside of the church participate in God's good, true and beautiful ways with the world? For too much of Christianity the answer has been more often, NO. A dualism has operated and the church has operated like a sect—albeit at times a puffed up empire—separated from the world.

What if sociality is a fundamental constituent of creation rather than an add-on (through a doctrine of redemption) or by product of the need for efficient organisation and pragmatic endeavours to meet a multiplicity of needs? This would require a careful rethinking of the Christian doctrine of creation and redemption and as a consequence, the life of the

---

9. Mark Chapman, 'The Social Doctrine of the Trinity: Some Problems', in *Anglican Theological Review*, 83/2 (2001): 239–54.
10. For example, Leonardo Boff, *Trinity and Society* (Maryknoll NY: Orbis, 1988).
11. Daniel Hardy, 'Created and Redeemed Sociality', in *Being the Church: Essays on the Christian Community*, edited by Daniel Hardy and Colin Gunton (Edinburgh: T&T Clark, 1989), 21–47.

church in the world. Where sociality belongs to those 'necessary notes of being'[12]—unity, truth, goodness, beauty—then the deep relationality we observe in creation—in the animal kingdom, human society and in the symbiotic life of the natural environment—is no accident or evolutionary surprise but a form of life inherent in the very nature of things, creation and persons. Sociality belongs, on this account, to creation as such and is to be attributed to God's work of creation. This ought not be surprising given the character of the triune God whom Christians worship and follow. Indeed created sociality is exactly what we ought to expect from a trinitarian account of creation and human social life. Such an approach invests the whole world with new possibilities for community and we ought not be surprised that human society, beyond the boundaries of the ecclesiastical world, abounds with instances of the operation of such a created sociality.[13]

However as we are well aware natural community is not necessarily ideal in its operation or purpose. Genuine created sociality, if it is reflective of the sociality that belongs to God, will necessarily be in constant stages of transformation. Created sociality is also a potential to be achieved as human community is assimilated to the holiness of God, a movement concentrated in the offering of worship.[14] There is then a necessary redemptive moment in all social life so that created sociality becomes an emergent redemptive sociality. In other words we might want to inquire into the dynamics by which a 'faithful sociality'[15] is sustained in a world where broken communities and unholy ways subvert the deeper intentions and purposes of the divine creativity of the God and Father of Jesus Christ. In this context the Christian community has a story to tell and a form of life to practise that can bear witness to and be an instantiation of the holiness that belongs to the triune life seen in the life of Jesus and the Spirit. This calling of the ecclesia is not a judgement of the church upon the failure of the world but more a response to the abundant graciousness of God who bestows a rich sociality upon the world.

12. Hardy, 'Created and Redeemed Sociality', 24f.
13. Hardy's discussion of sociality has been critiqued by Colin Gunton in *The One the Three and the Many: God, Creation and the Culture of Modernity*, The 1992 Bampton Lectures (Cambridge: Cambridge University Press, 1993), 219–23.
14. Daniel Hardy, *Finding the Church: The Dynamic Truth of Anglicanism* (London: SCM, 2003), chapter 1.
15. I am grateful to conversations with Lynlea Rodger at St Mark's for this phrase.

Such reflections of a theoretical kind might feed a practical ecclesiology in the service of new religious community.[16] Such an approach would not negate God's faithful sociality in the world but rather point to it and express it as a true praise of God. If MacIntyre is correct in his assessment of the contemporary scene then the new St Benedict he waits may not be a lone person but an eschatological movement manifest through a new form of common life in the Spirit. This Spirit of holiness will be christomorphic and in this way trinitarian. It will represent a calling of the church to recover the secret of its own life and bear witness to the created and redeemed sociality which is God's gift in Christ and the Spirit.

The above reflections emerge for me from MacIntyre's lament about the decomposition of Western society and his hope for a new St Benedict. The church is in travail from the top down and the bottom up. And there seems to be no shortage of remedies in the ecclesiastical market place: church growth, emerging church, purpose-driven church, new monasticism. Undergirding much of this is the overwhelming sense that the church has to move from dysfunctional and closed forms of religious community into a more creative and open space. The search is on, at least in some quarters, for new forms of community that draw upon the rich tradition of Christianity, but in an alternative way. If you are concerned for the viability and flourishing of religious life in the twenty-first century then it seems to me you will need to be focussed on the form of communal life we live. For the Kingdom of God will not survive with Robinson Crusoes dotted all over the place.

When St Augustine said in the opening paragraphs of his famous *Confessions*: 'Our hearts are restless until they find their rest in thee' he could also have added—but alas didn't—'and with others'. It is a theme brought to my attention by the United Church Methodist scholar, Roberta Bondi who refers to the wonderful image of the desert monk, Dorothea of Gaza, who described the pathway to God as a movement from the perimeter of a circle to the centre of the Divine.[17] As one moved closer to the centre from the perimeter one was also brought closer to others on the same journey. To find our rest in God cannot happen without a corresponding growth

16. 'It is of great importance, therefore, that the foundations of the possibility of society be intelligently grasped, and the possibility thus revealed acted upon. Only thus may the direction of society be identified, and pathological deviations discovered and remedied' (Hardy, 'Created and Redeemed Sociality', 22).

17. Roberta Bondi, *To Pray and to Love: Conversations on Prayer with the Early Church* (Minneapolis: Fortress Press, 1991), 14f.

in community with one another. The theological task is to clarify for the church why this is necessarily the case.

Monasterium as future church

In a letter written in 1935, Dietrich Bonhoeffer, entertained a vision of a future church:

> the restoration of the church will surely come only from a new type of monasticism which has nothing in common with the old but a complete lack of compromise in a life lived in accordance with the sermon on the mount in the discipleship of Christ. I think it is time to gather people together to do this.[18]

This form of life together no doubt had echoes from his earlier experiment in the seminary at Saffenwald where future leaders were prepared for the Confessing Church. Of course it is not possible to have a *new* monasticism 'which has nothing in common with the old'. But what is it about the old that might continue? Did Bonhoeffer imagine that the point of continuity resided in the 'complete lack of compromise in a life lived in accordance with the sermon on the mount in the discipleship of Christ'.

Throughout history there have been numerous examples of new religious movements associated with new communities of faith. Indeed it might be an interesting thesis to test the correlation between the impulse to Christian mission and the emergence of new religious communities. Monasticism was never one thing and the remarkable diversity of religious orders and communities needs more careful attention in our contemporary situation. Bonhoeffer's proposal might not be that unusual or strange. Rather, he might simply be reminding the church of the radical basis for its own renewal as witnessed in history. Certainly there are many examples in our present day of new experiments in religious community. In January 2006 I attended a workshop on new monasticism at Mt St Bernard Abbey in Leicestershire. It was a relatively small gathering of twenty people from all over the United Kingdom. Participants came from across

18. Dietrich Bonhoeffer to his brother Karl-Friedrick, 14 January 1935. See *Bonhoeffer for a New Day: Theology in a Time of Transition: Papers presented at the Seventh International Bonhoeffer Congress, Cape Town, 1996*, edited by John de Gruchy (Grand Rapids, MI: WB Eerdmans, 1997), 48.

the ecclesial traditions: Roman Catholic, Anglican, Baptist, Evangelical/Charismatic Independent Churches. Participants also came with a range of previous experiences: founders of the Northumbrian Community, newly-established independent churches, traditional monastic settings (Benedictine), evolving mainline churches; Iona Community. Men and women in leadership with a concern for the future of religious community gathered for three days to hear presentations from practitioners, and theologians of religious community. The workshop was organised by *Monos*, a network established to connect people interested in new monasticism.[19]

Later at a conference in Durham I met an Anglican layperson who is a member of the new Roman Catholic ecumenical order, Chemin Neuf, near Lyon, France.[20] This community of 1300 people worldwide includes all denominations, men and women, ordained and lay. It is lead in Chartres by a Lutheran woman! The local Roman Archbishop has given permission for full eucharistic hospitality to be extended to all members of the community. Leaders from all denominations preside at eucharistic gatherings. Some people live together in traditional settings and some live in their own houses. They all come together once a week and are also encouraged to remain members of their local church faith communities for Sunday worship. In Lyon the community has members who are training for the Roman priesthood. They live together with others and undertake theological studies at the local Jesuit University. They also undertake other ordination studies within the community.

The contemporary experiments in new religious community connects with the deeper tradition of Celtic models of monasticism. Ian Bradley's discussion of Celtic models of monasticism for the contemporary world[21] offers an historical account of the development of monasticism in the Celtic tradition. In particular I was struck by the variety of monasticism in its evolution. It has included desert, community (*cenobitic*), single and married monks, lay and ordained. And people seemed to have differing relationships to the cenobitic models of community life. The origins and development of the minster model of church out of monasticism seemed particularly relevant to our times:

19. See <http://www.monos.org.uk/>. Accessed 15 March 2011; for articles and books on the subject, see also <www.newmonasticism.com>. Accessed 15 March 2011.
20. See <http://www.cheminneuf.org/spip/rubrique.php3?id_rubrique=260>. Accessed 15 March 2011.
21. Ian Bradley, *Colonies of Heaven: Celtic Models for Today's Church* (London: DLT, 2000), chapter 1.

> before the development of the parish it is now accepted that in England pastoral care was organised through large 'parishes' served by teams of priests and other clergy operating from important central churches—these churches are familiarly called minsters, translation of *monasterium*.[22]

The *monasterium*, in its role as minster, played a central role in the pre-parochial era, that is, before the eleventh and twelfth centuries. The strongly monastic character of the pre-parish system generated a team model of ministry that was both collegial and communitarian. The minister, as precursor to the cathedrals, was a powerful centre of ecclesial life in the church before the English parish system. The collegial and communitarian model of ministry is fostered was associated with a rich and diverse range of ministries. Indeed the word *monasterium*

> covered a huge range of different communities, from tiny settlements of two or three hermit's huts to townships of several thousand people. Monasteries could be made up of entirely of hermits or anchorites, of those living a cenobitic or communal life or of a mixture of both solitaries and monks living in community. They could be single-sex institutions or communities of both sexes, some of whose members led celibate lives and others of whom were married. Some monastic communities had just one priest attached to them were largely made up of non-ordained monks, others had no members under monastic vows and were essentially teams of regular clergy undertaking a largely pastoral role in the surrounding area. Within some of the larger monasteries, solitary hermits lived and prayed alongside married monks; professed monks and nuns coexisted with lay brothers and sisters; regular and secular clergy, ordained and non-ordained, men and women, shared their common life with the many pilgrims, penitents and other guests who regularly stayed in the *hospitum*.[23]

This brief description of England before the consolidation of the parochial system is important in reflection upon our present context. It may well be the case that with the decomposition of the western church the earlier

22. Richard Sharpe, cited in Bradley, *Colonies of Heaven*, 4.
23. Bradley, *Colonies of Heaven*, 7.

minister model of ecclesial organisation and mission will re-emerge. It is a revolutionary old idea. But it will occur in new ways. Already the notion of revamped minister type models underpins much of what people mean when they talk about new communities of faith.[24] Unfortunately lack of understanding of the history of the church means that often we are ignorant of and thus unable to draw upon a longer wisdom and we assume that we are creating communities *de nouveux*. It is also the case that the tradition of the *monasterium* seems to be but one option among a diverse range of possibilities for reinventing the church.

Monasticism within the 'emerging church'

Our reflections so far need to be brought into relation to the discourse on emerging church. Is new monasticism one form of this latter development or something quite different even alien? Certainly there is a lot of talk about new forms of church, planting new congregations, and so on. But what are we to make of forms of new church in, for example, the recent publication, *Mission Shaped Church*?[25] Maybe 'emerging church' speak (USA) is a very different thing from 'mission shaped church' speak (UK). It seems such a mixed bag these days. 'Fresh expressions' are everywhere!

Some questions arise: could you spot a church that was emerging if you saw it? From where would it be emerging—out of paganism? Would it have been formerly a dead church that had come alive again—resuscitated like Lazarus? Or would it be a church plant that had never existed before—created *ex nihilo*, as in Genesis? What are the criteria for 'emerging church'? Is it an 'under 40s only' church? Is a pre-requisite that traditional liturgy has been dispensed with? Or perhaps Hill Song material is the staple diet of the music? Does it depend on where the worshippers gather such as a school house or coffee shop, compared to a traditional building. Or maybe they aren't into worship but only meeting together. Is incense allowed in the emerging church or will it kill it off? What about candles and other symbols? Is one of the criteria that the priest or minister wears open neck shirt or blouse, or perhaps goes a bit more up market in accountants attire; basically anything but an ecumenical alb with associated

24. For example, in the Diocese of Canberra and Goulburn the development of 'hubs' for new mission initiatives has similarities to an early phase in the development of a minister model within a diocesan framework.

25. Graham Cray, *Mission Shaped Church: Church Planting and Frresh Expressions in Changing Contexts* (London: Church House Publishing, 2004).

ecclesiastical stuff like a stole and chasuble? Are emerging churches essentially free of the shackles of denominationalism or can they be a part of it? And who owns the language of emerging church? Who are the gatekeepers of the religious rhetoric that is now floating around the church? Finally, where would you say your church would sit on the emerging church scale, say 1 to 10 (10 being right out there as a leader, 1 being a member of the submerging church)? Perhaps in the post-modern the emerging church can be any or all of the above? And how long does it take for a church to emerge, what will it look like and what will it be called when it has emerged—a non-emergent church or 'established church'?

I am keen to know who or what constitutes the emerging church. I also want to know which churches or parts of the church qualify and what are the criteria. In particular I wonder about how new religious communities with intentional links to earlier religious orders or monastic traditions fit within the emerging church spectrum.

Recently I have been thinking about the submerging church; the church on the way down rather than up. There are at least two senses in which the Western church is submerging. First, and most clearly, there is the church that is literally dying. We hear pronouncements about it regularly, usually in relation to someone else's church patch. I was reminded of the submerging church when I was walking in the Snowy Mountain's National Park recently. The fires of 2003 had destroyed the once-beautiful gums and all that was left was an ashen grey wooded area. This, I thought, is the fate of much of the present church. But the church is submerging in a second and positive sense. The sense of going underground is appealing. The catacomb churches of early Christianity are a vivid example of mission via another route. In another vein the early monastics became a prophetic movement within a dying and conformist church culture. They literally disappeared from sight. Here submerging is associated with resistance, hospitality and subversion in a non-violent manner. But it doesn't register on the radar of a national church census, synod debate about new church structures for mission nor does it attract funding. Perhaps a catacomb ecclesiology is needed as a compliment to the quest for new visibility and relevance. Both emerging and submerging churches may contribute to the mission of Christ. The new St Benedict spoken of by Macintyre may be as much at home in a truly submerged church as one that was emerging.

So what counts as a fresh expression of the coming church? Could a theological institution qualify? And what about chaplaincy ministry in education, prison, hospital, industry? Where do these ministries fit within the emerging church? What about the rural church? In particular how do we see the relationship between the mission focus for an emerging church and the newer forms of monasticism? How are the mission action strategies of some parts of the church in dialogue with other sections that seek new forms of monastic and prophetic life with an emphasis on contemplative life and social action? Are they all aspects of the emerging church? Do they register, and who decides? I confess to a certain ambivalence about emerging church talk. I wonder if some of the rhetoric 'emerges' from the deepest reaches of Western angst fuelled by the chronic anxiety or perhaps melancholy of Western institutional life.[26]

I say I am ambivalent because I am all for the emerging church. But usually it comes from the Spirit of Christ and it will totally surprise us. Right now, some seem to have privileged information about 'lo it is here and lo it is there'. But you hear the sound of the Spirit and you do not know where it comes from or where it is going. So it is with everyone born of the emerging church. Institutions, sector ministries, parishes, informal and formal networks of people, theological communities, even cathedrals may belong to the emerging church! The really reassuring thing is that God will decide where God's church is a sign of the age to come. The church is simply called to feed its pilgrims and the aimless wanderers of the twenty-first century. It needs its downs as well as its ups to do that: its basement ministries, parish outposts, chaplaincy networks and new monastic communities. The critical issue will be how such new developments embody God's particular way of creating and sustaining human community in the world.

Marks of the new monasticism

Some marks of a new monasticism are outlined in a recent important set of essays.[27] It may be as well to name them here:

1. Relocation to abandoned places of empire
2. Sharing economic resources with fellow community members
3. Hospitality to the stranger

26. Proposal of Lynlea Rodger in a paper given at new monasticism seminar, St Mark's National Theological Centre, Canberra, 24 June 2006.
27. *School(s) for Conversion: 12 Mark's of a New Monasticism*, edited by The Rutba House, (Oregon: Cascade Books, 2005).

4. Lament for racial divisions within the body of Christ and our communities combined with the active pursuit of a just reconciliation
5. Humble submission to Christ's body, the Church.
6. Intentional formation in the way of Christ and the rule of the community along the lines of the old novitiate
7. Nurturing common life among members of intentional community
8. Support for celibate singles alongside monogamous married couples and their children
9. Geographical proximity to community members who share a common rule of life
10. Care for the plot of God's earth given to us along with support of our local economies
11. Peacemaking in the midst of violence and conflict resolution along the lines of Matthew 18.
12. Commitment to a disciplines contemplative life.

Each of these marks has been developed into a chapter by different members of Rutba House who come from across the ecclesial spectrum. The editors note that the essays:

> are an attempt to show how some Christians in the church in the United States feel the Spirit leading them to creative ways of life that may provide the hope of new possibilities for faithfulness. In this sense the new monasticism hopes to spark ecumenical conversation in churches across the country about how we should live together as the pilgrim people of God sojourning in a place and time where the powers of darkness still struggle to maintain their fading dominion.[28]

The marks of new monasticism, as identified above, point to a grassroots ecumenism and prophetic witness. Recovery of these things goes hand in hand with the fundaments of *monasterium*: hospitality, prayer, theology and service. Are the marks of a new monasticism consonant with the ancient creed's affirmation of 'one holy, catholic and apostolic church'? It does seem that in every age the traditional marks of the church have to be re-interpreted. In the ecumenical climate of Post-Vatican 2, Hans Küng attempted to find common ground among the churches for their mission and future. In characteristic style he stressed the concrete real-

28. *School(s) for Conversion*, 10.

ity of the church as the locus for the reappropriation of the traditional marks. Thus we are not surprised when he referred to unity in diversity, catholic in identity, holy in sinfulness and apostolicity through witness.[29] Division, failure and the paramount importance of joint witness provided the framework for his interpretation of the marks.

From the Reformed wing of the church, Jürgen Moltmann, developed unity in terms of freedom, catholicity as partisanship, holiness in poverty and apostolicity in suffering.[30] Moltmann offered a theologically innovative interpretation of the marks against the background of a renewed emphasis upon pneumatology and eschatology encapsulated in the title of his work, *The Church in the Power of the Spirit*. How might the marks of a new monasticism connect with these contemporary interpretations? The credal marks provide the basic frame of reference for the life and mission of the church. Their reinterpretation in each generation occurs at multiple levels from the macro (for example, Küng and Moltmann) to the micro or more intermediate levels found in new religious movements such as new monasticism. Thus the larger conceptual frames identified by Moltmann—freedom, partisanship, poverty and suffering—receive concrete expression in, for example, the marks of ecclesial life identified by the Rutba House community. Hence 'catholicity in partisanship' finds concrete expression in 'relocation to abandoned places of empire' and 'holiness in poverty' involves 'sharing economic resources with fellow community members'. The correlations between developments in wider ecclesiology and its practical expressions at the ground is part of the process by which theology serves the interests of a practical ecclesiology. In this way new ways of being the people of God through new monasticism can be critiqued in order to improve practise. In this way theology contributes to a ground-up approach to new apostolic communities of the one, holy and catholic church.

Of course there is much to explore in the above and this chapter is only a beginning. However, to connect the above chapter to my own recent context I confess to more than an interest in how a place like St Mark's National Theological Centre might orient itself more intentionally in the direction of a religious community along the minister lines but in a new setting. The great advantage St Mark's has is a strong and foundational commitment to the task of theology and the life of the church within a

29. Hans Küng, *The Church* (London: Search Press, 1976), 264–359.

30. Jürgen Moltmann, *The Church in the Power of the Spirit* (London: SCM Press, 1977), 337–61.

public space. This means it is not in the desert tradition but rather right in the middle of things. This accords with an earlier European monasticism which, as far I can see, provided essential glue for social, ecclesial and intellectual life of earlier times. Not everything is transportable nor desirable.

Perhaps what we want is a new minster model focussed around theological study, prayer, hospitality and mission. The minsters and monasteries were not simply missional in work and orientation, they constituted a mission by their very life and practise. They also operated as a hub for mission in the local region. It was an infinitely better model than one priest looking after six to ten churches because it took community seriously as a powerhouse for mission and pastoral care. The Chemin Neuf community is attractive because of its link to the work of theology and scholarship as well as its ecumenical and lay focus.

It is, among other things, the possibility of bringing the study of theology into the cauldron of new mission through its place in a new monasticism that I find both attractive and potentially revitalising for the mission of the Church. New monasticism as a locus for theological vitality is one of the enduring needs of an ecclesial community after virtue.

Part Three

Discipleship: Pilgrims on a Common Journey

Chapter Ten
Discipleship and Divine Simplicity: A Conversation with Karl Barth[1]

The Ways of Discipleship

This essay on discipleship was an attempt to develop some of my earlier doctoral research on simplicity in relation to the theme of discipleship. Karl Barth proved an engaging—as ever—companion for this exercise. Theologically the concept of simplicity provides a basis for a rich and diverse discipleship in the world. But there are false tracks in simplicity which lead to fundamentalism.

The imperative of simplicity

Few words seem to offer so many complexities as does *simplicitas.*[2] In the biblical tradition simplicity (*haplous*) is associated with singleness and undividedness of heart for God, and personal integrity and straight forwardness in all relationships as befits those of the Kingdom of God. This evangelical *simplicitas* is linked to that humility, poverty and childlike innocence in which Jesus rejoices: 'I thank you, Father, Lord of heaven and earth, for you have hidden these things from the wise and understanding and revealed them to babes' (*nepiois*; Matthew 11:25, compare Luke 10:21). The ethical, moral and religious dimensions of this evangelical *simpliticas* find their deepest theological rationale in the simple God who

1. Originally published as 'Barth on Divine Simplicity', in *Karl Barth: A Future for Postmodern Theology*, edited by Geoff Thompson and Chris Mostert (Adelaide: ATF Press, 2000).
2. See for example, 'Simplicity', in *The New International Dictionary of New Testament Theology*, edited by Colin Brown, volume 3 (Grand Rapids, MI: Zondervan, 1986) 571f; William Hill, 'Simplicity of God' in *New Catholic Encyclopedia of Theology*, edited by Staff Catholic University of America, volume 13 (Washington & New York: McGraw Hill, 1967), 229–32; S Payne, 'Simplicity', in *The New Dictionary of Catholic Spirituality*, edited by M Downey (The Liturgical Press, 1993), 885–89.

is wholly and undividedly trustworthy and faithful, and who accordingly calls forth similar trust and simplicity in life.

Throughout the history of the Christian tradition the simplicity of this God has been heavily influenced by a Neo-Platonic metaphysic of the absolute simplicity of the divine being entirely free from all composition.[3] However, preoccupation with the ontological status of simplicity has, under the pressure of Enlightenment rationalism, given way to epistemological concerns. Here simplicity assumes primary significance as a parameter invoked, whether consciously or not, as a criterion in the structuring of knowledge.[4] In this respect the philosopher of science, Elliott Sober, has noted that the desire for theories in science, 'in large measures reduces to a desire for simplicity'.[5] He further notes the 'chaos of opinion' concerning simplicity and comments that

> diversity of our institutions about simplicity is matched only by the tenacity with which these intuitions refuse to yield to formal characterisation. Our intuitions seem unanimous in favour of sparse ontologies, smooth curves, homogenous universes, invariant equators and impoverished assumptions.[6]

These remarks suggest that the appeal of simplicity involves aesthetic as well as ontological and epistemological considerations. They also point to the elusiveness and, it seems, the inherently controversial nature of simplicity. Indeed, another philosopher of science, Mario Bunge, refers to the 'myth' of simplicity, arguing that the concept, though useful at some stages in the structuring knowledge, fails as a reliable criterion of truth. Bunge thus reverses the scholastic dictum, *simplex sigillem veri* (simplicity is the seal of truth).[7] From this perspective simplicity as conceptual economy is thus a sign of transitoriness, of falsity being superseded by a lesser falsity. Simplicity may have aesthetic appeal but have little ontological weight.

3. See for example Karl Barth's discussion in *Church Dogmatics* Cd-Rom volume 2 (Logos Research Systems) part 1, 332–50 and 440–61. The references to Barth on simplicity hereafter appear in the text in the form (CD volume/part/page).
4. Nicholas Rescher, *Cognitive Systematisation* (Oxford: Blackwell, 1979), chapter 1.
5. Elliot Sober, *Simplicity* (Oxford: Clarendon Press, 1975), 168.
6. Sober, *Simplicity*, Preface.
7. Mario Bunge, *The Myth of Simplicity: Problems of Scientific Philosophy* (Englewood Cliffs, NJ: Prentice-Hall, 1963).

This suggests that consideration of the ontological status of simplicity seems a highly problematic exercise. For a start it seems counter-intuitive given the fact that increasing penetration of reality discloses increasingly higher degrees of complexity. There is, as indicated earlier, a certain resistance to this recognition. As one theologian has noted, 'We are too fond of simplicities and the comfort they bring to face how deeply complexity reaches into the issues which we discuss'.[8] It seems that the sciences of the twenty-first century will be developed on the basis that we are 'part of an ever-changing, interlocking, nonlinear, kaleidoscopic world'.[9] The supposition of such an inner complexity which cannot be known without similar complexities in the structuring of knowledge[10] suggests that theology must divest itself of the simplicity ideal, except perhaps as a purely pragmatic strategy. On this account simplicity is a purely human construct, of some heuristic value in the ordering of knowledge but, as noted earlier, deserving of distrust as a measure of truth. Nevertheless the appeal of simplicity exercises a powerful and enduring attraction. Indeed, as Alfred North Whitehead recognised in his famous maxim—'seek simplicity and distrust it'—the appeal of simplicity seems to be an enduring preoccupation of the human spirit in its search for understanding and meaning.

Today, this search is undertaken in conditions of high risk and danger; the modern world has taken on a decidedly 'menacing appearance'.[11] Issues to do with trust, personal relations and identity have to be renegotiated within the context of abstract systems of security. The possibility of achieving some degree of personal and social harmony (control?) amidst the complexities and chaotic eruptions of modern life seems daunting. Risk of failure in these 'local projects' is intensified given other potential global catastrophes which 'provide an unnerving horizon of dangers for everyone'.[12] It's no surprise that simplicity life and thought exercises a powerful attraction in such an environment and assumes something of

8. See Daniel Hardy, 'The Future of Theology in a Complex World', in *Christ and Context: The Confrontation between Gospel and Culture*, edited by Hilary Regan and Allan Torrance (Edinburgh: T&T Clark, 1993), 22.
9. M Waldrop, *Complexity: The Emerging Science at the Edge of Order and Chaos* (London: Viking, 1993), 333.
10. See Daniel Hardy, 'Rationality, The Sciences and Theology', in *Keeping the Faith: Essays to Mark the Centenary of Lux Mundi*, edited by Geoffrey Wainwright (London: SPCK, 1989), 282.
11. See Anthony Giddens, *The Consequences of Modernity* (Oxford: Polity Press, 1990), chapter 4 for the following discussion.
12. Giddens, *The Consequences of Modernity*, 125.

status of a foundational axiom of modern efforts to recover wholeness and integrity within a divided and complex world. This general social and cultural importance of the appeal simplicity gives added force to what Joseph O'Leary refers to as the 'imperative of simplicity'. O'Leary notes that this 'thirst for first hand contact with the heart matter'[13] occurs in any radical questioning after religious identity. The force of this simplicity imperative has long been recognised as a feature of the Christian tradition as such. However, the attempt to grasp 'the heart of the matter' through recovery of a 'primordial simplicity'—developed historically, existentially or through some form of naturalism—is understandable but full of pitfalls. Primarily it disregards the radically contingent nature of Christian identity and its corollary that is, that 'the path to the simple' is never simple. It seems that distrusting simplicity may be good advice. However, as Karl Barth noted, a deeper problem concerns the originating impulse to seek the simple 'It is very understandable, that complex as he [sic] is and suffering from his own complexity as he does, man would like to be different, ie simple' (CD 2/1/449). Barth viewed the free and unfettered fulfillment of this drive for the simple as generative of human idolatry and sin. His discussion of simplicity, and in particular divine simplicity, is important in its own right and also because it offers some clues for the practice of Christian discipleship in the complexities of modern life.

Divine simplicity in the tradition

Barth's discussion of simplicity occurs within the long tradition of reflection on the nature of the divine simplicity. Indeed, as indicated earlier, the concept of God as absolute simplicity has exercised a significant impact on the development of the Christian doctrine of God from early in the tradition.[14] The roots of the doctrine of divine simplicity can be traced to Greek metaphysics where the supposition that ultimate reality is simple has been articulated within Neoplatonic and Aristotelian frameworks. According to Plato everything composite—that is, made up of parts—was necessarily divisible and consequently mutable or destructible. As Wolf-

13. J O'Leary, *Questioning Back: The Overcoming of Metaphysics in Christian Tradition* (Minneapolis, MN: Winston Press Inc, 1985), 205 and more generally 204–12.

14. See, for example, W Pannenberg, *Basic Questions in Theology*, volume 2 (London: SCM, 1971), 165–73. For recent discussion on divine simplicity in philosophy see T Morris, *Our Idea of God: An Introduction to Philosophical Theology* (Notre Dame: University of Notre Dame Press, 1991), 113–18.

hart Pannenberg points out, the Platonic doctrine of God as the ultimate and hence immutable origin (first cause) leads to the supposition of the absolute simplicity of God's essence; without qualities or properties.[15] The correlate to absolute simplicity is the radical incomprehensibility of the divine being.

Given the axiomatic strength of the doctrine of divine simplicity in Patristic theology it was clear that any reconstruction of the doctrine of God in light of the Christian revelation would present significant difficulties. Indeed William Hill suggests that the early centuries of trinitarian and christological reflection can be understood as an attempt in Christian theology to show how 'neither the Incarnation of the Word nor the real distinction of the divine persons is in any wise injurious to God's simplicity'.[16] On Hill's account the controlling question is clear: How might the Christian revelation be understood *within* the received doctrine of divine simplicity? Such an approach was full of danger. Thus when Arius distinguished between Christ as 'creature' and the divine 'Ungenerated One' his real mistake was not so much in lowering the status of the Son but rather inappropriately exalting the Father over the Son.[17] In doing so Arius preserved the absolute simplicity of God at the price of displacing or nullifying an emerging Christian consciousness in respect of the doctrine of God. The Arian controversy could, from this perspective, be understood as an attempt to think through the received doctrine of divine simplicity in the light of the Christian gospel of God. In this respect the Nicene Creed's affirmation of the *homoousion* of the Father and the Son suggested a quite radical and novel reconstitution of the simplicity of God, for the sake of the ontological coherence of the Gospel.[18] On this account affirmation of God's simplicity entailed less a denial of composition and division and more a recognition of God's rich and integral wholeness. Such a conception belonged to the evangelical significance of the *homoousion*. Barth recognised this when he spoke of the church clarifying its mind about the simplicity of God by reference to the *homoousion* of the Son and Holy Spirit with the Father and the unity of the divine with human nature in Jesus Christ (CD 2/1/446).

15. Pannenberg, *Basic Questions*, 167.
16. Hill, 'Simplicity of God', 230.
17. See Frances Young, *From Nicea to Chalcedon* (London: SCM, 1983), 63f.
18. See the discussion of *homoousion* by Torrance, *The Trinitarian Faith* (Edinburgh: T&T Clark, 1988), 132–45.

However, developments in trinitarian theology indicated the difficulty, if not the impossibility, of satisfying the demands of the doctrine of divine simplicity and at the same time doing justice to the surprising novelty introduced in the doctrine of God through the life, death and resurrection of Jesus Christ in the power of the Holy Spirit. In the West this tension between the biblical tradition of the simplicity of God and an alien metaphysic of divine simplicity can be discerned in Augustine and traced through the medieval tradition as expressed in, among others, Anselm, Aquinas and Ockham.[19] This tension remains in Barth's own illuminating discussion to which we now turn.

Barth on divine simplicity

Barth considered divine simplicity in the context of his discussion of the perfections of God in volume two of the *Church Dogmatics*.[20] In his insightful discussion two kinds of simplicity emerge; a false simplicity that takes its cue from a general idea of simplicity and a genuine divine simplicity determined by the revelation of the Lord of Glory. In the context of his discussion of the perfections of divine freedom Barth considers the natural human tendency to absolutise the uniqueness of God. Whilst 'we must say that God is the absolutely One . . . we cannot say that the absolutely one is God'; this latter and very natural human tendency evidences itself in monotheism, 'an idea which can be directly divined or logically and mathematically constructed without God' (CD 2/1/448). For Barth monothesim is 'the religious glorification of the number 'one', the absolutising of the idea of uniqueness' (CD 2/1/448). Thus in Barth's view there is a great gulf between the way in which Islam and Christianity proclaim that there is only one God.

In precisely the same way that it is quite false to say that the absolutely one is God so too with the notion of the simplicity of God: 'the assertion of the simplicity of God is not reversible in the sense that it could equally well be said that the simple is God' (CD 2/1/449). He notes that whenever human beings have 'begun to worship the unique as a deity, they have always more or less consistently tried to describe it as the simple as well'

19. See R La Croix, 'Augustine on the Simplicity of God', in *The New Scholasticism* 51 (1977): 453–69; M Adams, *William of Ockham*, 2 volumes, chapter 21; C Hughes, *On a Complex Theory of a Simple God: An Investigation in Aquinas' Philosophical Theology* (Ithaca & London: Cornell University Press, 1989), 166–70.
20. See footnote 2 above.

(CD 2/1/449). However, when the simple is equated with God this generates a natural yet mistaken understanding of divine simplicity (derived from the metaphysics of Ancient Stoicism and Neo-Platonism) and made determinative for Christian theology (CD 2/1/329). It leads to a view of the simple as 'an utterly unmoved being, remote from this world altogether, incapable of sound or action, influence on or relation to anything else' (CD 2/1/449). Such a view of the simple, abstracted from all that is complex, is correlated to a world that is necessarily autonomous and over which the absolutely simple has no 'mastery'. Alternatively, a relation between the simple (unconditioned) and the world (conditioned) is posited such that the latter becomes essential to the former thus generating a dialectical identity of the two. This leads to the abandonment of the absolute simplicity of the 'would-be-simple' and with it 'that in which we were seeking the divinity of God' (CD 2/1/449). This, in Barth's view, was the fate of the orthodox doctrine of God as it developed in the early church, and in medieval theology through to Hegel and Schleiermacher, at least 'to the extent that its basis was the concept of the *ens simplicissimum*' (CD 2/1/449). An 'absolutised idea of simplicity' thus leads to either a god no longer sovereign over and free for the world, or a god so co-mixed with the world that genuine simplicity is forfeited.

This false track on simplicity evidenced itself in the traditional discussion of the attributes of God. Under the pressure of a strict nominalism all predications of the being of God (for example, Ockham's 'attributal perfections') constitute mental constructs and descriptions to which there is no corresponding reality in God who is 'pure simplicity'. In a milder form the multiplicity of perfections attributed to God are expressive of a vision of God necessarily constrained by the limits of human existence. This could lead to the 'accommodation' view of Calvin in which the enumeration of God's perfections did not describe God's inner life 'but in relation to us, on order that our acknowledgment of him may be more a vivid actual impression than empty visual speculation'.[21] However, full recognition of God's perfections was continually thwarted or undermined by the 'alien proposition that the being of God meant at bottom God's *nuda essentia* whose simplicity must be conceptually the first and last and real thing' (CD 2/1/329). The properties of God inevitably assume a purely secondary significance. By beginning from a generalised notion of God, 'the idea of the divine simplicity was necessarily exalted to the all-controlling prin-

21. Calvin, *Institutes of the Christian Religion*, 1.x.2; available at <http://www.reformed.org/books/institutes/books/book1/bk1ch10.html>. Accessed 15 March 2011.

cipal, the idol . . . devouring everything concrete . . . [Accordingly] when we speak of God, we must mean essentially only the simplicity and not the richness, at best the simplicity of richness, but at bottom only the simplicity' (CD 2/1/329).

The false track on simplicity was, in Barth's view, symptomatic of the 'fundamental error of the whole earlier doctrine of God' (CD 2/1/348) which began first with God's being in general and then considered God's triune nature.[22] By beginning with the revelation of the personal triune God, Barth argued that the notion of God's simple being is given its proper foundation. Formally this means that whilst God is absolutely simple, this simplicity 'can only be God Himself—and not "God Himself"—interpreted by the idea of the absolutely simple, but God Himself in His self-interpretation' (CD 2/1/457). Thus, characteristically Barth points to God's self revelation attested in Scripture as the absolutely simple One, uncomposed and indivisible. Breaking the idolatrous simplicity of human imagining requires the recognition that 'the simplicity of God *is His own simplicity*' (CD 2/1/458; my italics). Barth's discussion of divine simplicity belongs to his inquiry into the revelation of the being of God as the one who loves in freedom. The utterly simple God is thus to be located precisely in the place in which the prophets and apostles found and were found by God—'in God's self-demonstration given by Him in His Word and work' (CD 2/1/459). Materially God's Word and work throughout the Bible are self-demonstrations of God's trustworthiness, truthfulness and fidelity. God's simplicity consists in this, for God 'is trustworthy in His essence, in the inmost core of the His being. And this is His simplicity' (CD 2/1/459). As such God's simplicity is both foundational for life and known only by faith in the God who is trustworthy. God's trustworthiness and faithfulness converge and concentrate in Jesus Christ in whom 'is the Yea and the Amen of the one God' (CD 2/1/460). Ultimately then God is trustworthy and true because Jesus Christ is the true and faithful one of God. The simplicity of God thus reveals its inner grounding in the God of the doctrine of the Trinity and Christology: 'the unity of the triune God and of the Son of God with man in Jesus Christ is itself the simplicity of God' (CD 2/1/446).

22. Compare Jürgen Moltmann, *The Trinity and the Kingdom of God* (London: SCM, 1981), 16ff.

Divine simplicity under two forms: God's love and freedom

Clearly for Barth, to speak of the divine simplicity is not to posit an abstract, impersonal absolute; rather the true and genuine simplicity of God—God's indivisible, indissoluble and inflexible being—is the implicate of the being of the God who loves in freedom. God's simplicity is demonstrated and confirmed in God's covenant of loving faithfulness with the creature. God's essence, revealed in God's act, is trustworthy; this is God's simpleness. The fulfillment of the covenant of love in Jesus Christ reveals the nature of God's simple being: 'indivisible' (whole and integral), 'indissoluble' (secure and indestructible) and 'inflexible' (unrelenting and unyielding) in faithfulness and truth. The simplicity of God is, in this way, transposed from bare essence to dynamic act, from the realm of metaphysics to implicate of revelation. God loves and so reveals who God is: the absolutely simple one. The ontological status of the simplicity of God is confirmed but only through particular concrete personal acts of love. Accordingly for Barth divine simplicity is above all else an ethical category.

Precisely because God loves *in freedom*, the simplicity of divine love has its necessary correlate in God's freedom. Being simple—wholly and undividedly God—in all distinctions, even in God's triunity, entails not only God's essential oneness and uniqueness but also designates God as 'incomparably free, sovereign and majestic' (CD 2/1/445). Accordingly, God's simplicity is God's Lordship; even in the triune life and 'the whole real wealth of His being' God remains 'unconditionally One'. Barth is quite clear: *'for every distinction of His being and working is simply a repetition and corroboration of the one being'* ((CD 2/1/445; my italics). The implication of such simplicity is that God's relation to the world cannot entail any 'combination, amalgamation or identification'; nothing must be so interpreted 'not even the incarnation of the Son of God in Jesus Christ'; even in the oneness of God with the creature in Jesus Christ 'God does not cease for a moment or in any regard to be the one, true God' (CD 2/1/446).

In Barth the simplicity of God is thus manifest from two perspectives: God's love and God's freedom. Formally of course simplicity as indivisibility is relevant in both domains. However, it is far from clear how the strong christological and ethical grounding for simplicity as faithfulness—'the real meaning and basis' of God's simplicity—informs the simplicity by which God is incomparably free, sovereign and one through all multiplicity. Is it possible that, having located the true and genuine basis for divine simplicity—one conducive to a rich trinitarian simplicity—a remnant of another alien simplicity doctrine remains the service of Barth's strong assertion of the freedom and aseity of God? Might not Barth's discussion and deployment of the simplicity postulate evidence an ambiguity that has been discerned in the monist tendencies of this doctrine of the Trinity? This is hardly surprising, for Barth himself recognised that the 'battle for the recognition of the simplicity of God was the same as for the recognition of the Trinity and of the relation between the divine and human natures in Jesus Christ' (CD 2/1/446). And again, 'the unity of the triune God and the Son of God with man in Jesus Christ *is itself* the simplicity of God' (CD 2/1/446; my italics). Problems in one area will necessarily manifest themselves in different guise in other related areas.

To follow the simple God

Our brief excursus of this major area of Christian theology as developed by Karl Barth highlighted both the importance and the difficulty of breaking through to a rich and adequate understanding of the true simplicity of God. Christian theology still struggles to cope with the fecundity, sheer novelty and complexity of the God of the Gospel. Insofar as Barth's point holds good, that 'the unity of the triune God and of the Son of God with man in Jesus Christ is itself the simplicity of God', it is possible to formulate a concept of God as *a being of maximal economy*, whose simplicity is concentration of plenitude.[23] This seems to accord with Barth's own best intentions as evidenced in his remarkable discourse on the perfections of God. God does not merely possess the 'wealth' of his perfections—their multiplicity, individuality and diversity—God 'is this wealth'. The conclusion Barth draws from this is critical: God is '*in essence* not only one, but multiple, individual and diverse' (CD 2/1/331). His concern is to break the 'undialectical understanding' of the inner being of the *simplicitas Dei* which results in an 'empty and unreal' divine simplicity. For Barth, the simple being of God 'transcends the contrast of *simplicitas* and *multiplicitas*, including and reconciling both. We can only accept and interpret God's *simplicitas* and *multiplicitas* in such a way as to imply that they are not mutually exclusive but inclusive, or rather that they are both

23. Compare Sober, *Simplicity*, who proposes a notion of simplicity as relative informativeness, that which requires the minimum extra information, that is, that which is maximally informative is the most simple. High quality simplicity signifies maximal concentration.

included in God Himself' (CD 2/1/333). The discussion of divine perfections reveals itself at this point as a search by Barth for that harmonious dynamic of God's dialectical simplicity (CD 2/1/348). Clearly on this account simplicity and plenitude (rich complexity) are correlated, a point expressed eloquently by Barth when he noted that, 'Consideration of the divine attributes can but move in circles around the one but infinitely rich being of God whose simplicity is abundance itself and whose abundance is simplicity itself' (CD 2/1/406). Barth was in no doubt, the doctrine of the Trinity, as plenitude in simplicity, was the Christian doctrine of God.

The project envisaged by Barth, of reconceiving the triune simplicity of God, remains on the theological agenda. Precisely because it is the truth of God's simple being that is sought, simplicities that offer genuine epistemological insight and possibilities for godly discipleship ideally engender a dynamic in Christian life and thought that befits God's own trinitarian simplicity. The supposition here is that the nature and dynamic of the simplicity of God is generative of a correspondence at the level of Christian discipleship. Here, in the face of the 'menacing appearance' of the modern world, the appeal of simplicity easily succumbs to precisely the same danger as observed in the doctrine of God. The barren simplicity of an impersonal deity is transferred into forms of discipleship that are similarly barren and impersonal. The monist drive in the doctrine of God re-emerges in forms of discipleship that 'succeed' through domination or self-enclosure. This is most evident in various forms of religious fundamentalism. A more genuine and therefore radical Christian discipleship entails a prizing open of new possibilities amidst the complexities and confusions of modernity, of so willing the one thing that one is willing for anything for the sake of Jesus Christ. There is a richness to this kind of discipleship which cannot be reduced to a singular form but which is constrained only by the gospel of God's triune simplicity. To find a simplicity of life in correspondence with the simpleness of such a God is the other project that remains on the ecclesial agenda at the end of the second millennium.

Chapter Eleven
The Mystical Way for a New Age: William Law as a Test Case[1]

Disciple as Mystic

In an age when the fire of the religious instinct seemed not to burn so bright the eighteenth century Anglican mystic William Law's entry into the heart-land of God was refreshing, sustaining and controversial. Law discovered that beyond the formal structures of his inherited Christianity there was a Spirit of love and prayer located in the heart of the believer in union with God. Law and John Wesley were contemporaries and although they clashed they represented powerful though different directions for Christian discipleship that remain relevant. This essay offers followers of Jesus some wisdom and warnings on the ancient mystical way and discipleship that has to be crafted experimentally.

The mystical turn and human transformation

No longer do we Australians live in a monochrome religious culture, if we ever truly did. Today, more than ever, we are aware of the rich tapestry of religions present in our culture. In this new context the question of Christian identity assumes a new and urgent importance and finds expression in, among other things, a concern to articulate the uniqueness of the gospel. A particular difficulty with this task today is that it has to be executed in relation to efforts by those of other faiths to clarify their own religious identity. Self-consciousness of this religious context is not an optional extra. However, it is far from clear how Christian theology can find the Way which gives strength to its own inner life and also propels it beyond itself into fresh conversations and shared lives in this country.

1. The present essay was originally published as 'Finding the Way in an Age of Religious Pluralism: The Relevance of William Law and the Christian Mystical Tradition', in *Pacifica* 9/2, June (1996): 145–63.

Given the above it is perhaps unsurprising that theology finds itself in a new period of experimentation; new strategies for response are being explored. The present paper represents a brief excursus into an important element within the Christian tradition which has significance for those in Australia of other religious traditions and perhaps none at all. In particular, I wish to focus on the Christian mystical tradition as it came to form in the life and theology of the eighteenth century Anglican divine, William Law (1686–1761). This has all the hallmarks of a leap back into the ark if not the dark, so a brief explanation is warranted.

First, I have, for some years, been interested in Law as an example of how people undergo change *within* their own religious tradition in a way that facilitates a healthy movement across established ecclesial boundaries. In other words Law, like many before and after him, discovered new resources within his religious inheritance that not only provided personal nourishment but also constituted a powerful, though not unproblematic, theological response to social, cultural and ecclesial pressures of his day.

Second, whilst it is simply impossible to make any quantum leaps from the mid-eighteenth century to our late twentieth century Australia it is my view that there are certain theological dynamics at work in Law's pilgrimage into the Christian mystical tradition that have an enduring value for our own day. This becomes particularly important given the significance of the mystical element in most contemporary religions and the resonance of the mystical way, broadly understood, with the quest for an Australian spirituality that spans the spectrum from a secular pop mysticism (the local book shop variety) to the more traditional Christian type that is undergoing a contemporary renaissance. From this point of view it is incumbent upon Christians to sharpen their understanding of a feature of their own tradition that has proved enduring, controversial and open to significant distortion.

Thirdly, this inquiry might offer a way of opening up the particular character of the Christian gospel, but in a way that provides an impetus for deeper conversations with a whole range of other religious traditions and so-called 'irreligious' Australians, whose hunger for the things of the Spirit has hitherto remained unsatisfied.

Realistically these hopes far surpass the capacities of the present article but they at least indicate an intention and program that others, in their own way, no doubt share. In the first part of the article I will outline Law's spiritual and theological journey. A shorter, second section will consider Law's mysticism within the religious pluralism of our own context. Such an article does not allow or require a full-scale critique of Law nor a discussion of the nature and meaning of mysticism. Rather, I presume Law's own important and widely recognised engagement with Christian mysticism[2] and seek to find there resources for a fuller understanding of the theological dynamics of this tradition and its relevance for today.

Part 1: A theological narrative of the life of William Law

The Christian tradition under stress

By the end of the seventeenth century deep rifts between God and the world had opened.[3] The inherited symbols of the Christian tradition had become opaque. A universe understood sacramentally, in which it was supposed that nature, history and human life mediated God's presence had, in the course of seventeenth century developments in science and natural philosophy, given way to tight mechanistic conceptions of the universe. Important in this latter development was the attempt to provide very general and simplified explanations of things, and to eliminate unpredictability. These developments were symptomatic of a rationalist frame of mind which generated oppositional ways of understanding and excluded large chunks of reality. This generated sharp divisions between, for example, the natural and supernatural, and faith and reason. Evidence of this was to be observed in the tendency to compartmentalise and isolate doctrines pertaining to natural religion, as distinct from supernatural revelation. This seriously undermined the inner coherence and dynamic of Christian theology. What was required was a fresh reintegration of doctrine in relation to Christian discipleship. This would necessarily have to include those elements of religious experience—'those, namely, which involve an acknowledgment of paradox, even of irrationality at the heart of things, certainly of transcendence or 'otherness'; of God not merely as deified Reason but as mysterium tremendum'[4]—which eighteenth century

2. For a recent introduction to Law see W Keith Walker, *William Law: His Life and Thought* (London: SPCK, 1973). Gordon Rupp, *Religion in England* 1688–1791 (Oxford: Oxford University Press, 1986), 218–42, provides an excellent critical discussion. See also the perceptive but sympathetic discussion of Law by Austin Warren in *William Law: A Serious Call to a Devout and Holy Life and The Spirit of Love* edited by Paul Stanwood, The Classics of Western Spirituality (London: SPCK, 1978), 11–32.
3. For general background see F. Brehier, *The Seventeenth Century* (Chicago & London: University of Chicago Press, 1966).
4. Basil Willey, *The Eighteenth Century Background: Studies on the Idea of Nature in the*

Deism had ignored. In short, what was required was an alternative way of believing and living the Christian faith.

William Law's response to this situation was radical and controversial. It involved a renewed stress on the redemptive activity of God immanent in the world, a moral rigour derived from an evangelical call to holiness of life, and a sense of wonder as the human response to God as 'All Love'. Law's renewed concentration upon God as 'soul presence', vivifying interior human life and generating human capacity for love and obedience in the moral sphere, constituted a powerful response to the crisis of orthodoxy in early enlightenment thought. Law's appropriation of the 'inwardness' tradition in Christianity[5] eventually expressed itself in a form of ecclesial mysticism. In this sense Law's mature theological position represented a radical transformation of his inherited High Church tradition to what might be termed a 'soul-realism'. God was most real as a dynamic interior presence. This development in Law's theological pilgrimage involved a move from one understanding of Christianity to another. A vigorous and highly embodied High Church ecclesial tradition gave way to a theological understanding of Christianity in which reality was reversed: God was most intensely and richly present in interiority. However, to trace the development of Law's mystical theology brings into view a way of being Christian which has remained both alluring and controversial in the history of Christianity, a fact reflected in the sharply divided responses to Law in modern Christian thought.[6] Such an inquiry also raises questions about the viability of a way of living which exerts considerable appeal in

---

Thought of the Period (London: Chatto & Windus, 1974), 84.

5. Rupp, *Religion in England* (207) notes that 'inward religion' was the common term for mysticism in the eighteenth century. Stephen Sykes discusses the dialectical relation that obtains between the inwardness and externality traditions in Christianity. The former—'the reiterated appeal to that inner spiritual reality of personal lives transformed by God'—operated as a critique of the ever-emerging institutional markers of the faith, for example, creeds, doctrines, church structures, and liturgies. See Sykes, *The Identity of Christianity: Theologians and the Essence of Christianity from Schleiermacher to Barth* (London: SPCK, 1984), 231ff.

6. For example, compare the favourable assessments of Law by J Hoyles, *The Edges of Augustanism: The Aesthetics of Spirituality in Thomas Ken, John Byrom and William Law* (The Hague: Martinus Nijohoff, 1972) and William Inge, *Studies of English Mystics* (London: John Murray, 1906), 124–72 with the rather negative views of W Grinsbrooke, 'The Nonjurors and William Law', in *The Study of Spirituality*, edited by C James et al (London: SPCK, 1986), 452–54, and Martin Thornton, *English Spirituality: An Outline of Aesthetical Theology according to the English Pastoral Tradition* (London: SPCK, 1963), 282.

contemporary religious life. A theological narrative of Law's life can be conveniently, though somewhat artificially divided into five phases.[7] A brief discussion of these phases will provide a foundation for assessing Law's mystical way in our contemporary context.

Tradition in transformation: a personal journey

Phase One: *High Church Traditionalism*

Law began his theological life as a vigorous apologist of High Church Anglicanism.[8] His entry into the arena of Church controversy was occasioned by the controversial Bishop of Bangor, Benjamin Hoadly (1676–1761) who had, during the early decades of the eighteenth century, vigorously attacked the Nonjurors—those clergy of the Church of England who had refused to take the Oaths of Alliegence and Supremacy to William and Mary and were subsquently deprived of their livings. Hoadly had also denounced what he considered to be the pretentious claims to authority espoused by the High Church party, and disparaged the importance of church communion, sacramental ordinances and episcopal ordination. For the latitudinarian Hoadly, private judgement guided by unbiased reason was a more reliable guide to truth than tradition and dogma; sincerity alone was sufficient as the touchstone of faith. In Hoadly's view God did not favour a person because they belonged to a particular communion but because they had chosen that communion honestly. The entire question of particular communions was relativised by Hoadly's 'universal invisible church'.

Law, like many, viewed Hoadly as one who had secularised the faith. In Law's view Christ's Church on earth could not but be visible despite the fact that those who were finally to be saved remained unknown. Since Christianity was a 'method of life necessary for salvation', external communion, which was one's profession of Christianity, was a necessity for, 'we can no other way appear to be Christians' (1\168). Law succinctly captured the essence of his inherited tradition: 'For Christ as truly comes to Christians in Institutions, as he came to the Jews in Person; and it is as dangerous to disregard him in the one Appearance, as in the other' (1/158). The highly

7. Each of these phases reflect developments (sometimes overlapping) in Law's spiritual and theological journey and, as the article will show, help to identify some of the important changes in his actual historical journey in faith.

8. See William Law, *Three Letters to the Bishop of Bangor*, in *The Works of the Reverend William Law* MA, 9 volumes [1762; reprinted for G Morton 1892], volume 1. Hereafter references to this work appear in text as volume number\page reference, that is (1\168).

embodied ecclesiology presupposed here was, in Law's mind, entirely dissolved by Hoadly's 'novel' doctrine of sincerity alone as the basis of God's favour. The criterion of sincerity gave no basis for differentiation between the merits of the competing visible and particular communions. Within Law's ecclesiology 'the whole question' turned on a right and safe choice in this regard. To be in a particular communion was the way of being in the Church of Christ; it implied, said Law 'our embracing Christianity' (1\180). Hoadly's 'Universal Invisible Church', based on the criterion of sincerity alone was, in Law's view, simply 'no church' (1\ 90).[9]

Law's understanding of Christianity in this first phase was clearly indebted to his High Church tradition.[10] It accorded with a highly embodied ecclesiology focussed on the institutions and profession of ecclesia: 'Christianity itself is a *Matter of Fact* only conveyed to us by *historical Evidence*' (1/79). The fundamental doctrines of the faith, the testimony of Scripture and tradition all belonged to the fabric of the institution, being measures against which loyalty to the truth could be assessed. Within this environment the process of ecclesial purification operated through vigorous reassertion of established institutional markers—creeds, rites and offices. The arid and static nature of this position became apparent to Law only as he began to search for more satisfying and dynamic ways of living a godly life within Christianity's institutional forms.

Phase Two: *The Transposition of Doctrine into Ethics*

In 1723 Law entered the house of Edward Gibbon as chaplain and private tutor to Gibbon's son, Edward. It was during this time that Law's *Serious Call to a Devout and Holy Life* (1729)[11] was composed. In this famous work Law explored the possibilities for dynamic Christianity within an inherited tradition, which included not only the Caroline divines, but also seventeenth-century French spiritual writers. This work was an attempt to

9. For a critique of Law's response to Hoadly, especially on the controversial notion of 'sincerity', which Law may have taken out of context, see Rupp, *Religion in England*, 97ff.

10. Stephen Hobbhouse identifies the Bangorian letters as 'The First phase' of Law's churchmanship, quite at variance with the spirit and temper of that which follows, that is, 'The Period of the Serious Call' (see *William Law and Eighteenth Century Quakerism* (London: George Allen & Unwin, 1927), 255).

11. Full title: *A Serious Call to a Devout and Holy Life: adapted to the State and Condition of all orders of Christians*. The text used is that appearing in *The Ancient and Modern Library of Theological Literature*, volume 10 (London: Griffith, Farran, Brown & Co, ND). Hereafter references given in text as SC, followed by page reference.

refocus Christianity in piety, that is, 'a life given, or devoted, to God' (SC 13).[12] Christianity, in its most real form, still concerned externals: 'this alone is Christianity, a uniform, open, and visible practice of all these virtues' (SC 18). He had in mind humility, self-denial, renunciation of the world, poverty of spirit and 'heavenly affection'. It was a call designed to undermine the formalism and barrenness of a 'polite age' in which, he noted, 'we have so lived away the spirit of devotion' (SC 277). It was a *serious* call, for it was a challenge to live a life witnessing a return to God.

It was a question for Law of what Christianity should look like anywhere and everywhere at all times. Law's answer was simple; it should appear as a life of regular, uniform piety under God. This call was a radical one for an age that made strong professions of Christianity on certain occasions but repeatedly betrayed those professions in its disregard for true devotion in ordinary life. The evangelical tenor was clear: 'Either this piety, wisdom and devotion is to go through every way of life, and to extend to the use of everything or it is to go through no part of life' (SC 52).

This was Christianity at the level of praxis. Doctrine was here transferred into the ethical mode. In an age in which world and church had become inextricably enmeshed, renewal would be effected only by a true and radical devotion that penetrated life in its entirety. Accordingly, one held on to and participated in the doctrines of the gospel, and felt and truly believed them as one implemented them in practice: 'If, therefore, a man [sic] will so live, as to show that he feels and believes the most fundamental doctrines of Christianity, he must live above the world; this is the temper that must enable him to do the business of life, and yet live wholly unto God' (SC 41).

But what fundamental doctrine was it in Law's mind that required realisation in practice? In the *Serious Call* the doctrine of the cross was central, for in it was focused the character of the true spirit of Christianity, a way of death and crucifixion to the world. This was the spirit of Christ, true Christianity. 'The history of the Gospel is chiefly the history of Christ's conquest over the spirit of the world' (SC 182). Only those that

12. Law's perceptive portrayals of the various characters that make up the *Serious Call* was no doubt greatly influenced by his life on the Gibbon estate at Putney—the family and their middle-class guests, businessmen and their wives. More importantly, however, Hobbhouse, *Law and Quakerism*, (260f) suggests that the spirit of the *Serious Call* points to Law having undergone 'something of the nature of a conversion' after the Bangorian Letters (some evidence indicates 1720) that involved a shift from a religion focussed on rites and ceremonies to a life of devotion.

lived in that spirit were true Christians. Law perceived that the central doctrines were most properly held as they were manifest in practice. Thus Law suggested that 'if the doctrines of Christianity were practised . . . it would be as easy a thing to know a Christian by his outward course of life, as it is now difficult to find anybody that lives it' (SC 20).

Implicit in this evangelical call to perfection was an attempt by Law to develop a more refined correspondence between the life of piety and the presence and work of the Holy Spirit of God in human life. Far from a reduction of the gospel to moralism, the *Serious Call* indicated an attempt to recover the centrality of practice in the definition of Christianity. 'This, and this alone, is Christianity; an universal holiness in every part of life' (SC 99). The Reformed doctrine of justification by faith was transferred into the practice of a holy life. Moreover, for Law, this righteousness of life was sharply Christocentric: 'We are to be like him [Christ] in Heart and Mind, to act by the same Rule, to look towards the same End, and to govern our lives by the same Spirit. This is an Imitation of Jesus Christ, which is as necessary to Salvation, as it is necessary to believe in his Name. This is the sole End of all the Counsels, Commands and Doctrines of Christ, to make us like himself'.[13] To be formed in this way was to be an imitation of love itself.

Law's understanding of Christianity was still focussed upon the externals of faith. However, the locus of this embodiment had shifted from institutional forms to the all-encompassing life of piety. This shift had reorientated the doctrinal tradition towards discipleship. Furthermore, the way of discipleship suggested in the *Serious Call* did implicate Law in a move towards interiority which would later intensify. Devotion did, after all, arise out of a life 'hid in Christ'. It was the inner intentions of the heart, orientated towards a God of infinite love and goodness, that were embodied in the practice of piety.[14]

---

13. This quotation is from Law, *A Practical Treatise upon Christian Perfection*, in *Works*, volume 3, 216. Compare SC, 227.

14. Thus Rupp, *Religion in England* (228f) notes that the *Serious Call* was 'not simply morality, but that without which morality becomes impossible and meaningless, the new life which God pours into the hearts of those who unreservedly commit themselves to him'. In relation to Law's own spiritual development a debate continues as to whether the *Serious Call* represents a 'pre-mystical' stage or whether traces of Law's later mysticism can be discerned there. In this respect R Tuttle states that 'most would agree that these treatises [*Christian Perfection* & *Serious Call*] especially the latter represent a transitory stage in Law between a highly ethical period and a highly mystical period beginning in 1732' (*Mysticism in Wesleyan Tradition* (Grand Rapids,

Phase Three: *On the Edges of Interiority*

Law's focus on the life of devotion and the inner intentions of the heart came more sharply into view in 1731–32 in a series of pastoral letters to a lady[15] contemplating a change of her ecclesial allegiance from Anglicanism to the Roman communion. Law referred to 'the spirit of Christianity' as residing in the 'infant simplicity of resignation to God'. This was the essence of piety and it consisted in an 'implicit faith and total resignation of ourselves to the adorable Providence of God' (9/249). This was a 'state of mind' which 'covers all our imperfections, sanctifies all our endeavours, makes us holy without any holiness of our own, makes our weaknesses as serviceable to God as our strength, and renders us acceptable to God at the same time that we do nothing worthy of him' (9/249). Law's reader was enjoined to lay hold of this temper in such a way that everything could become 'fresh occasions, of committing yourself to God by a faith without bounds, a resignation without reserve' (9/246). Such true devotion and piety of heart was, for Law, the way of finding, living-in and feeding from 'Divine Truths'. The way of resignation was the way through the uncertainties and fallibilities of human reason into the truth.

Such humility, faith and resignation to God was the means by which the mind was led into the 'truest deepest knowledge of the mysteries of God'. Law rightly perceived a natural reciprocity between the object of faith and the life of resignation, the former nourishing piety, the latter the means of tapping the vision. It was in this context that Law exhorted his reader to recognise that God was to be 'All in All', not just in the next life but in the present. To find God thus was to be 'full of the honour and glory of God.' Law understood, with great clarity, that the emergence of a creative and open self was a corollary of the fully conscious act of renunciation, rather than the annihilation of the ego. To live 'out of oneself' was to live in an enriched relation to God. Law had captured a far richer focus here. 'We must consider, that the Infinite Wisdom, Goodness, and Perfection of God, is the fathomless object of our faith and adoration and not of our comprehension' (9/234). Resignation to a God who was 'All in All'

MI: Francis Asbury Press, 1989), 68f).

15. Law, *Letters to a Lady*, in *Works*, volume 9. The lady in question was Mrs Elizabeth Dodwell, daughter of the Nonjuror Henry Dodwell (1641–1711). Law wrote three letters between May 1731 and September 1732. Though not intended for publication the letters show Law's power as a spiritual advisor and, as Walker notes, they 'show how far he [Law] had come from the position of the *Serious Call* wherein he states that reason is our universal law' (*William Law*, 88).

was not therefore a retreat into the self but entailed a dynamic orientation towards a rich and nourishing object of faith, an alternative way of coming into relation with God which required a letting go of all external supports for faith. What emerged was an uncompromising Christian discipleship quite at variance with the spirit of the age. Law was exploring at the edges of interiority, in a stage of theological transition.[16]

Phase Four: *Penetration to the Real*

In Law's writings from the late 1730s his espousal of a more radical Christian life was taken up with greater intensity in the light of his reading of the seventeenth-century Lutheran mystic, Jacob Boehme.[17] Boehme's thought, often bizarre, obscurantist and anachronistic (for example, his seventeenth century alchemic symbolism) exercised a powerful attraction for one such as Law who was in search of a 'system' to satisfy the desires of his heart (the mystical reality) and his need for intellectual certainty. Law selectively borrowed and assimilated Boehme's philosophy and deployed it to sharpen his critique of latitudinarianism. In this respect Law perceived two kinds of idolatries that afflicted the Church. In addition to the prevailing and direct idolatry of deism, there was a species of idolatry that had arisen from within Christendom of those 'who, though receiving and professing the Religion of the Gospel, yet worship God not in Spirit and in Truth, but either in the Deadness of an outward form, or in a Pharisaical carnal Trust and Confidence in their own opinions and Doctrines' (6/206). Such were the 'nominal', 'historical' or 'literal' Christians. They had only the 'name' of gospel mysteries, the 'image' of the truth. As regards the reality, 'the true life of the new birth, they oppose and reject as heartily as the Deist does the outward Form and Letter' (6/206). Both kinds of idolatry were destructive of the Christian faith. Both indicated a failure to appreci-

16. See Walker, *William Law*, 87.

17. Law's major works during this period are to be found in volumes 5, 6 and 7 of his works. For brevity sake only volume and page number are given in this article. The impact of Boehme on Law has been the subject of a number of studies. For a general discussion see Walker, *William Law*, chapter 10; and Rupp, *Religion in England*, 232–40. Rupp notes that Law's first contact with Boehme was from 1733–35 though in 1737, in dispute with Hoadly on the doctrine of the eucharist, Law discusses Boehme at length and later still, in 1740, Law acknowledged his debt to the whole mystical tradition including Boehme (see Rupp, *Religion in England*, 234). Austin, observes that the general opinion is 'that Law selects from Boehme, omits the too esoteric, and gives a simplified version of the system' (*William Law*, 26). Tuttle sums it up well: 'Law, via Behmen in 1737 *chose* a route deeper into mysticism' (*Wesleyan Tradition*, 116).

ate the true nature of Christianity. The rationalism of deism had explained away the truth of the gospel and the lack of depth of nominal Christianity led to a view of Scripture doctrines that allowed 'more height and mystery in the expression than in the thing itself' (6/160).

Law's assessment of the situation presupposed a radical engagement in the controversy at the heart of the English Enlightenment between 'inner light' and 'outward Enlightenment'.[18] So much of the controversy between deist and divine had operated at the level of 'outward Enlightenment' and to this extent it was impoverished by the sterility of Lockean philosophy. Some years later Law could summarise a generation of religious controversy thus: 'For I had frequently a Consciousness rising up within me, that the Debate was equally vain on both Sides, doing no more real Good to the one than to the other, not being able to imagine, that a Set of scholastic, logical Opinions about History, Facts, Doctrines, and Institutions of the Church, or a Set of logical Objection against them, were of any Significancy towards making the Soul of Man either an external Angel of Heaven, or an external Devil of Hell' (7/153). This was nominal religion. As one interpreter of Law has noted, at this level there was 'no difference between the Christian, with or without the Trinity, and the Mahometan'.[19]

Law considered that the method practised by the modern defenders of Christianity implied a failure to recognise 'this great and decisive Truth, that Christianity is neither more nor less, than the Goodness of the Divine Life, Light and Love, living and working in my Soul' (7/117). On this account infidelity was present wherever the gospel had not been embraced with the heart with a corresponding dying to all that was earthly within and without. Accordingly, infidelity was compatible with 'verbal Assents and Consents to everything that is recorded in the New Testament'; it did not matter whether the infidel was a 'Professor of the Gospel, a Disciple of Zoraster, a Follower of Plato, a Jew, a Turk, or an Opposer of the Gospel-History' (7/152).

Law's defence of the gospel made redundant a whole range of modernist apologetics. The ground of argument was shifted from evidences and reasons to a basic distinction between real and nominal Christianity, between the spirit and the letter. One could either embrace Christianity as a 'sinner' or as a 'scholar'. The former way alone was taught by Christ: 'To be a defender of Christianity, is to be a Defender of Christ, but none can defend Him . . . than so far as he is his follower' (8/212). Law desired

18. Hoyles, *Edges of Augustanism*, chapter 7.
19. Hoyles, *Edges of Augustanism*, 101.

to be pragmatic, his concern was to recapture and awaken true piety, to establish 'real regenerate living members of the mystical body of Christ' (6/204).

For Law this was effected by a turn inwards. What was needed was a divine light to shine *within* to give true and full knowledge of the gospel. This was the light that arose with saving faith, which Law characterised as a hunger, thirst and complete 'given-overness' to the goodness and mercy of God in Christ Jesus. Such resignation to God effected the new birth of the Kingdom of God within; one became a 'true inward Christian', a true 'enthusiast', 'possessing all that one believes' (6/200). This was the evangelical core of Law's message as he had found in Boehme.[20] Yet it was precisely this core that John Wesley had taken issue with Law over, particularly in the light of his Aldersgate conversion of 1738 and his rejection of Law's mystical way.[21] Law's doctrine of the mystical divine spark and, in Wesley's view, the consequent failure to reckon with the depth of original sin; Law's recommendation of passive inner resignation to God, of trust through the 'dark night' of the soul without the assurance of justification; of a call to holiness without the power to realise it (in Wesley's view), all signalled for Wesley the Pelagian and legalistic tendencies in mysticism manifest through an 'inner' rather than an 'external' works-righteousness. Law, it seemed, embraced Boehme and the mystical way, Wesley 'was driven deeper into the Reformed tradition'.[22]

As important as the dispute with Wesley was, and in a sense remains, Law's achievement in the area of theological method ought not be overlooked. Law had recovered a correspondence between the interior form of faith and its linguistic expression. Christian doctrine was properly related to its founding reality. In this 'affectional transposition of doctrine'[23]

20. As Austin states, 'But the doctrine of Boehme, chiefly, when stripped of its alchemy and theosophy, is good Evangelical Protestant mysticism', though Austin goes on to note that Law 'attributed to Boehme much which he had already read in the earlier mystics but was earlier not ready to accept' (*William Law*, 26).

21. Tuttle provides an excellent up to date discussion of the Wesley\ Law dispute including important assessments of earlier studies by Eric Baker, *A Herald of the Evangelical Revival* (London: Epworth Press, 1948) and Brazier Gren, *John Wesley and William Law* (London: Epworth Press, 1945); see Tuttle, *Mysticism in Wesleyan Tradition*, (113–33).

22. Tuttle, *Mysticism in Wesleyan Tradition*, 116. What of course is interesting for Tuttle is the continuing influence of the mystical tradition on Wesley.

23. The phrase is Jaroslav Pelikan's to describe the recovery of the centrality of 'practice' in the definition of Christianity and hence the 'experimental' basis of Christian doctrine in the eighteenth and nineteenth centuries in Europe. See *The Christian Tradition: A*

one necessarily spoke of the Trinity from a penitent heart. Here was the vision of Church purified and interiorised. It was not a human creation but occurred as Christ was incarnated within the believer. The soul's communion with the Trinity was the one essential for blessedness of life. Participation with other Christians in the communion of saints was only *indirectly* achieved through participation in God. The believer no longer dwelt within the Church; rather the Church was immanent within the individual. Consequently, 'All Ways and Opinions, all Forms and Modes of Divine Worship, stand on the Outside of Religion' and as such they were 'helps' to the Kingdom, to be considered as 'gates' or 'guides' to that 'inward life' (6/223).

Phase Five: *The Divine Superabundance*

In 1740 Law retired to the village of his birth, King's Cliffe, later to be joined by the widow Hutcheson and Hester Gibbon. It was from this semi-monastic life of King's Cliffe that all of Law's mystical writings were composed.[24] In perhaps his most important writing of this period, *The Spirit of Love* (1752–1754),[25] Law's spiritual vision was transfixed and nourished by a God who in himself 'can be neither more nor less, nor anything else, but an eternal Will to all Goodness' (8/1). It was, in Law's view, more possible for the sun to give darkness than for God to give anything but goodness. This goodness, which was 'the whole nature of God' was an 'infinite Plenitude, or Fullness of Riches . . . an UNIVERSAL ALL' (8/61).

The characteristic feature of this Spirit of love was one of *overflow.* Thus the Spirit of love was eternal, unlimited and unbounded, an 'ever overflowing Ocean' of divine attributes, flowing as 'streams breaking out of the Abyss of Universal Love', a Trinity of Love for ever and ever giving forth all God's gifts giving 'Life to all Nature and Creature'(8/35). This was the Spirit of love which, said Law, had only one desire, 'to propagate itself', seeking nothing 'but its own increase'.

History of the Development of Doctrine, volume 5 (Chicago: Chicago University Press, 1971–88), 127ff & 146–62.

24. Such a context provided Law with great freedom to write though the relative isolation of his life from other critical minds meant that the later works of his life exemplify many of the characteristics of such an environment containing often brilliant insights, frequent repetition and large chunks that remain obscure and unusable.
25. The other important mystical works of this later period were *The Spirit of Prayer* (1749) and *The Way to Divine Knowledge* (1752) though his *An Humble, Earnest and Affectionate Address to the Clergy* (1761), picks up many of his late-life concerns.

Such a being of overflowing love confronted all wrath, evil, hatred and opposition 'only to overcome it with all its Blessings', in such a way that 'everything is as Oil to its Flame' (8/4). Accordingly Law located wrath not in God but in the creature, in its 'emptiness', 'want', 'impoverishment' and self-imposed 'exile'. It was the result of the individual's loss of the power of the Spirit of love (8/42). Wrath arose out of disorder. It was to be likened to a sore in the body that only erupted when the body was not in a right state (8/39). This view appeared to contradict many Scripture passages that attributed wrath to the Deity. The thrust of Law's argument was that the only experience of God available for human beings in their lostness—living according to nature without the life of God—was an experience of God as consuming fire (8/55). Yet God, argued Law, had no wrath in himself but continued to be one and the same 'infinite Fountain of Goodness, infinitely flowing forth in the Riches of his Love upon all and every life' (8\55).[26] Human sin was thus not the occasion for divine wrath but rather mercy, exemplified by the good physician who, out of love and care for the patient, necessarily administered that which was unpalatable and severe in order to restore health.

Accordingly, Law rejected a long established view of the atonement that had employed forensic categories and interpreted Christ's death as an offering paid to God to satisfy the just demands of his righteousness. In common with the mystical tradition Law moved in an entirely opposite direction. Forsaking the fabric of forensic terminology he re-orientated the traditional Scripture categories for atonement (ransom, sacrifice, price, propitiation) towards the natural sphere of human life. Since this was where wrath and sin arose, this was where the redemptive categories belonged. Thus, it was no longer God's righteousness that needed to be satisfied but humankind's original lost righteousness—that which rightly belonged to his 'paradisiacal' natural humanity. Redemption was neither an alteration of God's state nor a satisfaction of his righteousness, but rather a 'raising' of righteousness in humankind. Christ given for us was 'neither more nor less than Christ given into us' (8/74). The atonement was an event not 'outside' but 'within' the human being; a view it should be noted that was quite central to Wesley's break with Law's mysticism.[27] For

26. In Wesley's view the unbalanced exaltation of love and the mystic emphasis on a human response of love and self-discipline failed to take account of the full extent of human sin and the call to repentance. In other words Law, in Wesley's view, placed sanctification before justification. See Tuttle, *Mysticism in Wesleyan Tradition*, 118f.

27. 'The mystical substitution of this internal subjective element for faith in the atoning

Law medical rather than forensic categories predominated. Christ was the good physician, the 'natural remedy'. Christ eternally 'qualified' to be the redeemer, and 'actualised' this in the process of his incarnation and death (8\96). Christ brought perfection to the natural form and he achieved this in a natural way, by overcoming in his natural life all that the first Adam had lost.

Law believed that such a scheme of redemption was in accord with the requirements of the natural order of things. There was no appeal here to some supernatural redemption being effected from without through some transaction between God and Christ. On this account Christianity alone qualified as the one, true, 'natural religion'. It was a 'religion that had everything in it that the natural state needed' (8/91). The ground was thus, in Law's view, swept away from under the deist, who was justifiably critical of an unnatural scheme of redemption which imputed into the character of the Deity a wrath requiring appeasement. Such a view revealed an ignorance of the most fundamental doctrine of the gospel. If held, it could easily become in some a pretext for licentiousness and infidelity, in others, a source of superstition and fear. Perhaps most importantly, such a view, by falsely transferring responsibility away from human beings to God, obscured the calling of the Christian to an absolute resignation to God and renunciation of the world. In this way the demands of truth and piety were falsely ruptured.

As the logic of this stance was further unravelled, it filtered through the web of a doctrinal tradition. The familiar doctrines of election and reprobation underwent significant modification. Election and reprobation were no longer related to particular individuals or divisions of people, but rather referred to everyone as they were constituted according to their earthly and heavenly nature. A person, according to his or her earthly nature, was reprobate. Election belonged to a person in so far as he or she had the heavenly seed of the Word of God. In this scheme of redemption, that which was elect was brought to full birth, that which was reprobated perished. This was Law's hermeneutical key to the Old Testament passages which spoke of the election of Abel, Isaac and Jacob and the reprobation of Cain, Ishmael and Esau. All that was said of them was 'only as they are figures of the earthly Nature, and heavenly seed in every Man. For nothing is reprobated in Cain, but that very same which is reprobated in Abel,

work is the crucial issue in Wesley's break with mysticism', according to Tuttle, *Mysticism in Wesleyan Tradition* (116) who goes on to note that Law's soteriology 'lacked any concept of a substitutionary atonement'.

viz, the earthly Nature; nor is anything elected in Jacob, but that very same which is elected in Esau viz, the heavenly Seed' (8\103). The Spirit of love had an appropriate and quite particular doctrinal form for Law. Overflow at the level of language cast the tradition in a new and arresting light.

Law, the mystic Christian, had charted a way back to the origins of faith and theological creativity. On his account true Christian discipleship could not be 'rationally apprehended' nor 'historically known' but was only 'experimentally found' (7/262). Yet such a way could be dangerous, open to all kinds of wild excess and arbitrariness. To find God experimentally was a matter of being rightly bonded to God. In Christian redemption this re-bonding was achieved. A double movement was involved: from one side the heavenly divine life offered itself again to the 'inward' person; from the human side came a hope, faith and desire, a 'hungering, and thirsting, stretching after, and calling upon this Divine and Heavenly life' (7\190). Thus the turn inward was *simultaneously* a movement of the heart to its centre in God and the emergence of that centre into the foreground of a person's willing, desiring and thinking. In this double turning the divine-human bond was actualised. Presupposed here was an original reciprocity between the divine and human life which constituted the basis of interior apprehension of God. However, the turn inwards was not simply a retreat into subjectivism. Law recognised that there was a kind of turning inward which was nothing more than a turn of the self to its own will and reason as seen, for example, in fanciful imaginings of the deist.[28] True inwardness demanded a different orientation in which the will and desire were directed towards God.

However, the experimental way did not render human imagination null and void. As Law himself had stated, 'In Will, Imagination, and Desire, consists the Life, or fiery Driving of every intelligent Creature' (6/197). As such, Law considered imagination and desire 'the greatest reality we have . . . the true Formers and Raisers of all that is real and solid in us' (6/134). The fall was not occasioned by the intrusion of imagination into human life, but more properly by a failure in its direction. Indeed, Law's view of

28. Thus, in the *Spirit of Love* (8\93) Law argued that deism was false, 'a fanatic product of pure Imagination . . . because it quite disregards the *Nature* of Things, stands wholly upon a *supernatural* Ground', going above and contrary to the 'Powers of nature'. The self-seeking rationalism of deism failed to identify the mode of God's presence in the world. As a result the god of deism was the product of a fanciful projection. Elsewhere Law noted that the turn inwards, in so far as it was not directed to the divine will, could 'only have such a life, Spirit and Blessing from God, as a *Thistle* has from the *Sun*' (6\62).

an original 'paradisiacal' reciprocity between God and human life drew creative human capacity, particularly the God-directed imagination, into a vital link with the creative activity of God. A correspondence was presupposed: 'Our own Will, and desirous Imagination, when they work and create in us a settled Aversion, or fixed love of anything, resemble in some Degree, the Creating Power of God, which makes Things out of itself, or its own working Desire. And our Will, and working Imagination could not have the Power that it has now even after the Fall, but because it is a product, or Spark of that first Divine Will or Desire which is omnipotent' (6/72). The imagination was thus at the centre of human creative capacity, giving shape and form to reality. The regeneration of this capacity was therefore critical for godly life.

Clearly Law's experimental way had a regenerative effect on human life. The mystical way was not simply the pathway to right apprehension of God but also the means to a recovery of the lost or hidden, and true self. It was in fact the recovery of that holy humanity originally derived from Christ and restored in redemption in the form of a person's 'heavenly will'. This was not an arbitrary subjectivism but rather the recovery of a rightly formed and animated subjectivity. Hence for Law, 'nothing is the Way to God, but our heart. God is nowhere else to be found; and the Heart itself cannot find Him, or be helped by any Thing else to find Him, but by its own Love of Him, Faith in Him, Dependence upon Him, Resignation to Him, and Expectation of all from Him' (8/128).

Such, for Law, was the 'simplicity of faith'. The turn inwards in patience, meekness, humility and resignation was a turn to Christ. It was thus simultaneously praise of God and conversion to God. In this simple turning the Spirit of prayer (which Law depicted as the desire of the soul turned to God) became the occasion for the celebration of the 'marriage feast'. Here humankind entered into the highest state of union with God, referred to by Law as 'the BirthDay of the Spirit of Love in our Souls' (8/131). The Spirit of Prayer and the Spirit of Love coalesced in resignation to God. The form of this meeting was the impress in the soul of the image and likeness of the holy Trinity.

The apprehension of faith entailed both a right engagement of self with God (in other-directedness), and knowledge of the right self (the heavenly will) that is, a double and interrelated knowledge of God and self. What the self discovered was that its life and reality were derived from God. In this discovery the self was not annihilated but released from its own narrowness and rigidity.[29] Mystical union did not entail loss of identity but its transformation and freedom. Law's achievement was to universalise the possibility of living as a Christian in the Church. The one simple way was not only absolutely necessary, it was also absolutely possible, and possibly irresistible.

Part 2: Law and the contemporary scene

Most obviously this overview of Law's theological pilgrimage has highlighted the dynamics of personal transformation, some of the critical developments in Law's embrace of Christian mysticism and the implications this had for his handling of the inherited theological tradition. Through the five phases of his journey we observe his opening into successively richer and fuller forms of religious life. His spiritual and theological development would make for a very interesting analysis in the light of modern understandings of the dynamics of change and stages of faith. Fundamentally we observe a maturing in his faith expressed through deeper insight into the presence and work of God in his life and a growing freedom in faith expressed through a deeper appreciation of his connectedness in the Spirit with all Christians, and especially those who had already, in their own way, set out on the mystical way.

For Law the uniqueness of the gospel was to be identified in its capacity to bond people together regardless of their particular ecclesial affiliation, status in life or educational attainment. However, it was Law's conviction that, in his context, this bond could only be fully realised as religious life recovered its 'soul'. In this respect the move to interiority was a recovery of what Baron von Hugel later referred to as 'the mystical element of religion'.[30]In this manoeuvre Law overcame the barrenness of the prevailing institutional Christianity and discovered a richer form of life with God.[31] Furthermore, in so far as this form of life entailed a recovery

29. For further discussion on this issue see the perceptive comments on Law by P Grant in *The Literature of Mysticism in the Western Tradition* (London: Macmillan Press, 1983), 93.
30. Baron von Hugel, *The Mystical Element of Religion as Studied in Saint Catherine of Genoa and Her Friends*, volume 1 (London: JM Dent & Sons, 1927), chapter 2.
31. Space does not permit an adequate critique of Law though some of Wesley's disputes with Law have been referred to earlier and in our present context relate to the enduring appeal of mysticism as a contemporary form of self-help. This is not intended to be a harsh judgement but it remains a danger. However, it is as well to note that there are certain other difficulties that will eventually have to be faced by those who pursue the

of a sacramental understanding of the world, in which the divine presence was mediated through nature, history and human life, it would be reasonable to expect that the mystical way might have an important role in the renewal of the sacraments within religious life. This is a topic that goes beyond the confines of this article but well worth pursuing in its own right.

This mystical element in religion has been an enduring and controversial feature of the Christian tradition. Some of the reasons are not difficult to discern and can be located in the potential disruption and challenge the mystical way poses for rigidly structured and powerful institutional forms of religion that are resistant to change and have heavy investments in preserving the status quo. However, in such a context the mystical way simply stands as a constant reminder that there is in fact a dialectical relation in Christianity between what has been referred to earlier as the tradition of inwardness and a vigorous externality tradition. The operation of this dialectic generates an inevitable conflict within Christianity and of course the possibility of constant reformation and creative advance in new contexts.

The mystical way remains an option for many today and significantly complicates notions of religious plurality in Australia. Clearly our context is not simply one of a variety of different religions but rather different religions with significant internal differentiations. Moreover, to the extent that such internal variation includes what has been described above as a dimension of inwardness, it is clear that there exists another level beyond the recognised institutional forms and practices, which both links the different religions and generates further variety.

Perhaps there is a depth religious experience of God that bonds all those who, for example, take the plunge and pursue the mystical way in religion and discover with Law the reality of God as the 'Abyssal all'; Boehme's *ungrund*, the 'ground of all things'. Certainly this possibility has

---

tradition of Law and the mystics. For example, it is not clear how the way of personal renewal within crumbling institutional structures offered by mysticism can in fact generate the sort of communal life that might be expected within a Christian tradition which proclaims the gospel of a God whose *communio* of being finds concrete expression in human communities of reconciliation. For in such communities people do not simply participate in community *indirectly* through God—as in Law and the mystical way more generally—but are bonded with the divine life *in and through the bonds with each other and corporate sacramental life.* Can then the mystical way generate new community in which sacraments are have a renewed importance? This is a major issue. The other obvious challenge is somewhat related and concerns the capacity of Law's mysticism to shed its Neoplatonism and give a full and proper account of bodily life which is not so fixated on the renunciation of the material order.

operated as an important presupposition for both Catholic and Protestant theologians in the past.[32] In a context of religious pluralism such an approach has a natural appeal and may prove worthwhile and enduring. However, George Lindbeck has raised questions about the assumption of a primary experience of God common across the religious spectrum.[33] He has argued that it is the communities of faith with their own quite particular stories, grammar and symbols that provide access to and generate forms of experience of God that are simply not transferable. Lindbeck's proposal is important and requires further theological testing. In this regard theologians of the Church have a responsibility to attend more carefully to the dynamics of the Christian mystical way.

In an age of so much 'pop mysticism' the form and inner vitality of the specifically Christian mystical tradition needs far greater attention. It is precisely here that the case of William Law might be of value as we discern the Way today. Here I would point to the recovery by Law of a sense of the presence of God in human life. In the context of barren and sterile nominalism in religion Law's recovery of the category of presence was critical for the vitality and wholeness of Christian faith. This was precisely the category that had been lost in eighteenth century Deism. The transcendent God had, under the pressure of a powerful rationalism, disappeared from view, so to speak. Certainly, such a God had proved increasingly resistant to access. The forms of religion had been emptied of significance; they no longer mediated God's presence but rather God's absence. The outward forms had, in Law's own words, the character, at best, of 'venerable remains' of the 'ministration of the Spirit'. Law had recovered God's saving presence, not by strong reassertion of a naïve, 'simple' presence but by recovery of the domain in which the very desire for 'presence' was relevant to human life that is, in the experience of absence.[34] In this region of human subjectivity Law had identified the hunger and thirst for a presence which seemed unavailable. Yet what had proven unavailable at one level, Law recovered at another. Moreover, this mystical way recovered not merely God's presence but the reciprocity between divine absence and

32. In a general way Rahner, Lonergan, Tillich and Tracey follow this line which can be traced in modern theology to Schleiermacher's theological program.

33. George Lindbeck, *The Nature of Doctrine: Religion and Theology in a Post Liberal Age* (London: SPCK, 1984), 32.

34. See the important discussion of the relation between God's presence and absence in Karl Barth and contemporary thought by Walter Lowe, *Theology and Difference: The Wound of Reason* (Indiana University Press, 1993), chapters 1 and 2.

presence that obtains within the doctrine of God in the Christian tradition. Law's mysticism had charted a pathway into the fullness of life with God. At the heart of this was neither an experience of God's 'simple' presence *or* 'simple' absence, but the experience of the fullness of divine being who was nothing but overflowing gracious love, incarnated in Christ and enlivened by the Spirit. Thus, could Law state: 'we know the Trinity in ourselves' (5/82). It was the sheer abundance of God's particular triune presence that gave rise to the elusive and alluring absence of the Spirit of Love who in turn enticed and called one deeper into the Spirit of Prayer. In other words, the quite unique and particular character of the God present for faith generates the mystic believer's experience of an unsurpassable presence which includes an irreducible absence. The former constituted the presupposition of Wesley's doctrine of assurance whereas the latter required Law's doctrine of faithful resignation to God. The conditions for such religious experience can be located in the quite radical mode of God's presence that comes to form in the Christian doctrine of the Trinity.

Law's project looks decidedly modern, even perhaps post-modern. In a world where the experience of God's absence provides the backdrop for much religious and theological discourse; where the forces of religious fundamentalism engage in massive reassertion of God's presence in quite rigid and binding forms; where many still harbour the hope of a presence that sustains; whilst the vast majority have capitulated to the 'Kingdom of Nothingness'[35], the Christian mystical tradition is a reminder that there is another way through the many competing religious claims of our day both within and across the religious divides. Perhaps the intuitions of our poets and theologians are on track when they speak of an 'Australian mysticism'.[36] However, the form it takes will be critical. Simply to proclaim that 'my way is as good as yours' and 'anything will do' points more to a lack of nerve than real freedom of spirit. At precisely this point Christians have a responsibility to imaginatively and faithfully braid the riches of their inheritance of the mystery of the gospel with contemporary life. This will have to be done with sensitivity and openness, both of which require a new buoyancy in the same Spirit of Love who makes a world of difference in every context. Perhaps we will find, like Law, new and surprising bonds in the same Spirit who raised Jesus from the dead.

35. Manning Clark's well-known phrase, quoted by John Thornhill in *Making Australia: Exploring Our National Conversation* (Millennium Books, 1992), 169.

36. See, for example, Tony Kelly, 'Australian Mysticism' in *A New Imagining: Towards an Australian Spirituality* (Melbourne: Collins Dove, 1990), chapter 8.

Chapter Twelve
The Passions: A Cautionary Note for Disciples

Passionate Discipleship

Most of the difficult struggles and tensions we live with are the common lot of human beings. This essay returns to the ancient and neglected theme of the passions. The early church spiritual writers had quite a bit to say about the passions and how they needed to be properly directed for a life of love and hope. Our contemporary appeal to the passions offers a more positive spin but it was not always so. I find much that resonates on the theme of the passions with contemporary insights from psychology, spiritual direction and general wisdom. If we are to be passionate disciples then we might as well know what that could look like and what St Paul really meant when he spoke of crucifying the passions.

The passions: A personal note[1]

This topic rarely surfaces today. Indeed, interest in the 'passions' seems to have disappeared from our cultural discourse. As we shall see in this essay we are more familiar with the language of the 'emotions'; their intelligence and significance in our lives. Specifying the relationship between the passions and the emotions is more difficult, but more of that in a moment. This paper arose out a quest to explore and understand the significance of the passions in my own life and work. I discovered over many years that the energies of my life could be harnessed for good or ill, or could overwhelm me in ways that could at times induce depression and/or paralysis. Could such experiences be relevant to the passions? This was an important question for me. There was another dimension to the passions that I wanted to understand better. This concerned the almost endemic split in

1. I am grateful to my daughter Ruth for reading and commenting on an earlier draft of this essay and encouraging me to make it more personal and concrete.

Christianity between the body and the soul and the long-standing negative assessment of the body. This split could be traced like a red thread throughout the history of faith. It was troubling for me as a theologian and at a personal level. I had discovered in mid-life that my own heritage had strong roots, to my surprise, in Primitive Methodism on one side and Scottish Presbyterianism on the other. These traditions had melded into a middle-of-the-road sacramental and society orientated Anglicanism of my childhood. I came to value the different threads in my own spiritual life. However, I also came to recognise that my inherited spiritual traditions could quite easily fall prey to an incipient moralism which only endorsed and encouraged the body/soul split. This meant that when I heard the words of the Apostle to 'crucify the sinful nature with its passions and desires' (Galatians 5:24) I heard this as a call to renounce life in the body as an inherently dangerous and unwelcome existence. I knew I was not alone in this. I also observed that one could react in an entirely opposite way and in the name of celebration of the body justify all kinds of unhealthy behaviour—as far as I could judge!

For the above reasons I have more than a passing interest in the passions. This essay is an attempt to unravel some of the issues surrounding the theme. After a preliminary discussion of the concept of the passions in contemporary literature I return to the ancient tradition on the passions and take a closer look at what became known as the 'deadly sins'. I have found this more concrete approach illuminating and surprisingly relevant in answering questions about human well being and what it means to follow the God who loves beyond measure, a God who loves the whole of us, not just selected parts. In this sense I am searching for a way to deal openly with the passions and clarify what the Pauline injunction to 'crucify the flesh with its passions' might entail and importantly what it does not require. I take this to be a critical matter for those who want to live a life of freedom and joy amidst the challenges and tensions of life on planet earth. The disciple of Jesus is called to precisely this kind of life and so this inquiry has something of the character of a cautionary note for would be disciples.

Passions, emotions and desire: some contemporary insights

In everyday use the word 'passion' conjures up a variety of images and ideas: intense emotions (for example, anger) and habits of mind. We often speak of someone playing sport with plenty of passion. We may remark that a person has a passionate desire to serve the poor. You hear the statement: 'they were passionate lovers'; or 'someone has a passion for chocolate or motorbikes'. In contemporary culture 'passion' is regularly used to refer to any strong emotion usually in a positive sense. It seems to have attained the status of a virtue.

This approach to the passions seems to inform the American philosopher, Martha Nussbaum recent work *Upheaval of Thought: The Intelligence of the Emotions*.[2] Nussbaum offers a *tour de force* of human life and the emotions which 'shape the landscape of our mental and social lives'.[3] For Nussbaum the emotions are not alien forces but highly discriminatory responses to what is of value and importance. In particular, she explores compassion and love and in the process discusses pride, disgust, mercy, revenge, shame, fear, grief and anger, to name but a few. These emotions have cognitive as well as affective elements. Her work is remarkable for its breadth and clarity. What about the passions in relation to emotions? In a book of 800 pages the index gives the clue: on 'passions', see 'emotions'. Clearly for Nussbaum the two terms are synonymous and assessed in a positive light. The only negative assessment on the passions occurs in her use of the phrase 'the bondage of the passions'[4] in relation to Spinoza's theory of the emotions.

Popular usage offers a positive twist on the passions and links it closely to intense emotions. However, etymologically the concept of passion is more nuanced and interesting. Passion comes from the Latin *passi* (*passin*, *passus*) pertaining to sufferings or 'an undergoing'. In the past it was often related to the sufferings of Jesus or a martyr. From Late Latin it was also associated with sinful desire. Synonyms are fervor, fire, zeal, ardor. These nouns denote powerful, intense emotion. It is the sense of being overwhelmed or a suffering undergone that is critical. Hence being subject to the passions has traditionally been understood as an experience of being overwhelmed. This often involves inner disturbance and loss of control. The ancients viewed this as a failure of practical reason to check and steer primal forces of desire and repulsion. Whatever we may think of this assessment one thing seems to be clear. There has been a serious disconnect between the passions and practical reason and a consequent loss of a more integrating account of the relationship between the passions and reason.

2. Martha Nussbaum, *Upheaval of Thought: The Intelligence of the Emotions* (Cambridge: Cambridge University Press, 2001).
3. Nussbaum, *Upheaval of Thought*,
4. Nussbaum, *Upheaval of Thought*,

It has also led to confusion about the role and function of the passions in our life.

In 1984 the philosopher and psychiatrist Roberto Unger wrote a book, *Passion: An essay on Personality*[5]. He noted that 'passion' has often been viewed negatively and understood as a threat to reason. 'The passions lead people to act in ways that they themselves in more reflective moments would reject as unrealistic or too risky. They prompt people to violate their own standards of self-interest. They involve us in relationships that go far beyond what our everyday assumptions about the world take to be possible.'[6] Unger continues: 'for all their capacity to surprise, however, the passions can rarely be defended as devices of a utopian prospect—the outward signs and instruments of a deliberate effort to change the established world. They are more like a recurrent darkening of sight than an alternative vision.[7] The key here is the phrase, 'a recurrent darkening of sight'. It is as if the passions can overwhelm us with the result that we think, feel and act in ways that 'violate their own standards of self-interest'. This picks up a consistent theme in the ancient tradition, which we shall come to in a moment. Unger's work was an attempt to reinterpret the ancient tradition of the passions. It was more in line with Nussbaum and other contemporary writers who view the passions as strong emotions, not necessarily negative, which reveal to us truth about the self and the world. The result is a generally positive assessment of the passions. Certainly these days the passions appear as an attractive dimension of the human life. Indeed we often lament the loss of passion(s).[8] We admire those who seem to have it, signifying as it often does, energy and strength of character.

Robert Solomon's examination of the passions addresses the 'myth of the passions' that consigns them to second place in relation to notions of 'cool' rationality and makes them the subject of 'unchallenged critical abuse'.[9] Solomon sets out on a different tack arguing that the passions 'are the defining *structures* of our existence, in fact, *identical* to the intellectual structures'.[10] For Solomon the passions are essentially emotions bearing

5. Roberto Unger, *Passion: An Essay on Personality* (The Free Press, 1986).
6. Unger, *Passion*, 101.
7. Unger, *Passion*, 101.
8. The twentieth century Spanish play writer Fedierico Garcia Lorca refers to Greek theatre overflowing with a passion that seems to have been lost in contemporary western theatre. See Ian Gibson, *Federico García Lorca* (London: Faber & Faber, 1989).
9. Robert C Solomon, *The Passions: Emotions and the Meaning of Life*, second edition (Indianapolis, Indiana, Hackett Publisher, 1993), preface 19.
10. Solomon, *The Passions*, 5.

life's meaning rather than 'dangerous and disruptive forces'.[11] For this author human life 'has its meaning in our passions and nowhere else' and as such 'the passions are not to be separated from reason; they are to be welded together in a single unit'.[12] Solomon wants to map out a new 'rational romanticism' that gives a more adequate appraisal of the importance of the passions for the meaning of our lives. Passions as emotions 'are judgments, not blind or irrational forces that victimise us. Emotions are the life forces of the soul, the source of most of our values . . . the basis of most other passions'.[13] On this approach 'moods are but generalised emotions' and emotions, rather than distorting reality and leading us astray are responsible for it, create our interests and our purposes.[14] As such the passions ought not be played off against reason but constitute the subject matter of our reasoning. Thus he concludes that what 'is called "reason" is the passions enlightened, "illuminated" by reflection and supported by a perspicacious deliberation that the emotions in their urgency normally exclude'.[15] Solomon's approach does not lead him to an undifferentiated approach to the passions, as if all were equally acceptable. Indeed he recognises that the constitutive emotions of life can not only generate self-understanding but also be pathological.[16]

Solomon's more positive appraisal of the passions is echoed in Unger and more powerfully in Nausbaum. Common to all three is the desire to move beyond an ancient psychology with its overly simple distinction between reason and the passions. What is sought is a more nuanced and sophisticated account of the passions in the light of modern psychology. Furthermore, in contemporary discussion the passions seem to have undergone a transposition into emotions which are understood as constitutive of meaning and self-understanding.

The foregoing developments can be observed in recent discussions of emotions, desire, the senses and the passions in the area of pastoral psychology and Christian spirituality.[17] Thus Robert Roberts refers to a

11. Solomon, *The Passions*, 10.
12. Solomon, *The Passions*, 15.
13. Solomon, *The Passions*, 15.
14. Solomon, *The Passions*, 15.
15. Solomon, *The Passions*, 15.
16. See his discussion in the final chapter of the book, 'The Emotional Register'.
17. Timothy J Gorringe, *The Education of Desire* (London: SCM, 2001); Philip Sheldrake, *Befriending our Desires* (London: Darton, Longman and Todd, 2001); Robert C

passion as 'a concern that can give a person's life a centre, can integrate and focus the personality and give a person "character"'.[18] He appeals to Kierkegaard's notion of 'essential passion' to identify that which makes a 'genuine human being', that is, the kind of person we are supposed to be.[19] While Roberts can also speak of instances where a passion 'is positively *im*moral'[20] for this writer the passions are fundamentally positive dispositions and/or character traits. What about the emotions? For Roberts emotions 'are literally *pass*ions in an older sense of the word—that is, undergoings, events that happen to us, rather than *act*ions that we perform'.[21] Roberts wants to speak positively about 'Christian emotions' being based on a 'Christian passion' concerning desire for God's Kingdom.[22] But exactly how is 'desire' related to the passions and the senses (taste, touch, smell, hearing, sight)? Philip Sheldrake sees desire as foundational for our life and can speak of a continuum in desire from 'faint wishes' to 'powerful passions'.[23] The matter becomes sharper when he differentiates different levels of desire, the deepest being 'authentic desire' that opens us up to God's love.[24] In Timothy Gorringe's exploration of the senses he recognises that in the biblical tradition desire is overwhelmingly viewed in a negative light.[25] In his nuanced and insightful discussion the senses appear to function as the media through which desire is manifest. Whether or not such desire becomes a passion depends on the form and content of the desire. On Gorringe's account the human project becomes one of educating our desires in order that they might be orientated to the love of God.[26] His discussion of desire and the misuse of the senses has significant overlap with an earlier ages' inquiry into the passions. Roberts, Sheldrake and Gorringe exemplify, in different ways, a more positive assessment of the passions in relation to desire, emotions and the senses. In this respect they are in company with contemporary voices from other disciplines. It is noticeable that their examination of desire, emotions and the senses remains, for the

Roberts, *Spiritual Emotions: A Psychology of Christian Virtues* (Grand Rapids, MI: Eerdmans, 2007).

18. Roberts, *Spiritual Emotions*, 17.
19. Roberts, *Spiritual Emotions*, 18.
20. Roberts, *Spiritual Emotions*, 18.
21. Roberts, *Spiritual Emotions*, 22.
22. Roberts, *Spiritual Emotions*, 31.
23. Sheldrake, *Befriending our Desires*, 20.
24. Sheldrake, *Befriending our Desires*, 29.
25. Gorringe, *Education of Desire*, 85.
26. Gorringe, *Education of Desire*, chapter 4.

most part, unrelated to their own inherited tradition of discourse on the passions. It seems to have slipped out of view. As welcome as such insights are it is also worth noting that the conceptual structure for understanding the passions developed by contemporary commentators does not negate the significance of the passions but rather intensifies the analysis, albeit with a different repertoire of language. It is in the process of deciphering the dynamics of the emotions that the most interesting and rewarding insights are to be found concerning human behaviour, its motivations and effects. Whether it is emotions or passions it becomes crystal clear that, precisely because they have such a constitutive role in the meaning and direction of our lives they exert immense power for good and ill. It is precisely at this point that contemporary insight on the passions feeds off an ancient wisdom which has more to offer than is usually recognised. To this longer tradition I now wish to turn.

'Face to face' with the passions: the ancient tradition

In turning to the ancient tradition of the passions I am aware that this was never a topic for detached critical assessment in earlier times. It was invariably an inquiry related to deeply personal and pastoral concerns, about one's well-being and what made for a good life. What part did the passions play in this quest? Coming to terms with this in my own life has been a continuing challenge. For example, finding ways to recognise and release the affective and emotional dimensions of my life has raised questions for me about the underlying passions, how they are hidden or suppressed but yet what power they exert. How such things might be linked to faith in God, prayer, conversation and healing (for example, of memories) has been important to me. It is at this point that the ancient tradition might, I believe, have something of value to say. Indeed it may be that the tradition on the passions offers some surprising insights which have largely been ignored in our modern world. My chief companion here is an American United Methodist theologian Roberta Bondi. In a remarkable little book, *To Love as God Loves: Conversations with the Early Church*,[27] Bondi uncovers the ancient tradition of prayer, love and the passions. In particular she considers the writings of those counter-cultural misfits of the early church who left the habitations of 'normal' society for a differ-

27. Roberta Bondi, *To Love as God Loves: Conversations with the early church* (Minneapolis: Fortress Press, 1987).

ent life, the early desert fathers and mothers. They went in search of a deeper life with God. What they discovered was wisdom not only about the Divine but also about themselves and life in the world. Wherever they went would-be disciples followed them; people thirsty for wisdom, hungry for true and lasting friendships. The desert fathers and mothers came face-to-face with the 'passions'. Bondi's inquiry reveals that our monastic forebears would not speak of a 'passion for life'. For them the word passion carries a negative meaning most of the time. Why? Because for them a passion has, as its chief characteristic, what we have already noted as the 'perversion of vision and destruction of love', 'a recurrent darkening of sight' For the monastics a passion may include a strong emotion, a state of mind, an habitual action, anger, forgetfulness, gossip, and depression.[28] .

This ancient approach meant that strong emotions, which accompany love, lead to love or express love, are never passions. A strong desire to serve the poor is not a passion. Mercy, hospitality, and remorse so strong that it causes a torrent of tears—none of these belong to the passions because of their relationship to love. On the other hand, over-religiosity, scrupulousness about one's own righteousness, indifference to the well-being of others, judgmental attitudes, all these are passions that blind us to love. The point here is that a proper integration of reason and passion enables increased capacity to love.

The early monastics did not invent this approach to the passions but in line with popular psychology they went back to Plato and Aristotle. One of the most frequent metaphors to illustrate human life and passions was a charioteer driving a chariot pulled by two horses. The two horses are the basic impulses or life forces within us. They enable us to interact with the world, drawing things into us (desire, the 'appetitive'), and pushing ourselves against other things (anger, 'spirited'). These two horses are far more than surface emotions: I want that car, dress, home, and so on; I am angry with that person. Rather, they are two sources of energy, one bringing the world to us, the other pushing against it. So desire (anger, sexual attraction), repulsion, compassion and contempt are fuelled by such drives. For the ancients these impulses are blind. We share these instinctual forces with the animal world. We cannot do without them. When they function as they are meant to, they are good horses for the chariot.

Driving the chariot is reason. But the 'reason' referred to is not what we come to associate with the term. The ancient notion of reason is richer

28. Roberta Bondi, *To Love as God Loves*, chapter 2.

and deeper than merely capacity for logical thought. Reason includes the capacity for seeing the world and responding to it (not a cold rational operation). Reason enables us to respond to the world not simply at the level of physical needs and desires but consciously and in a manner that honours the human person as a sentient being capable of discerning goodness and acting accordingly. The illumined reason enables us to see and know God, to see as God sees, to love God and others.[29] So acts of compassion, forgiveness, worship, and insight into others, all stem from reason fuelled by the appetitive and spirited energies of life. If reason is overthrown by the horses, the result is chaos: the energies of desire and anger become the source of power for destructive passions. Human personality is turned over to these passions; passions assault, victimise and overwhelm the self. In this way the passions can grip our life and we become blind to their impact and influence. Furthermore, such passions can never be satisfied, they remain insatiable. In our times we know this by different names: addictions, compulsive disorders. The cycle of desire is continuous and lifelong.

As a result in the ancient tradition the passions are in need of reform and direction (not negation!) from reason. Reason enables us to see clearly, and serve the good and true. The one who lives like this lives in love. Thus we have on the one hand passions which blind us to love and truth. On the other hand reason, serving love, opens our eyes to truth. So for the ancients 'love is never blind', rather love is the way to see truly and act virtuously. The passions blind us to seeing truly. It is easy to make a mistake at precisely this point. It is the passions un-integrated with reason that cloud the vision and distort the truth. In like manner reason, disconnected from the elemental life force of the passions, generates a barren and vacuous world. But how does this measure up with the enchantment of love spoken of by William James?

> Every Jack sees in his own particular Jill charms and perfections to the enchantment of which we stolid onlookers are stone-cold. And which has the superior view of the absolute truth, he or we? Which has the more vital insight into the nature of Jill's existence, as a fact? Is he in excess, being in this matter a maniac? Or are we in defect,

29. This understanding of reason that has been largely lost in the modern period, along with the emergence of an overly rationalistic logic. But this was patently not the way in which the category of reason operated in earlier times.

> being victims of a pathological anesthesia as regards Jill's magical importance? Surely the latter; surely to Jack are the profounder truths revealed; surely poor Jill's palpitating little life-throbs are among the wonders of creation, are worthy of this sympathetic interest; and it is to our shame that the rest of us cannot feel like Jack. For Jack realises Jill concretely, and we do not. He struggles towards a union with her inner life, divining her feelings, anticipating her desires, understanding her limits as manfully as he can, and yet inadequately too; for he is also afflicted with some blindness, even here. Whilst we, dead clods that we are, do not even seek after these things, but are contented that that portion of eternal fact named Jill should be for us as if it were not. Jill, who knows her inner life, knows that Jack's way of taking it— so importantly—is the true and serious way; and she responds to truth in him by taking him truly and seriously too. May the ancient blindness never wrap its clouds about either of them again! Where would any of *us* be, were there no one willing to know us as we really are or ready to repay us for *our* insight by making recognisant return? We ought, all of us, to realise each other in this intense, pathetic, and important way.[30]

James suggests that the blindness of the enchanted lover is the way to see and appreciate the deeper truth about another. Does he thus confirm the maxim that 'love is blind' and that 'reason' is an unwelcome intrusion? And is this simply that 'intense, pathetic and important way' in which we are humans? This has echoes of Solomon's earlier positive appreciation of the passions as constitutive of the meaning we attach to self and others. However, Solomon was also clear that this role of the passions did not negate reason but presumed a deeper integration. Something similar seems to be operating when James refers to Jack's insight into the 'concrete' person of Jill that is the real Jill. This appreciation and acceptance of the other 'in the concrete' presumes a synthesis beyond the disjunctions of blind love, passion and reason.

Modern psychology and ancient understandings of the person are very different. This is reflected in different understandings of the passions as

30. William James, *Talks to Teachers on Psychology* (London: Longmans, Green and Co, 1908), 267.

discussed earlier in this essay. But even after Freud's inquiries into the conscious and unconscious (the *id, ego, superego*) there remains the common recognition of the power of the underlying energies of desire and anger, 'the longed for' and 'the movement against the world'. Much more could be said. The passions have a developmental process of their own. Temptation is not a passion or sin for the ancients. It is so only when it takes root and becomes an obsession. Abba Poemen was once asked about what 'do not repay evil for evil' meant. He responded by outlining how a passion grows:

> Passions work in four stages—first, in the heart; secondly, in the face; thirdly, in words; and fourthly, it is essential not to render evil for evil in deeds. If you can purify your heart, passion will not come into your expression; but if it comes into your face, take care not to speak; but if you do speak, cut the conversation short in case you render evil for evil [31]

Finally, Bondi notes that the ancient monastics spoke little about sin and about God being displeased or hurt by our sin. Rather it is we who are caught in the passions. 'It is we who are God's image who are injured'[32]. God's character is mercy, for God sees us as we are and comes to us in our weakness. How then does this play itself out in the concrete realities of life in the body? I turn now to this matter with a brief account of the 'deadly sins'.

Passions and the 'deadly sins'

In earlier centuries the concept of the 'deadly sins' was the way in which the passions were usually discussed. What is a passion? How could you recognise one? Is there a dynamic in the passions that requires unmasking? Why makes the 'deadly sins' so deadly? How can we harness the passions in order that our lives may be strengthened with new energy and commitment? I believe there is value in such an inquiry, however brief, in order to put some flesh and bones on the idea of the passions as they operate in our lives. My concern is about identifying the way the elemental drives of life can be skewed and distorted and 'violate our self-interests' and the well being of others. In this section I follow Roberta Bondi's en-

31. Bondi, *To Love as God Loves*, 70.
32. Bondi, *To Love as God Loves*, 70.

gagement with the early monastics and the recent interpretation of the 'deadly vices' by the Oxford philosopher Gabriele Taylor.

Taylor provides an insightful and contemporary analysis of the so-called 'deadly vices' or as we are perhaps more familiar, the traditional 'deadly sins'.[33] Taylor discusses what it means to be 'in the grip of' or 'possessed by' deadly vices such as pride, envy, covetousness, anger, gluttony lust, and sloth. She highlights the disabling and self-destructive nature of the vices; the way in which the vices protect the self from painful discoveries; the manner in which the vices interfere with the order and harmony between reason and passion, and the distance and fracture the vices create between people. She notes, following Aquinas, that 'the overall defect was said to consist in inadequate control of reason over the passions, and the 'passions', in one form or another, seem indeed to be essentially constitutive of these vices'.[34] Whereas some vices—pride, envy, anger—'share their name with those of emotions; others—lust and gluttony—seem crucially concerned with indulgence and pleasure; sloth similarly involves a form of self indulgence, and covetousness implies limitless desire'.[35] She can speak about 'ordinary vices' and an 'excess of vices'.[36] On this account the vices constitute the 'passions' undirected by reason. In this sense 'passion' is a catch-all concept and Taylor helpfully shows how it is related to contemporary discussions of the will, action, moods, dispositions and emotions. To put some more flesh on the passions I want to consider for a moment the traditional deadly sins or vices as particular instances of the manifestation of the passions. The lists of the passions have been quite fluid, though the medieval church codified them into the seven deadly sins.[37] Much earlier the fourth-century monk, Evagrius Ponticus, reflected on the passions. Bondi, following Evagrius' list, discusses the passions. I want to briefly consider her approach and also draw upon Taylor's more recent work.

33. Gabriele Taylor, *Deadly Vices* (Oxford: Clarendon Press, 2006).
34. Taylor, *Deadly Vices*, 13.
35. Taylor, *Deadly Vices*, 13.
36. Taylor, *Deadly Vices*, 8f.
37. For a discussion of the development of the 'seven deadly sins' see Solomon Schimmel, *The Seven Deadly Sins: Jewish, Christian and Classical Reflections on Human* Psychology (Oxford: Oxford University Press, 1997).

Gluttony

The first sin of Adam and Eve was gluttony. The desire for an unnecessary variety in food was often associated with obsession with food that went beyond physical needs. In this passion food controlled the monk. Another desert theologian, John Cassian, spoke about three kinds of gluttons. First was the monk who broke his fast before the appointed hour and would sneak into the kitchens in search of food. Second was the monk who ate at the appointed hour but gorged himself. Finally, there was the monk who was extremely fussy about what food he would and would not eat. Not surprisingly on this interpretation gluttony appears as a passion common to many! An obsession with the enjoyment of the senses of the palate can blind someone to other things in life. Taylor sees the addiction to food as an indicator of the desire for nourishment. 'The glutton does not feel himself to be self-sufficient; on the contrary, in his view his self needs to be nourished'.[38] But what exactly is lacking for the self? 'What he [the glutton] wants is some more long-lasting pleasure or comfort, a health-giving and heart-warming pleasure. If this is what he needs then this is what he lacks.'[39] Of course, the pleasures of the palate can never deliver the long-lasting nourishment and affection sought by the glutton. The desire is insatiable and its social and political dimensions are evident. Whilst a culture of gluttony searches for elusive self-nourishment most of the world is starving and remains undernourished. This vice can significantly impact on the well being of others.

Impurity

Evagrius refers to this passion as 'lusting after bodies'. It drove the monastic that was committed to celibacy to engage in sexual acts. It could cause one to leave monastic life for marriage. So celibacy was an act of faith and sign of hope in God's promises in the face of death. Giving in to lust meant the abandonment of hope. This is not our world but 'lusting after bodies' is now made a lifestyle and celebrated. What has been lost are notions of fidelity, intimacy, sustainable relationships and appreciation of how friendship and intimate relationships evolve and mature over time.

Taylor notes that in the medieval tradition the vices of gluttony and lust, being sins of the flesh rather than the spirit, were considered 'less culpable than sins of the spirit', more 'warm-hearted sins' that, accord-

38. Taylor, *Deadly Vices*, 99.
39. Taylor, *Deadly Vices*, 99.

ing to Kant, could encourage social intercourse.[40] Taylor's consideration of lust includes an analysis of sexual desire and the underlying drive for union with another implicit therein. At the heart of this dynamic are the key elements of conquest and possession. But the satisfactions are fleeting. 'The particular partner of the moment deserves full attention since she represents all womanhood. But since she represents all womanhood any other representative will do as well, so there can be no reason for fidelity.'[41] Taylor suggests that this 'gives some support to the Kantian view that the lustful merely use their partners, and will cast them aside "as one casts aside a lemon which has been sucked dry"'.[42] Relationships for the lustful are neither significant nor enriching. 'They reflect a very meager self', that is, a sexual conqueror.[43] 'But even this identity is not secure, for the image of himself has to be constantly renewed. His search for confirmation as powerful is therefore doomed, and the lustful, like other vicious characters, turns out to have needs which are frustrated by his very attempts to meet them.'[44]

Avarice

The person who is blinded by avarice is unwilling to share resources because they are driven by an overriding desire for personal security. Evagrius says this comes from fear of the future. If I give away now, what will happen when I am old? This passion also makes people unwilling to accept help from others. The greed which causes blindness, causes people to believe that possessions actually provide more security than they do. Rampant materialism driven by the blindness of this passion is a feature of our modern western world. We are also familiar with the shame that comes from receiving charity and a culture contemptuous of those in need. But they are the very ones that Jesus had compassion for. The miserly avaricious are blind to the needs of others. Their investment in self-security ('the self assured of its possession') and personal protection is overwhelming. It results in a misdirected self-love which 'prompts a second, namely, the self-deception needed to protect the first self-love from being seen to be misplaced'.[45] Obsessive aquisitiveness conceals the deep

40. Taylor, *Deadly Vices*, 99.
41. Taylor, *Deadly Vices*, 105.
42. Taylor, *Deadly Vices*, 105.
43. Taylor, *Deadly Vices*, 107.
44. Taylor, *Deadly Vices*, 107.
45. Taylor, *Deadly Vices*, 39.

insecurities which haunt our age and drive our lives. It generates a delusional state that we are hanging on to something of great value. The quest for a self-protective love through possessions is a chimera; no such self exists. The avaricious are doomed to frustration; they can never possess enough to satisfy a sense of self which is fundamentally false. The self is not self-generated but a gift to be received and shared. This is the proper basis for the assurance sought.

Depression

For the ancients this was one of the most debilitating passions. When depressed we can't see ourselves as beloved children of God. Our way of seeing ourselves, our past lives, our accomplishments, the way of seeing others around us, are all distorted and coloured grey. There is no energy to fight this distorted vision. Evagrius linked this passion to grief for what has been given up for the sake of the monastic life. Behind it lies regret that the monk would never have a partner, family, or children. Of course the reasons for depression are complex but whatever the reason depression leeches out everything positive from our perspective on life. This certainly accords with my own experience and it has been instructive for me, if not a little arresting, to locate depression within the passions.

Taylor refers to depression as a 'mood' which 'is not "about" any aspect of life in particular, and no particular event can be picked out as an explanation'.[46] This suggests that '"seeing everything as black" is at least a partial description of what depression amounts to'.[47] In this sense depression can become a 'standing mood' or 'frame of mind' but it does not fit easily into the matrix of vices developed later in the tradition. However, it is not an exaggeration to state that the last century and our present time, particularly in the West, is a period marked by depression and its companions, despair and hopelessness. In this sense depression has a grip on people and provides a fundamental frame of reference for self-understanding. It represents a debilitating condition, complex in its causes, often resistant to amelioration and distortive of life generally. However, because we tend to view depression as something that happens to us, it does not fit easily with the idea of a deadly sin as such. Yet the matter is probably far more complex and the question of human responsibility ought not be lost sight of. In fact depression may be an important but

46. Taylor, *Deadly Vices*, 14.
47. Taylor, *Deadly Vices*, 14.

neglected instance of the loss of harmony and balance between reason and the passions. Evagrius may have a point and contemporary insights into the plasticity of the human brain and capacity for change may offer ways to live beyond the grip of depression.[48]

Anger

This was referred to as 'the most fierce passion', destructive in nature and more so than any other passion. It could involve a great danger of self-deception because we are only correcting the other for their own good. Our angers explode often because we fail to find ways to deal appropriately with this passion. Some anger is quite justified and does not immediately come into view in relation to the passions. The aggressive anger which is characterised by excess is the key to this passion. It manifests itself in two forms: outward explosive anger and the suppressed resentful anger. The former can be a blind impulsive reaction to any kind of perceived hurt and can cause great harm to others. The latter is a more deliberate anger in response to a perceived injury. It can be highly destructive as it hibernates and gathers toxic proportions. In this respect Aristotle refers to the bitter; 'those who suppress their animosity and keep up their anger for a long term'.[49] Underlying this vice is the sense of being undervalued, unappreciated, ignored or that one's wishes and expectations are not being given their due weight. From this point of view anger seems related to defence of a person's view of their position. Beyond protection the anger is designed to re-establish the sense of self. Have the angry an accurate assessment of their self-image? This is the deeper issue. To the extent that their self-evaluation is false or inaccurate the angers will be more severe in order to shield the self from its own delusion regarding its low self esteem. This is particularly so for the resentful whose angers become self-frustrating:

> the agent's desire to be properly valued by others and consequently by themselves cannot be fulfilled through the means which they adopt. As in other deadly vices, there is confusion in their evaluations, for they wish to impress their own worth on others, but are not sufficiently convinced of that worth to have the courage to take the relevant steps. A disclosure

48. Norman Doidge, *The Brain that Changes Itself*, revised edition (Melbourne: Scribe Publications, 2010).
49. Taylor, *Deadly Sins*, 85.

> of their feelings may after all reveal the world's assessment of them to be correct. Painful and frustrating though their position may be, keeping their feelings to themselves is still seen as a form of self-protection.'[50]

Anger as a passion is played out in personal lives and at the macro level between nations and the mayhem and destruction of wars.

Acedia

In the Middle Ages this was identified with sloth or laziness. But it is more accurate to see it as boredom with the ordinary; 'the days seems 50 hours long'. Life loses its savour and someone else is to blame. This is a passion of the old and young; a teenager's favourite word is 'boring'. Acedia is debilitating, it is associated with a restlessness: we hate our jobs; tire of our partners; take up dangerous hobbies; spend money; gamble. The constant change covers the emptiness of our lives. It is possible to spend our life trying to find ultimate meaning in non-ultimate things: work, marriage, friendships, hobbies, material pleasures. Whilst sloth has been considered an 'obsolete emotion', Taylor's consideration of this vice highlights the complexity of this deadly vice.[51] She associates sloth with indolence and boredom and highlights its basic characteristic as a fundamental lack of engagement with life. The result is a joyless, depressed and lifeless demeanor. 'Once these moods have a grip, states of hopelessness and despair, or alternatively states of fatigue and weariness, are a natural consequence.'[52] Taylor concludes: 'sloth is a paralysing vice. The slothful carry the burden of a useless self . . . periods of relative contentment cannot disguise sloth as an obstacle to leading any sort of life at all, and so an obstacle to functioning as an agent. In this consists its harm.'[53] Thus the slothful live an impoverished existence because they lack the capacity for active engagement as a person in the world.

---

50. Taylor, *Deadly Sins*, 91.
51. Taylor, *Deadly Sins*, 17ff.
52. Taylor, *Deadly Sins*, 24.
53. Taylor, *Deadly Sins*, 30.

Vainglory

Those who suffer from this passion require praise or recognition so much that all their actions are determined by their need. In the monastic tradition sufferers from this passion needed to be observed in their ascetical practices. This is an insidious passion of our own time and has strong associations with narcissistic behaviour. It particularly afflicts people in the caring professions who are trained to please others. For such carers their sense of self-worth becomes tied up with their capacity to help and be appreciated by others. Clergy are often in the grip of this passion. The problem with vainglory is that it will wear you out. Burnout is a common experience in our modern day and may have some interesting connections to this powerful passion. This vice is often associated with envy and covetousness. These vices manifest in those whose lack of their own worth and consequent need for constant affirmation easily transforms into envy of those who are perceived to have what they lack. It generates rivalry, competition and destructive behaviour. 'What is to be destroyed, if only by belittling it, is not the good in question, but is the position of the possessor of that good.'[54] The sour grapes syndrome belongs to the vice of vainglory and its companion envy. The latter is a 'self-protective emotion or attitude'. What it protects 'is a self that she herself does not think much of . . . she protects the, in her own view, defective self by further attempting to protect the appearance of an esteem-worthy self which she and others can, deceptively, be expected to respect'.[55] This is designed to avoid self-directed hostility. The insatiable need for affirmation hides a fermenting self-hatred which is directed towards others. The real need is for an esteemed self but it remains elusive.

Pride

This passion is deep-seated and all-pervasive. It is also contested in the modern era. Hume considered that not all pride was vicious. Some have praised it as a virtue while others have labeled it the deadliest of sins. 'So it has been regarded as both a wholly desirable virtue and a thoroughly destructive vice'.[56] Taylor identifies three forms of vicious pride: conceit, vanity and arrogance. 'While the vain need others to reflect a flattering image of themselves, the conceited use them as that against which their own

54. Taylor, *Deadly Sins*, 45.
55. Taylor, *Deadly Sins*, 49.
56. Taylor, *Deadly Sins*, 70.

superiority may be measured'.[57] Taylor notes that for Kant arrogance is 'the pride which pretends to an importance which it does not possess.'[58] Arrogance seems to be more deadly in so far as it is 'wholly self-referential'.[59] Whilst the vain and the arrogant both substitute illusion for reality the arrogant 'are indifferent to admiration and approval from others'.[60] Those most at risk of arrogant pride are the heroes, saints and martyrs. 'They may strike others as being sinfully proud, and may themselves wonder whether their dedication to a cause is a means to self-admiration rather than an end it itself.'[61] The problem for the proud is that they live in a hermetically-sealed value world which they consider superior to others. But this assessment is without reference to others and hence lacks objectivity. Among other things this situation thwarts possibilities for self-development because the proud remain caught as they are in their own isolation and self-absorption. 'Given these features it is clear the proud must suffer from a shriveled self, being deprived of interrelationships and crucial types of knowledge. The contrast is great indeed between the fantasy self and what the self has turned out to be.'[62] As the ancients well knew, pride taints and diminishes everything it touches.

The list of the passions seems endless and they press to the root of our being. Our solace is in our common plight for, as the sixteenth-century Reformer Martin Luther reminded us, we are all in the same 'swamp'. The ancients knew the human blindness which affects us so deeply. They knew that, for the most part, we are not completely done in by our passions (though some are) and all of us sometimes.

Discipleship beyond the passions

The passions invariably turn us inwards in a manner that is self-centred. It is not surprising that the common thread among those subject to the passions is their 'self preoccupation', 'complemented by other indifference'.[63] Transformation is about moving from being self-centred to a properly centred self in the world with others and God. This is a process of healing

57. Taylor, *Deadly Sins*, 73.
58. Taylor, *Deadly Sins*, 74.
59. Taylor, *Deadly Sins*, 74.
60. Taylor, *Deadly Sins*, 74.
61. Taylor, *Deadly Sins*, 77.
62. Taylor, *Deadly Sins*, 79.
63. Taylor, *Deadly Sins*, 127.

and renewal. It can be spoken of as a form of self-transcendence. How does this happen? Minimally it requires an 'imaginative leap' in which the person can recognise that others have views and attachments worthy of respect. This recognition is more than mere 'head' knowledge. The irony of becoming a properly centred self is that this only happens in relation to others. An essential ingredient in this process is the capacity for sympathy. Why sympathy? Because sympathy is the capacity to see beyond the self towards others and their needs. As Taylor states, sympathy is 'the ability to represent to oneself another's state of consciousness beyond the merely self-referential context'; this opens the possibility for 'other regarding concern' and 'proper engagement in practical reasoning'.[64] When we are re-directed towards sympathetic engagement with others a healing and reintegration of the self begins. This process is continuous and fulfilled in personal love.

Much more needs to be said in relation to this dynamic of transformation but its inner logic resides in the fact that the vices can be understood as perverted forms of love and the associated loss of delight in another's existence. This accords with Bondi's earlier observations about the monastics' emphasis on recovering the capacity to love through recovery of an appropriate integration of passion and reason. The ancients recognised that to be caught in the grip of the passions is to be trapped in the self. This manifests itself in an inability to live an outer-directed life that recognises and respects others and has a proper regard for oneself (Romans 12:3). In this sense to be subject to the passions is to be moving in the wrong direction. As one theologian has said,

> Creatures are created to move towards God. When creatures somehow lose that towardness—becoming obsessive at some point, separating from the whole of things and serving only themselves—then the creation loses its order. To lack attraction to others and to God is to suffer the inertia of self-attraction: in Luther's terms, to be 'twisted into self'.[65]

In this context redemption involves the recovery of towardness to God and others. Attraction to God involves being untwisted in order that the true directionality of things is restored and the integrity of persons can be

64. Taylor, *Deadly Sins*, 130.
65. Daniel W Hardy with Deborah Hardy Ford, Peter Ochs and David F Ford, *Wording a Radiance: Parting Conversations on God and the Church* (London: SCM, 2010), 47.

restored. While this is a God-involving activity throughout it is difficult to track due to its interwovenness with the movement of the human spirit. Life beyond the passions is thus not denial of life but the recovery of its proper redemptive movement towards God, the world and others. This is one way at least to depict the basic dynamic of our lives as created in the image of God. As such it offers a clue to the challenge of being a disciple of one who lived a fully centred life in relation to God, others and the world.

Today the elemental power of the passions is evident in personal lives, in cultures, between races and nations. Nations suffer from their passions as much as individuals. The ancients knew these things and so do we in our clearer moments. But even more so the desert mothers and fathers knew about God's mercy and love. They knew that it was only as God's mercy touched them that their eyes were opened and the blindness of the passions could be countered. They could then see as God sees and strike out on a different direction in the chariot this time illumined by God's love. So too today; God is concerned for our own healing when we hurt others and ourselves when we fall prey to our passions.

The above reflections provide an important background for the biblical tradition of renunciation of self and openness to God. In the Gospel of Mark Jesus says: 'For whoever wants to save their life will lose it, but whoever loses their life for me and for the gospel will save it' (Mark 8:35). The Apostle Paul states: 'Those who belong to Christ Jesus have crucified the sinful nature with its passions and desires' (Galatians 5:24). These two different but related traditions have been often associated with approaches to Christian life that have unwittingly fostered a split between the body and the soul on the assumption that 'sinful nature' is co-terminus with the body.[66] However the 'sinful nature' is not the body as such but the whole self wrongly orientated. This insight has been absent for the most part and the focus has remained on negative assessments of the body. As a result the dualism noted above has denigrated bodily life and promoted an otherworldly approach to Christian life.

But does renunciation of self and crucifying the 'sinful nature' with its passions really justify such an attitude? This was my question at the beginning of the essay. Our reflections on the passions suggest not. As we have seen, the 'passions' are the energies of life wrongly directed and

66. Gorringe, *Education of Desire*, chapter 3 is particularly helpful on this. Gorringe notes the early church's attempts to break free from the body/soul dualism which is a feature of early Greek philosophy and culture. However the dualism persisted in various forms.

undisciplined. The passions arise when people lose their proper reference to love and mercy. When this occurs—as it does continually for frail human beings—we become subject to overpowering impulses and forces that express themselves as the passions. Putting to death the passions has been too quickly associated with the negation of those powers that give us life. The apostle wants to encourage the disciple to find freedom from the being overwhelmed and disorientated. This seems to accord with Gorringe's emphasis on the education of desire. I would link the death of the passions with baptism in which a person undergoes a transformation through burial and rebirth. The baptism of the passions is the critical thing. In this process the misdirected and uneducated passions are re-assimilated and integrated into our life in such a manner that they no longer overwhelm but serve the interests of love. The apostolic injunction to put to death the 'sinful nature with its passions and desires' is in fact the way by which people are freed to live with energy and happily with God and others. This is energy for life in the body in the world, not out of the body and disengaged from the world. This gels with my own experience over many decades, particularly in relation to depression. For me life beyond the passions has been an experience of being raised into freedom and light. In this sense the passions represent those forces which drag me downwards and de-energise and keep me self-absorbed. This is precisely what requires burial. This is not a recipe for denial and sublimation but rather recovery of true openness to self, others and God. This recovery of attraction towards God is a dynamic process in which our faltering movement towards God also involves being drawn by the Spirit of Love into love. Consideration of the passions reveals some fundamental issues to do with the way we live together. We are offered insights into the dynamics of our own fragile and broken world, and we are able to see more clearly than ever how much human beings need the mercy and love of God. Minimally our reflections point to the importance of patterns of life that foster nourishment, empowerment, value, self-esteem, humility and the gift of hope. The reason for mentioning these is that they correspond to the various passions outlined above. For example, true nourishment is precisely what the glutton is in need of. Bestowal of self-esteem is a counter to a number of the passions identified above. This would lead us into the tradition of the virtues and is a matter ripe for further consideration.

Reflection on the passions also offers a cautionary note for the disciple of Jesus. It is not so much a passionate discipleship but a discipleship in which the passions are properly directed by and to the love of God. In this sense to live with our passions rightly guided by love is fundamental to the human project. It charts the way for the emergence of a whole human being and a healthy and open society.

Chapter Thirteen
Unfinished Emmaus Journey: Discipleship for Pilgrims

A dynamic discipleship

To live a full and free life with others in God's world is the human project par excellence. There is a dynamism to such a way of life which is beautifully narrated in the Emmaus road story of Luke's gospel. In this story we are offered three critical strands for an ongoing and open-ended discipleship. These strands—word, sacrament and witness—are the focus for this essay and an appropriate conclusion for the reflections of this book.

A resilient discipleship

We live in a pressured, fractious and often violent world. We are all too familiar with the effects of disintegration in our personal lives and in wider society. As a result we seek peace and integration but it often remains a puzzle to us why such things seem so elusive or beyond our capabilities. We wonder whether we lack the patience and strength to craft a way forward, to remain on task and see something through to its conclusion. We are too aware at times that we lack the resilience required for the pursuit of peace and harmony; and for the sustaining and flourishing of life together.

Specifically, what resources build strength and resilience for the human journey? Google 'resilience' and you will find the concept relevant to an extraordinarily broad range of human life.[1] And when philosophers talk about human capability[2] it only makes sense if such capabilities breed resilience and endurance in the context of the difficulties and darkness

1. Books on resilience cover educational theory, childhood development, self-help and emotional intelligence, spiritual life, organisation and business behaviour, crisis intervention, engineering!
2. Martha C Nussbaum, *Women and Human Development: The Capabilities Approach* (Cambridge: Cambridge University Press, 2000).

that so quickly envelops our lives. Part of our difficulty with the idea of resilience is that we conceive it in fundamentally individual terms. It remains a quality and an achievement of the person. Whilst this may be true to some degree such an approach fails to recognise that resilience is fundamentally interpersonal and communal in character. Growing communities of resilience in the face of difficult and oppressive circumstances may be precisely what is required of the disciple of Jesus in the twenty-first century.

My interest in the present essay is to explore in a very preliminary way some of the critical elements that make for a resilient Christian discipleship. In this respect I have found the Emmaus road story from Luke's gospel both instructive and insightful. There are dynamics operating in this narrative that offer clues for an intelligent and sustained following of Jesus Christ.

Emmaus journey as paradigm for discipleship

Commentators on the Emmaus road narrative of Luke 24, both ancient and modern, seem to share a similar sentiment regarding this unique and well-known post-resurrection story. The Australian Roman Catholic scholar Brendan Byrne captures it well: 'The account of Jesus' appearance to the two disciples on the way to Emmaus is Luke's masterpiece. Rich in suspense, irony and play upon emotion, it offers a paradigm of Christian life and mission'.[3] It is the nature and character of this paradigm that I want to pursue briefly in this essay.

I note at the outset that the Emmaus story is not a stand-alone narrative. 'In Luke 24 the evangelist constructs a sort of triptych: three scenes involving events at the tomb in the morning (vv 1–12), on the Emmaus road in the late afternoon (vv 13–35), and in Jerusalem in the evening (vv 36–43)'.[4] Further, the Jerusalem scene is in three parts: proving of identity, commissioning and ascension. My particular interest is in the second and third scenes in the triptych for the light they throw on the way of discipleship. It is easy to miss the significance of the return journey to

3. Brendan Byrne, *The Hospitality of God: A Reading of Luke's Gospel* (Strathfield, Australia: St Paul's Publications, 2000), 186.
4. David Catchpole, *Resurrection People: Studies in the Resurrection Narratives of the Gospel* (London: Darton, Longman and Todd, 2000), 86. Compare NT Wright who says of Luke 24, a 'small masterpiece, designed as a closing scene for a large scale work of art', *The Resurrection of the Son of God* (Minneapolis: Fortress Press, 2003), 647.

Jerusalem on the Emmaus road. The two scenes highlight three key elements essential for a community of disciples: word, sacrament and witness. I argue in what follows that the intertwining of such a threefold cord generates resilience for the journey.[5] And this connectedness between the three elements is not incidental but quite deliberate on the part of the gospel writer. The theological connection between the two scenes is given even greater cogency when we recognise that the Emmaus road journey and Jerusalem upper room gathering both occur under the 'Shadow of Death'.[6] Ched Myers' reflections are apposite: 'As the exchange along the road makes perfectly clear, Jesus' execution presented a crushing blow to the movement he founded—a chilling Shadow of Death.'[7] The context is one of trauma, a far cry from the overly sentimentalised and domesticated portrayal in the church and in art.[8] This is the context in which we observe some significant narrative puzzles. There are in fact three.

A case of impaired vision?

The first such puzzle concerns impaired sight: 'but their eyes were kept from recognising him' (v 16). No doubt you have heard sermons on this and maybe preached on it before. 'But their eyes were kept'. What kept them ignorant of their companion?

If one of us had been in Jerusalem at the feast and then been caught up in the trial and crucifixion of Jesus the Nazarene and some other thieves, and this Jesus had been a personal friend, indeed someone you had pinned your hopes on for the liberation of Israel, and then these hopes had been cruelly dashed—we too would be understandably weighed down with grief and sorrow. The journey was 'a grief laden, scared stiff and contentious debriefing under the Shadow of Death'.[9] We can imagine the travellers, disconsolate, depressed, heads hung low, eyes to the ground. Perhaps they were also confused because of reports about the vision some of the women had, of an angel who said this Jesus was alive—what an absurdity. Why try to relieve grief with such a foolish thing? People under stress and

5. Ecclesiastes 4:12 'And though one might prevail against another, two will withstand one. A threefold cord is not quickly broken' (NRSV).
6. Ched Myers, 'Easter Faith and Empire: Recovering the Prophetic Tradition on the Emmaus Road, in *Getting on Message: Challenging the Christian Right for the Heart of the Gospel*, edited by Peter Laarman (Boston: Beacon Press, 2006), 5
7. Myers, 'Easter Faith', 3.
8. Myers, 'Easter Faith', 3, and Meyers' comments page 4, on the painting of the Emmaus Road by the famous Swiss pietist artist, Robert Zund (1827–1909).
9. Myers, 'Easter Faith', 5.

grief imagine almost anything. Grief does strange things to us. It disturbs our inner being and we can neither think straight nor act wisely. We are prone to all sorts of fantasies in our mind. No wonder their eyes were kept from recognising him.

The Greek text has the sense of 'their eyes were restrained, held back from'. It's a passive; they were prevented by something else, not necessarily of their own making. They couldn't see him. What's going on in the mind of the Luke the writer of the Gospel? Does he want to convey how tired and grief stricken Cleophas and his male companion[10] are as they walk to their village about eleven kilometres from Jerusalem? Perhaps, though I believe Luke intends to push the matter further. His concern is with a theology of vision rather than tired eyes and sorrowful hearts—at least at this moment in his narrative.

Their eyes were kept, held back, restrained by none other than the giver of sight to the blind. They might have been looking straight at him. Admittedly it was the late afternoon sun, but there was no way they were going to be able to see him. As the early church commentator Ephrem the Syrian stated: 'The Lord of the star appeared in his own person to the two who were travelling with him along the road, but his identity was hidden from them. His star too was like this, for its light appeared to all humanity [at his birth] while its pathway was hidden from all humanity'.[11] St Augustine suggested that their 'eyes were held from recognising him; their hearts, you see, needed more thorough instruction. Recognition is deferred.'[12] Their faith had evaporated and hope had been lost. The companion is seen but not recognised; the two travellers 'were walking along dead, with Life itself. Life was walking along with them, but in their hearts life had not yet been restored'.[13] Catchpole argues that non-recognition is 'of the very *esse* of the story' and it cannot be accounted for by the agency of Satan, nor are the travellers guilty of 'culpable failure'.[14] He notes that 'without non-recognition at the start there could be no moment of recognition at the

10. There is some conjecture regarding the identity of the unnamed companion but in all likelihood it was a male and not a female precisely because Luke wishes to fault the male disciples for dismissing the women's report of the risen Jesus. See Byrne, *Hospitality of God*, 188.
11. See Arthur A Just Jr, *Ancient Christian Commentary on Scripture: New Testament 111 Luke* (Downers Grove, IL: IVP, 2003), 378.
12. Just Jr, *Ancient Christian Commentary*, 378.
13. Just Jr, *Ancient Christian Commentary*, 379.
14. Catchpole, *Resurrection People*, 99.

end'.[15] This of course is to state the obvious but it does beg the theological question as to why they were able to see but unable to recognise Jesus. We might say that the 'spiritual senses' had not yet been attuned by faith to identify the risen Jesus. On this account recognition would involve a 'profound epistemic transformation'.[16] For theologian Sarah Coakley the conditions for this kind of seeing involve 'a radical dispossession of the Spirit' and 'demand a cumulative tangle of *practices*—meditative, sacramental, but also moral—in order to sustain this paradoxical form of unknowing/knowing'.[17] Transformative seeing thus reveals itself as a complex amalgam of divine gift and a cultivated and disciplined habit. We need to learn to see what is present. It resonates with our lived experience at many levels. It is well captured by the great astronomer of the eighteenth century, William Herschel, who, in responding to the accusation that his discovery of the planet Uranus had been 'accidental' and that the powers of magnification claimed for his telescope were 'illusory' responded:

> I do not suppose there are many persons who could even find a star with my [magnifying] power of 6,450; much less keep it if they had found it. Seeing is in some respects an art, which must be learnt. To make a person see with such a power is nearly the same as if I were asked to make him play one of Handel's fugues upon the organ. Many a night have I been practising to see, and it would be strange if one did not acquire a certain dexterity by such constant practice.[18]

There is evidently a natural disjunction between seeing and recognition which the Emmaus road travellers bear witness to. They are unable to recognise Jesus because they have not yet the requisite faculty of vision.

In the ensuing conversation Jesus asks the first *dumb* post resurrection question. He was a master at asking such questions in his ministry for example, do you want to get well? How many loves have we? Who touched me? Questions that seem foolish, and we know that because the disciples

15. Catchpole, *Resurrection People*, 99.

16. Sarah Coakley, 'On the Identity of the Risen Jesus: Finding Jesus Christ in the Poor', in *The Identity of Jesus Christ*, edited by Beverly Gaventa and Richard Hay (Grand Rapids, MI: Eerdmans, 2008), 301–19, 313.

17. Coakley, 'On the Identity', 316.

18. Herschel to William Watson, 7 January, 1982 in Richard Holmes, *The Age of Wonder: How the Romantic Generation Discovered the Beauty and Terror of Science* (London: HarperPress, 2009), 108.

always point it out to him. Invariably they are questions that open up conversation and provoke new thought and action. So on the Emmaus road he asks one: 'what are you talking about?' We know immediately this falls into the category of dumb questions because the disciples tell him so: 'are you the only stranger in Jerusalem . . . ?' They then go over the sad events and become even more disconsolate.

That's the cue, 'Oh, how foolish you are . . . and slow of heart—*kardia*. In Hebrew the heart is the seat of intelligence; in other words 'how dull'. Then he explains the scriptures; opens the very voice of God to them: the prophets, the suffering Messiah. He interpreted all the prophets and the things about himself that is, the messiah. And we are told their hearts were burning but 'still they didn't recognise the presence of the light'.[19] Couldn't recognise who it was. At this point St Augustine compares the two travellers to the penitent thief on the cross who 'believed straightaway and acknowledged him, while you [travellers] on the other hand have forgotten he is the author of Life'.[20] Evidently the instruction spoken of by St Augustine was not sufficient. Bock tries to make sense of this failure by drawing a distinction between Jesus 'opening up the truth' and 'his self-revelation' by which he means 'the breaking of the bread'.[21] But this seems forced. Something more than cognition was required in order to recognise Jesus.

The testing of spirits

Jesus 'walked ahead as if he were going on' (v 28). 'Pretend' is not too strong in this instance though it 'suggests that Jesus was hoping to stay with them and not journey on'.[22] Bock remarks that although the 'meeting was over' it was the 'sensitivity and interest' of the travellers that changes. But why? Is the 'pretence' of Jesus a Lukan 'literary foil for the disciples to urge him to stay with them; they so react out of a motive of hospitality for a stranger'.[23] The gospel writer is working at a number of levels and through the pretence Luke is hinting at some deeper psycho-theological veins running through the story. At this point the unknown traveller with the two is asking a searching question of hearts that, with hindsight we

19. See Just Jr, *Ancient Christian Commentary*, 380.
20. Just Jr, *Ancient Christian Commentary*, 380.
21. Darrell L Bock, *Luke Volume 2: 9:51–24:53*, Baker Exegetical Commentary on the New Testament (Grand Rapids, MI: Baker Books, 1996), 1918.
22. Bock, *Luke Volume 2*, 1918.
23. Joseph Fitzmyer, *The Gospel According to Luke (x-xxiv)*, (Garden City, NY: Doubleday, 1985), 1567.

already know have been burning. The question is simple: Do you want to go further with me? I don't mean along the dusty road; I mean do you want to travel further along the road I am opening up to you. It's an invitation to his companions to see whether they are satisfied or not. Here is the delicious irony of the narrative. They have come to their destination but in fact they have not yet reached their spiritual destination. The issue is whether they are spiritually hungry enough to press on. And in terms of the truth of Jesus and his Messianic significance in the life of Israel the whole saga has been opened to them. Do they not have everything requisite for faith and hope? But Luke will not leave the matter there. Faith is not yet born in the two. They have the word and their hearts are burning, ignited by his interpretation of the scriptures. They have it all, do they not?

But they urged him or pressured him in the sense of not taking 'no' for an answer.[24] The hospitable offer makes sense as it is becoming dark. And of course that must be the reason after all; it's dark and it's the right thing to do. Yet below the surface of the narrative the spiritual hunger of the travellers and their need for enlightenment drive their offer of hospitality. It remains unexpressed so we do not hear them say: 'please stay because we love listening to you and actually we must hear more'. The reward for their hospitality is recognition and the link is not unimportant. However, I suspect Luke the theologian is working at something else. The pretence of Jesus falls into the category of 'a try on' to see, as I said, if they are full yet, satisfied or do they want something more?

Recognition at last

Jesus 'took bread, blessed, broke and gave it to them; and their eyes were opened'. Eyes were opened by another; from without; not of their own making. Why in the breaking of the bread, at the first post Easter meal did they see? Why not along the road when the truth was spoken; why not when they first sat down together at meal; why after the bread was shared? Again Ephrem the Syrian, 'broken bread is the key to open eyes'.[25] From guest at the meal Jesus becomes the host. The recognition occurs immediately at the completion of the distribution but this is hardly an argument against a eucharistic interpretation of the meal.[26] And precisely at the moment of recognition Jesus 'became someone disappearing from

24. Byrne, *Hospitality of God*,189.
25. Just Jr, *Ancient Christian Commentary*, 381.
26. Catchpole, *Resurrection People*, 100.

them'.[27] Augustine said it well: 'He withdrew from them in body, since he was held by them in faith'.[28]

Not surprisingly the eucharistic significance of the Emmaus meal is a talking point among commentators.[29] Catchpole draws a distinction between 'a eucharistic way of describing an event and a eucharistic event itself in the strict sense of a sacramental rite'.[30] This helpful distinction enables us to see the gospel writer deliberately making some connections between the developing eucharistic celebrations of the early Church and this first post resurrection meal at Emmaus. St Augustine was in no doubt: 'The faithful know what I am talking about. They know Christ in the breaking of bread. It isn't every loaf of bread, you see, but the one that receives Christ's blessing and becomes the body of Christ'.[31] Fitzmyer says of the Emmaus meal, 'we are clearly confronted here with an abstract way of referring to the Eucharist, which was current in Luke's time'.[32] Nolland seems to hit the mark.

> There is no sense in which Luke is claiming that Jesus celebrated the eucharist with these disciples; rather Luke wants to make the point that the Christians of his day were able to have the living Lord made known to them in the eucharistic celebration in a manner that was at least analogous to the experience of the Emmaus disciples.[33]

Luke's audiences: yesterday and today

Luke the theologian is crafting a gospel for a post-resurrection church. Did he have a particular audience in mind or was it a gospel for all Christians? The matter has been the subject of renewed debate in gospel schol-

---

27. Fitzmyer, *The Gospel According to Luke*, 1568. Fitzmyer adds 'ie without physical locomotion'.
28. Just Jr, *Ancient Christian Commentary*, 382.
29. The Catholic scholars Fitzmyer and Byrne see stronger eucharistic allusions in the meal at Emmaus but the Protestant scholar Bocks clear that the meal is 'not a reenactment of the Lord's Supper' rather 'the meal simply pictures Jesus as raised and present with his disciples in fellowship' (*Luke*, 1919).
30. Catchpole, *Resurrection People*, 100.
31. Just Jr, *Ancient Christian Commentary*, 382.
32. Fitzmyer, *The Gospel According to Luke*, 1569.
33. John Nolland, *Luke 18:35-24:53*, Word Biblical Commentary, volume 35c (Dallas, Texas: Word Books, 1993), 1206.

arship.[34] A distinction has been drawn between the gospels being 'written *for* (initially) their community or *within* their communities'.[35] The latter emphasis gives a more universal intent than the former but the influence of the local conditions cannot be dismissed. The debate will no doubt continue.

In Luke 24 a narrative is being crafted for a community of faith that lives by word and sacrament. The Lord of the word who burns in the heart is the same Lord seen in the breaking of the bread. The same Lord broken open in word and sacrament. The Emmaus Road is a journey into a theology of word and sacrament. For Luke these two belong together. It was St Augustine who spoke about the word of God spoken and the Word of God visible, word and sacrament. The eyes were only opened when both word and sacrament coalesced.

Perhaps the solution to the puzzle of the Emmaus story may be found in an attempt by Luke the theologian to link the early church's experience of the scriptures with its developing liturgical eucharistic life.[36] From this perspective it is possible to hear the Emmaus story as a nascent theology of word and sacrament. This can be challenging for contemporary audiences that often see matters of faith quite differently. For example, where there are Christians whose focus is almost entirely on the written Word the Emmaus narrative can be disturbing. They may live in the word, listen to the word of God, discuss the word of God, grow with the word of God, have arguments about the word of God—in short they may be fully given over to the interpretation of the word. They may believe they do not need anything else. But the danger is they live in their heads—cognition is everything and doctrinalism lurks close by. We think with God and God burns in our hearts but the eyes are sometimes blind to God's presence. Yet being Christian is always more than a head thing.

On the other hand there may be Christians whose focus is on breaking bread like the first apostolic fellowship. They take every opportunity to do so. That's where they meet the risen Lord and their hearts burn within them. But the danger is that they can become preoccupied with the sacramental rite and neglect the vitalities associated with the living Word. In truth they ought never be pitted over against one another; I am for the

34. *The Audience of the Gospels: The Origin and Function of the Gospels in Early Christianity*, edited by Edward W Klink 111 (London & New York: T&T Clark, 2010).

35. *Audience of the Gospels*, 164.

36. This position would find sympathy with a number of the commentators engaged with above, namely, Byrne, Fitzmyer, Nolland and Wright.

bible; I am for the sacrament. Sacrament without word is empty and word without sacrament is blind.

Discipleship on the road again

We are not quite at the end of the discipleship road. It is eleven kilometres to Emmaus. And of course it is eleven kilometres back to Jerusalem. Word and sacrament are never completed apart from the life of witness. In fact word and sacrament are only half the story. The other half is the eleven kilometres back to Jerusalem. In this sense the Emmaus journey has a 'transitional role' in the narrative, particularly given the strong pull of Jerusalem for Luke. 'Journeying or returning to Jerusalem is juxtaposed to the theme of leaving the capital, and both create an evident narrative tension in the story. The two disciples, indeed, are journeying, but there is a general feeling that they move in the wrong direction'.[37] In terms of the foregoing discussion the disciples are not so much moving in the wrong direction towards Emmaus but rather the dynamic is multidirectional. This suggests a discipleship with an accent on travel and a wandering ecclesiology measured by the steps of Jesus.[38]

The return to Jerusalem is associated with witness and commissioning, neither of which would have been possible without the former journey to Emmaus. In short, the word was spoken and their hearts burned; the bread was broken and their eyes were opened and they gave their witness and Jesus appeared with a message of peace. The connections with the earlier mission in Luke 10:5 are clear.[39] The witness and commissioning continue the dynamic of the discipleship way at the Emmaus meal. 'The Jesus of Luke has constantly used meals to set the tone for his mission'.[40] The telling never stops as St Augustine crisply states: 'By telling what they

37. Octavian D Baban, *On the Road Encounters in Luke-Acts: Hellenistic Mimesis and Luke's Theology of the Way* (Milton Keynes: Paternoster, 2006), 206.
38. Following a pilgrimage to the Holy Land in 2007 the late Daniel W Hardy was struck by the simple fact that Jesus walked all over the land; he was a traveller with God and others on the land. It led him to speak of a travelling ecclesiology appropriate for pilgrims. See Daniel W Hardy with Deborah Hardy Ford, Peter Ochs and David F Ford, *Wording a Radiance: Parting Conversations on God and the Church* (London: SCM, 2010), 79–94.
39. Fitzmyer, *The Gospel According to Luke*, 1575.
40. Catchpole, *Resurrection People*, 129.

had seen, they added to the gospel. It was all said, all done, all written down. And it has reached us'.[41]

Unfinished Emmaus postscript

The three things are a unity: word (hearing), sacrament (seeing) and witness (sharing). In the dynamic interaction of these three elements of the Christian way the Lord of the way is present and active, willing the coming kingdom. Unfortunately the Church of Jesus Christ has been dividing up these intertwined realities for centuries, bickering and squabbling using sophisticated arguments and well-honed prejudices. In the process the divided church becomes blind to the presence of God. Energy and resilience for witness to the resurrection is lost.

The Emmaus road is a journey for the whole church. It is a journey into the very heart of the gospel (word and sacrament), and from that heart it is a journey into the very heart of others on the return journey. Many churches only purchase one-way tickets. Either they go to Emmaus and become enmeshed on the inside—in matters that are good and wholesome—but they fail to grasp the purpose of this journey. Some churches spend all the time scurrying back to Jerusalem with plenty of good advice for the rest of the world but hollow and noisy gongs inside; they haven't stayed with word and sacrament long enough to form the habits necessary for spiritual discernment.

The Anglican Church has ever been a church of word, sacrament and witness. As long as it remains committed to the whole twenty-two kilometres of its journey (Jerusalem/Emmaus return) and doesn't try shortcuts it will be faithful to the gospel. A church of the whole gospel, not half; certainly never merely a third; not a two strand church. Our lives move back and forth along the Emmaus road, hearing the living word of God, receiving the broken body of Christ, sharing our life with God and others. We are constantly being reminded that the only life we have as Christians is as a broken body of Christ. Anything else is pure fantasy. And it afflicts the Anglican Communion right now: fantasies about a pure and clean life beyond brokenness and fallibility. There is no such Emmaus Road Church on earth. And we are called constantly to make the return trip to Jerusalem, to the place of rejection, crucifixion to bear witness to the Lord who comes and stands among the people with a message of peace in a violent world. It is on the road back to Jerusalem that we meet the sick, tired, lonely, depressed, the perpetrators and violent, the penitent thief and the

41. Just Jr, *Ancient Christian Commentary*, 382.

stubborn unrepentant as well as the countless victims lying on the side of the road.

The church's ministry consists of three strands which form a threefold cord. It's the threefold cord that makes for a resilient church able to live the resurrection life; such a cord cannot be quickly or easily broken. Three strands: word, sacrament and witness are the key. This is why the Emmaus journey is so paradigmatic for Christian life and mission. The Emmaus road is the road less travelled in God's world; it is the Jesus road for a church shaped by the One who is the way, the truth and the life. It is along such a road with such a God that the faithful disciple travels.

Index of Biblical References

Index of Names

Index of Subjects

Lightning Source UK Ltd.
Milton Keynes UK
UKOW031636141111

182062UK00004B/9/P